D0934945

IN THE SHADOWS OF VICTORY

IN THE SHADOWS
OF VICTORY

America's Forgotten Military Leaders, 1776–1876

THOMAS D. PHILLIPS

CASEMATE

Philadelphia & Oxford

Published in the United States of America and Great Britain in 2016 by
CASEMATE PUBLISHERS
1950 Lawrence Road, Havertown, PA 19083, USA
and
10 Hythe Bridge Street, Oxford OX1 2EW, UK

Hardcover Edition: ISBN 978-1-61200-360-3
Digital Edition: ISBN 978-1-61200-361-0

A CIP record for this book is available from the British Library

Printed and bound in the United States of America

For a complete list of Casemate titles, please contact:

CASEMATE PUBLISHERS (US)
Telephone (610) 853-9131
Fax (610) 853-9146
Email: casemate@casematepublishers.com
www.casematepublishers.com

CASEMATE PUBLISHERS (UK)
Telephone (01865) 241249
Fax (01865) 794449
Email: casemate-uk@casematepublishers.co.uk
www.casematepublishers.co.uk

CONTENTS

PREFACE

History plays tricks sometimes. Its judgments can raise up events or issues or people, or diminish them, painting some in bright tones while casting others in shadows. It can exalt, or disparage, or ignore. During the course of America's existence, history has immortalized an exceptional few while making footnotes, at best, of others.

History, though, is neither a rigid nor an exact science. While enshrining some in the collective consciousness of the nation, it has overlooked others often equally as deserving.

This book is about some of those who have been overlooked; military leaders throughout America's history whose accomplishments have not been widely recognized. Although our nation owes them considerable debts, their services have been too little acknowledged and too seldom celebrated.

As all who study history understand, its verdicts are not immutable. Judgments sometimes change as new information reshapes perceptions of persons or events. Alternately, modem scholarship may revise interpretations of dated material, changing long-standing opinions of wars and battles and the people who fought them. Perhaps the stories in the book will cause readers to reflect further and discover heroes whose services to our country have been undervalued or overshadowed by more renowned contemporaries.

In preparing this book, I solicited comments and recommendations from the military history departments at the United States Military Academy, the United States Naval Academy, the United States Air Force Academy, Virginia Military Institute, The Citadel, and the University of Nebraska-Lincoln. I am particularly grateful to the faculty and staff at Virginia Military Institute, the United States Air Force Academy (most especially Lieutenant Colonel Douglas Kennedy), United States Naval Academy (Lieutenant Commander Jourdan Travis Moger), and Dr. Peter

Maslowski, University of Nebraska—Lincoln, for so graciously investing their time to provide detailed, thoughtful, comprehensive responses while identifying candidates for consideration.

General George H. Thomas, who commanded the Union's Army of the Cumberland during the Civil War, was the name most often mentioned by military historians. There was, however, nothing approaching a unanimous recommendation for any leader in any war. That outcome is altogether to be expected considering the different experiences, interests, and areas of expertise brought to the project by historians who contributed to it. It also accurately reflects the breadth of opinions regarding a most subjective, and at times highly controversial, issue.

Ultimately, though, the choices were mine alone. Discussions regarding them—those who made the list and those who did not—are welcomed. Indeed, the resulting dialogue may help shine needed light on deserving individuals whose contributions went above and beyond the call of duty but whose services to our nation are but little remembered.

One modest surprise resulted from this study: the identification of a few leaders whose major renown is associated with a specific war— General Winfield Scott as America's military leader during the War with Mexico, for example—who also rendered exceptional, though largely forgotten service during a different conflict (in Scott's case, the War of 1812 and, to a lesser extent, the Civil War). Examples are noted throughout the book.

At the end of each chapter, a 'Deeper in the Shadows' section with accompanying brief biographies identifies officers whose contributions, while perhaps a bit less consequential than those of colleagues chronicled elsewhere in these pages, are deserving of far more recognition that has thus far been accorded them.

This volume covers leaders "in the shadows" during the seven major conflicts that occurred during the first roughly one hundred years of the nation's existence. A second volume will continue the story beginning with the Spanish-American War and carry it through the wars in Iraq and Afghanistan.

Special thanks

I am especially indebted to Caxton Press for enabling me to draw from my works *Battlefields of Nebraska* and *Boots and Saddles: Military Leaders of the American West* in developing material for the Indian Wars of the American West chapter, and to Jeanne Kern for her usual wise counsel, friendship, and superb editing skills.

EXPLANATORY NOTES

Officer ranks

For more than a century after the nation's founding, brevet ranks were a feature of the American military. A brevet rank was a nominal promotion to a higher grade without commensurate pay or specific authority given as recognition for service or actions during a battle, campaign, or war. Thus it was not uncommon for an officer to hold two ranks: a permanent, official rank in the Regular Army and a brevet rank. The permanent rank was always lower than the brevet rank. The brevet rank was intended to be temporary, although many officers continued to be addressed by the higher brevet rank as a courtesy. George Armstrong Custer, for example, a lieutenant colonel in the Regular Army, was often referred to as "General"—a carryover from the brevet rank he achieved during the Civil War.

During the Civil War, the rank situation could sometimes be further confused by the fact that officers could hold brevets and actual, full ranks for service in both the Regular Army and the United States Volunteers. It was therefore possible to hold as many as four ranks simultaneously. For example, Ranald Mackenzie—who held commissions in both the Regular Army and the U.S. Volunteers—was a brevet major general of volunteers, an actual full brigadier general of volunteers, a brevet brigadier general in the Regular Army, and an actual Regular Army captain.

Where appropriate, I have tried to acquaint the reader with the actual and brevet ranks held by the officer whose story is being told. In the narrative discussion, when necessary to specify the officer's rank, I have attempted to consistently use the rank by which he was most commonly addressed at the time.

Army structure and terms

For much of its existence, from smallest to largest unit, the United States Army has been organized in companies, battalions, regiments/brigades, and divisions. In recent years, the term "brigade" has come increasingly to identify the Army's operational units above the battalion level. Through the Civil War and the wars with the Indians, such units were identified as regiments. "Cavalry troop" is a generic term typically given to a small force of horse soldiers. The term "dragoon" originally referred to mounted infantry and was then subsequently associated with light cavalry forces. Prior to the Civil War, the United States Army re-designated its existing dragoon units as cavalry regiments.

Military installations

Military installations were labeled "camps" if their intended occupancy was to be temporary (even if for an extended duration), and "forts" if the facilities were designated to be permanent. Those labels were sometimes changed. For example, the historic post in northwestern Nebraska was officially Camp Robinson for the first four years of its existence before being re-designated as a fort in 1878. "Post" is a more generic term associated with military establishments of all types.

References

In the Shadows of Victory tells the stories of more than 30 individuals and chronicles their activities in seven distinct conflicts. Space limitations in a book of this scope preclude the listing of a bibliography in the traditional sense. Publications related to the Civil War alone number more than 50,000 (of which 1,100 have been labelled as "essential" by one scholar). Therefore, in lieu of a traditional bibliography, I have compiled individual bibliographical lists, each focusing on a specific leader. These condensed lists may also serve as recommended readings for those interested in adding further to their understanding of the individuals who led forces during these extraordinary periods in our nation's history.

Similarly, traditional footnoting would have required the numbering of every third or fourth sentence and added further scores of pages to the text. Therefore—as have Robert Leckie, (*The Wars of America*) and others who have written in this genre—in the interests of space and readability I have confined reference notes to directly quoted material. In those instances, where different opinions exist regarding facts or numbers (quite often the case with casualty figures) the contending views are noted in the text.

Indian Wars of the West—Spelling

Names of tribal groups and Native men and women are sometimes rendered differently depending on the source. The name of one of the major tribes of the Sioux nation, for example, is spelled at least three ways in major texts: Oglala, Ogallala, and Ogalallah. In this and other cases, I have chosen the version that appears most frequently in recent scholarship. Interestingly, there even exists somewhat of a historic divergence in the spelling of the most famous of all Indian battles in the American West; i.e., Little Big Horn vs. Little Bighorn. Early references most often cite it as Little Big Horn. However, that rendering has changed over the years. I have followed the conventions of authors of recent major works on the subject, Nathaniel Philbrick (*The Last Stand*) and James Donovan (*A Terrible Glory*) as well as the *New York Public Library American History Desk Reference* and used Little Bighorn.

MAPS

GUILFORD COURTHOUSE

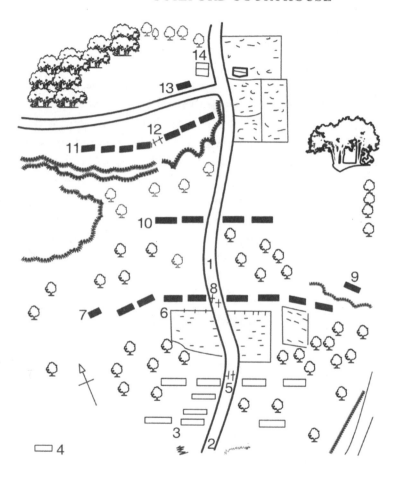

1. Salisbury Road
2. Cornwallis
3. Tarleton
4. British Troops
5. British Battery
6. Fence Line
7. American First Line

8. American Battery
9. Lee
10. American Second Line
11. American Third Line
12. American Battery
13. Greene
14. Guilford Courthouse

COWPENS

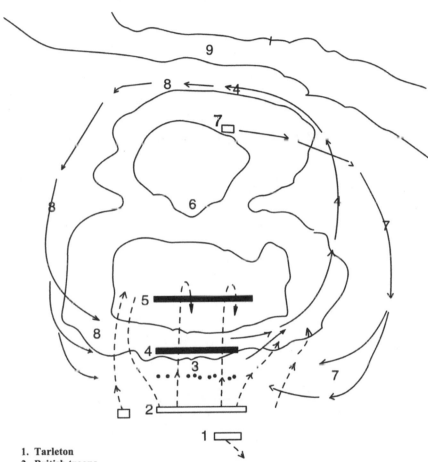

1. Tarleton
2. British troops
3. American sharpshooters in tree line decimate initial attack by British dragoons.
4. American militia (Pickens) fire two aimed shots then exit battle line to the left.
5. American continentals
6. Morgan
7. American dragoons (William Washiongton) sweep to the British right.
8. Pickens reforms militia units and attacks the British left.
9. Broad River

BATTLE OF LUNDY'S LANE

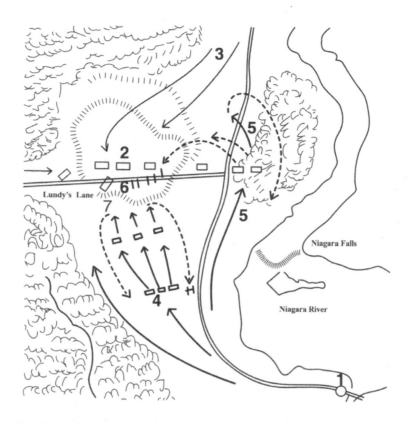

Lundy's Lane

Niagara Falls

Niagara River

1. MGen Jacob Brown replenishes following U.S. victory at Chippawa.
2. British BGen Phineas Riall occupies elevated ground along Lundy's Lane.
3. With U.S. forces on the move, LGen Gordon Drummond sends reinforcements.
4. U.S. forces under BGen Winfield Scott make first contact at 6:00 p.m.
5. Slowed by British artillery fire, Scott sends a flanking movement that unhinges the British left flank. Riall is captured. U.S. main force under Brown reaches field.
6. Drummond's center falls back, leaving his artillery uncovered.
7. U.S. bayonet charge captures guns and drives back British center. Three British counterattacks fail with heavy losses on both sides. Brown, Scott, Drummond, and Riall are wounded. The following morning, American attempts to drag the guns away, are thwarted when British reoccupy the battlefield. In the immediate aftermath, Brown withdraws to Fort Erie while British fall back to Queenston awaiting reinforcements, Subsequent siege of Fort Erie is defeated by Brown.

BATTLE OF MONTERREY

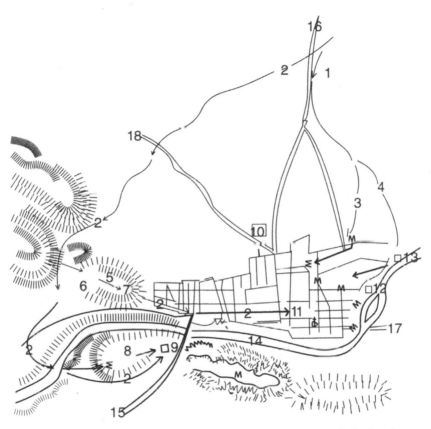

1. Taylor	7. Bishop's Palace	13. La Teneria
2. Worth	8. La Federacion	14. Santa Catarina River
3. Garland	9. Fort Soldado	15. Road to Saltillo
4. Butler	10. Citadel (Black Fort)	16. Road to Camargo
5. La Independencia	11. Plaza	17. Road to Caderetta
6. Fort Libertad	12. Fort Diablo	18. Road to Montclova
M Mexican Fortifications		

BATTLE OF NASHVILLE

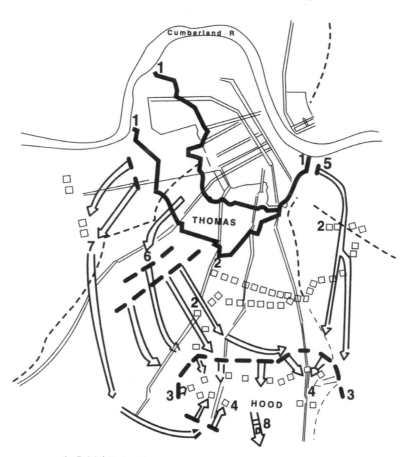

1. Initial Union line
2. Initial Confederate line
3. Union line at climax of battle
4. Confederate line at climate of battle
5. Steedman's division with U.S. Colored Troops, breaks through on the left.
6. The Union right wing swings like a massive hinge and attacks at an oblique angle across the Confederate front.
7. Wheeling movement by Union cavalry collapses the Confederate left.
8. With both flanks enveloped, Hood's army comes apart and flees the battlefield

THE BATTLE OF THE BLUE WATER

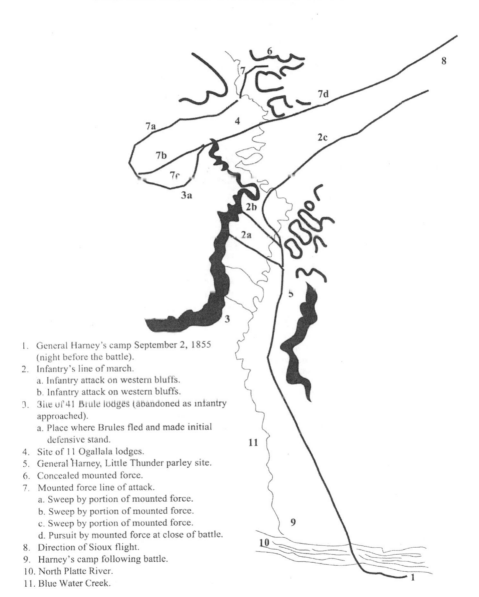

1. General Harney's camp September 2, 1855
   (night before the battle).
2. Infantry's line of march.
   a. Infantry attack on western bluffs.
   b. Infantry attack on western bluffs.
3. Site of 41 Brule lodges (abandoned as infantry
   approached).
   a. Place where Brules fled and made initial
      defensive stand.
4. Site of 11 Ogallala lodges.
5. General Harney, Little Thunder parley site.
6. Concealed mounted force.
7. Mounted force line of attack.
   a. Sweep by portion of mounted force.
   b. Sweep by portion of mounted force.
   c. Sweep by portion of mounted force.
   d. Pursuit by mounted force at close of battle.
8. Direction of Sioux flight.
9. Harney's camp following battle.
10. North Platte River.
11. Blue Water Creek.

REPUBLICAN RIVER EXPEDITION

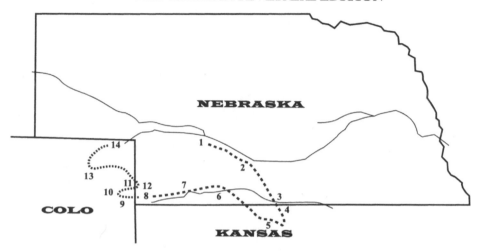

1. June 9: Carr departs Ft. McPherson.
2. June 12: A patrol scouting along Deer Creek chases a hunting party of 20 Indians.
3. June 13: Carr reaches Republican River.
4. June 15: Carr's force is ambushed while camped on the river.
5. June 16: Carr's scouts lose Indian trail on the North Fork of the Solomon River.
6. June 19: Carr moves back to the Republican River
7. June 19-29: Daily marches of 25-30 miles east to west along the river.
8. June 29-July 2: "Thickwood" rendezvous area. Troops are resupplied.
9. July 4: A patrol chases a 12-person war party.
10. July 7: Carr backtracks to find a better wagon route. The move may have been interpreted by Tall Bull as a retreat.
11. July 8: Small war party attacks three soldiers looking for a stray horse.
12. July 8: Cheyenne night attack on Carr's camp.
13. July 11: Battle of Summit Springs.
14. Mid-July: Expedition ends at Ft. Sedgwick, Colorado.

BATTLE OF WARBONNET CREEK

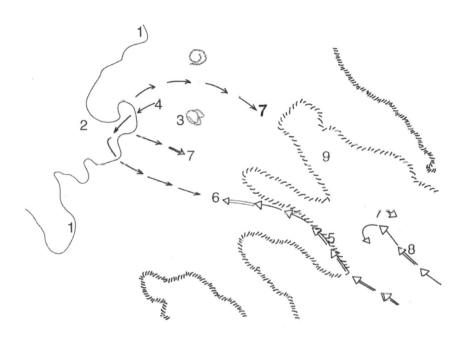

1. Warbonnet Creek
2. Fifth Cavalry bivouac area hidden behind tree line along creek.
3. Merritt's position atop the highest of the two conical hills.
4. Cody skirts behind hill and trees to attack Yellow Hair's party.
5. Route of Yellow Hair's advance party.
6. Site of Cody-Yellow Hair fight. Yellow Hair killed.
7. Fifth Cavalry attack led by Eugene A. Carr. Wings eventually form line abreast.
8. Advance and retreat of main body of Northern Cheyennes.
9. Series of low, finger-like ridges.

CHAPTER 1
THE WAR OF INDEPENDENCE

NATHANAEL GREENE

Afflicted with a limp so pronounced that some initially thought it should disqualify him from military service, Greene's extraordinary generalship in the Carolinas saved the South for the American cause.

America rightly identifies George Washington as the towering figure of the nation's War of Independence. Yet, without the services of one of history's most implausible military leaders the war might well have taken a different turn. Dimmed by the enormous shadow cast by Washington, the war-saving accomplishments of Nathanael Greene remain relatively unrecognized.

Greene was born July 27, 1742 at Forge Farm in Potowomut, Rhode Island, an isolated community on a peninsula fronting Greenwich Bay. One of the area's oldest families, the Greenes were modestly prosperous, operating saw and grist mills and a forge where Nathanael worked as a youth. In 1770, at age 27, he moved to Coventry, a village about six miles inland, to run a foundry his father had purchased. Though operating the forge aggravated his asthma, a life-long affliction, Greene quickly established himself in the community, building a home—a 2½-story dwelling called Spell House—and leading efforts to found the hamlet's first public school.

Little in his past marked Nathanael Greene for military leadership so exceptional that in the closing months of the war it surely bordered on genius. Greene often suffered from asthma and his appearance was characterized by a limp sufficiently pronounced that some of his colleagues at first thought it should disqualify him from military duty. Raised a Quaker, Greene was expelled from the faith before the war began, likely because of his interest and participation in military duties. His Quaker upbringing provided Greene with little opportunity for formal schooling. He was, however, intensely self-educated particularly in mathematics, law, and military history. A voracious reader, he purchased numerous texts dealing with strategy and tactics, and in essence taught himself the art of war. Even more remarkable perhaps is that in his most important role as Commander of the Southern Army, Greene never won an outright victory on any major battlefield.

Greene met Washington for the first time during the siege of Boston, where Greene had taken the Kentish Guards, a 1,600-man unit formed of men from his home region. The young Rhode Islander's exceptional competence was obvious to all and he quickly earned Washington's confidence, becoming one of his closest advisors. It was a trust he would retain throughout eight years of war.

Like Washington, Greene was one of the few American commanders who grasped immediately that the essential condition for American victory was to preserve an army in the field. Thus, in the South, Greene was content to draw the British away from their bases, engage them in chases, exhaust their supplies and fight at times and places of his choosing. After inflicting casualties that at times destroyed as much as a third of the British force, Greene typically chose to withdraw, leaving the ground to his opponent rather than risk losing his small army to acquire momentary possession of otherwise inconsequential real estate. So well-conceived was his strategy that by bleeding his opponents of troops, supplies, and endurance he caused British forces to withdraw from the Carolinas and Georgia, thwarting their attempt to sever the South from the rest of the American colonies. Eventually, the British commander, Lord Charles Cornwallis, moved north out of the Carolinas into Virginia—a trek that took him to Yorktown and to the final defeat that brought the war to a close.

American prospects in the South, dire from the beginning, had deteriorated steadily during the course of the war. The first American commander, Robert Howe, had lost Savannah. The second, Benjamin Lincoln, had lost Charleston and surrendered an entire American army in the process. The third, Horatio Gates, had been routed at Camden, South Carolina, nearly losing an army in a battle so horribly mismanaged that his leadership was most notable for his having been among the first to flee the field. Now, late in the fourth year of the war, the British were perilously close to effective control of Georgia and the Carolinas, and to separating the South from the middle and northern colonies.

Greene was appointed commander of the infant nation's southern forces in October 1780. It would turn out to be a fortuitous choice for Washington, who made the appointment, and for the revolutionary cause.

Greene was 38 years old when Washington's letter of appointment reached him. At five feet ten inches, he was taller than most of his contemporaries. Greene was solidly built with clearly defined features characterized most prominently by clear blue eyes and a high forehead.

After bidding goodbye to his wife Catharine ("Caty") in Philadelphia— it would be two years before they saw each other again—Greene traveled south, visiting governors of the states along the way, pleading for supplies and leaving liaison officers in place. These efforts were, at best, only minimally successful. States were reluctant to furnish scarce supplies to a national army.

Greene sent a senior officer ahead to map the terrain and identify favorable lines of march, retreat, and communication. Anticipating that the many rivers of the South would influence the type of campaign he intended to wage, Greene dispatched Thaddeus Kosciouszko to locate fords, build boats, and pre-position them at crossing points. In combination, these initiatives illustrated the qualities that would become the hallmarks of Greene's leadership: foresight, preparation, and planning. To those characteristics would soon be added innovation, a sense of anticipation on the battlefield, and skill at organizing and leading an army. All would prove essential.

When Greene arrived at Charlotte, North Carolina, to take command he found the wreckage left by Gates: a small, demoralized army, ill-disciplined and chronically short of supplies. Greene's initial force, numbering between 1,000 and 2,100 troops, was, like much of the American Army, underfunded and under-provisioned, lacking weapons, clothes, shoes, blankets, medical supplies, lumber, nails, and wagons. Morale was low to non-existent following a string of devastating losses.

As one of his first steps, Greene met with leaders of the South's guerrilla bands—the "Swamp Fox" Francis Marion, Thomas Sumter, Elijah Clarke, Andrew Pickens—eliciting their support. Marion, in particular, would come to render special services. In the months ahead the partisan forces along with Greene's superb cavalry commanders, Henry 'Light Horse Harry' Lee and William Washington, would launch raids on British and Loyalist outposts, supplies, and lines of communication, harassing and inflicting losses in men and material before vanishing into the interior of a country with whose vastness their opponents could never quite contend.

Greene's first move was unorthodox, but masterful in its conception and brilliant in its consequence. Although outnumbered two to one by British and Loyalist forces under Charles Cornwallis, Greene split his small army. Greene's maneuver caused Cornwallis, nearby at Winnsborough, South Carolina, with 4,000 men, to divide his own force in order to pursue the separated American columns. Greene believed his move might allow him to recombine his army at a favorable moment and attack the British wings one at a time. What actually took place was even more fortuitous. On July 17, 1781, the segment of Greene's army under General Daniel Morgan destroyed the force sent against it by Cornwallis. At Cowpens, South Carolina, in a brilliantly conducted battle, Morgan killed, wounded, and captured more than 900 of an 1,100-man force led by Banastre Tarleton, one of the British army's most capable and ruthless commanders.

Following the victory at Cowpens, Morgan's and Greene's forces recombined as Greene began a strategic retreat closely pressed by British units under Cornwallis' direct command. Greene's intention in retreating was to buy time to gather additional forces—at the time his army consisted of only 1,400 regulars and 600 local militia while stretching the British forces and exhausting their supplies.

Greene formed an elite light cavalry unit to hold off the advancing British in a series of sharply fought rear-guard actions and then used pre-positioned boats to cross rivers just ahead of his pursuers. Greene's retreat—"the race to the Dan"—across the breadth of North Carolina is considered a masterpiece in the annals of warfare.

Finally, in mid-February, with the British army only a few miles behind, using boats hidden along the river's banks and gathered from areas nearby, Greene crossed the Dan River into Virginia. The British arrived on the opposite bank not long after. The river was too high to cross without boats, and all the boats were on Greene's side of the river. Cornwallis gave up the chase. Greene and his army had escaped.

After a few days to replenish his supplies and secure promises of additional help, Greene re-crossed the river and went after Cornwallis. On March 15, 1781, on a field he had personally chosen, Greene brought his army to battle near Guilford Court House, a remote county seat in north central North Carolina.

The morning of the 15th dawned bright but cold in the late days of winter. Recent rains and snow had left the ground spongy and the nearby woods heavy with moisture. Early morning frost had burned off by the time the first shots were fired at about noon. The terrain selected by Greene was slightly rising ground near an abandoned court house. Now within the city confines of Greensboro, in March 1781 the landscape was mostly fields and some cleared areas flanked by occasional woods.

Cornwallis, approaching from the south, traveled along a north-south track, the Great Salisbury Wagon Road, that split the grounds of a large plantation before bisecting a fenced, wooded area a bit farther north. Past the fenced area the road emerged from the timber into an extensive open space of mostly cleared ground that ran toward the court house in a gentle upward slope. At the point, heavy forest bordered the road on the east.

Cornwallis formed his line of battle and at midday began moving across a plowed field toward the first American line about a quarter of a mile away. Greene had placed the first of his three defensive lines on the open ground just north of the fenced, wooded area. The second line, with two six-pound cannons in the center, was 200–300 years farther north. The third and final line was 400 yards back, closest to the court house. The first line was composed mostly of North Carolina militia, the second of Virginia militia, and the third by Continental regulars from Virginia, Delaware, and Maryland.

At this point in the war it had been the general experience of American commanders that the lesser trained and disciplined militia forces seldom held when faced with close attack by British regulars. In employing the militia forces at Guilford Court House, Greene adopted the stratagem used with great success by Daniel Morgan at Cowpens: he asked his militia lines to get off two aimed shots before retreating. They did so, many of them using fence posts to steady their aim before retreating in some disorder after the center of the line collapsed. Still, the 1,500 or so American muskets along the first line wreaked havoc on the British attackers. An officer with the 71st Highland Regiment thought that half of his unit had been knocked down by the initial wall of fire.

Greene's intention was to use his militia units to drain off the British advance before it reached his main line of resistance. The British attacked along the west side of the road, eventually forcing back Greene's first two lines while sustaining heavy losses—although Greene lost some effectiveness by placing his lines too far apart to fully support one another. Fighting was especially sharp at the second line before the British pushed around a flank and continued their attack in the direction of the court house.

When the battle reached Greene's third line, the struggle between the American and British regulars soon escalated into some of the most intense combat of the entire war. A painting depicting the fury of the battle at its height shows Greene mounted on a charger immediately behind the American line, directing blue-clad Continentals and militia in homespun garments against the oncoming Redcoats. In the background, William Washington's Light Dragoons outfitted in green uniforms race to the attack. As the armies surged back and forth, at one point two of Greene's cannons were lost and then recaptured in a violent counterattack.

As the savage fight continued, a British advance was repulsed by the 1st Maryland Regiment and Washington's horsemen. Portions of the British force were trapped and placed under simultaneous attack from two directions. With his army in retreat and its lines threatening to break, Cornwallis ordered British artillery to fire into the midst of the melee where forces from both sides were intermixed and struggling. The 'friendly fire' losses from his own shells killed several British soldiers but caused the Americans to break off their attack.

At this point, having destroyed more than a quarter of Cornwallis' army and not wishing to place his own force at further risk, Greene withdrew from the field. From a force that began the battle with about 1,900 men, British losses numbered 93 killed, 413 wounded and another 26 missing or captured. Greene lost 79 killed, 185 wounded, and 75 others wounded and captured. Additional numbers 'missing' are uncertain because of the propensity of some militia units to drift off after an encounter.

A torrential downpour began soon after the last shots were fired, further compounding the agony of an already horrific scene. Dead and dying soldiers from both sides lay scattered over the extensive battle area. Nearby families, many of them Quakers, helped doctors care for the wounded using farmhouses for many miles around as temporary hospitals.

After the battle, Greene withdrew his force into the more remote areas of North Carolina. Cornwallis chose not to pursue. Instead, still recovering from his severe losses and leading a force now depleted in men and materiel, he abandoned the interior of the state. Eventually, he arrived at Wilmington, a port city 100 miles distant where he could rest, recruit, and replenish his army. His decision later in the year to leave Wilmington and move north into Virginia would have major consequences for the outcome of the war.

Guilford Court House was a decisive battle. While Greene kept an army in the field and the revolutionary cause alive in the South, Cornwallis took his forces out of the area and put them on the path that led to Yorktown. The battle is remembered in other ways as well. Cornwallis described it thus: "I never saw such fighting since God made me. The Americans fought like demons." Greene's later words were more prosaic but also more telling: "We fight, get beat, rise, and fight again."

It was a pattern that would repeat itself.

In the days ahead, Greene and his army would fight, get beat, and rise again across North and South Carolina. After Guilford Court House they would wage three more substantial battles. In the conventional sense, they lost them all; but by those 'losses' the Americans wrested control of the South.

When Cornwallis moved north from Wilmington, Greene turned south. It was in some ways a surprising decision, but one that was of considerable strategic importance. Rather than trailing Cornwallis, Greene began a series of operations that would clear the interiors of Georgia and the Carolinas.

In April 1781 Greene's army fought at Hobkirk's Hill near Camden, South Carolina. They were beaten in a fight that cost the British a greater number of wounded and double the number killed. American losses were 19 killed, 115 wounded, 48 more wounded-captured, and an additional uncertain number captured or missing. British losses were 38 killed, 220 wounded and an additional, fairly small, number missing. Soon after the battle, Lord Francis Rawdon, the British commander, retired to Camden. There, flanked by Greene's forces on one side and militia units under Thomas Sumter on the other, and subjected to devastating raids on his supplies and lines of communication with the coast led by Francis Marion and "Light Horse Harry" Lee, Rawdon abandoned Camden and began a retreat that eventually took him to Charleston.

Greene used Continental regulars, local militias, and guerrilla forces in a concerted fashion in the campaign that led to Hobkirk's Hill. The British had possessed the town of Camden for a year and during their long occupation had constructed a chain of formidable breastworks around the city. When Greene approached Camden he saw that his force—only about 1,500 strong at the time—was too small to take the city by storm. Hoping instead to draw Rawdon into battle, he camped on Hobkirk's Hill, about a mile and a half away.

Five days later, on April 25, 1781, fearing that Marion and Lee were on their way to join Greene and having been misinformed that Greene's army was temporarily without artillery, Rawdon accommodated. In late morning, after skirting a swamp and avoiding a ridge occupied by Americans, Rawdon struck the Patriots' left flank. The British attack drove in the American pickets who nonetheless held up the assault long enough for Greene to set his defenses. After reforming his units, Rawdon moved up the hill on a narrow front against the main American force.

Greene countered with simultaneous attacks on both British flanks and by a head-on bayonet charge by two regiments. While those assaults were underway, he sent William Washington's cavalry to strike the rear of the British forces.

Greene's counterattacks, along with effective artillery fire, inflicted heavy casualties on the British. As the fighting progressed, two American officers leading the attack on the British left flank were struck down. When the American units on that side began to fall apart, Greene withdrew.

Washington's cavalry, meanwhile, raided a British commissary and hospital area, taking supplies and capturing 200 prisoners—a notable success, but one that delayed them from assisting in the main battle.

Rawdon withdrew to Camden the following day. Greene sent units to the battlefield to drive away a force of British dragoons and reoccupy the site. On May 9, Rawdon moved his forces out of the area

When Cornwallis moved north into Virginia, he left behind two British garrisons on the coast, at Savannah and Charleston, and three major outposts in the South Carolina interior—Camden in the center of the state, the town of Ninety Six in the west, and Georgetown in the east, midway between Wilmington and Charleston.

The battle at Hobkirk's Hill, and the concentration of American forces in its aftermath, caused the British to evacuate Camden. Meanwhile, Greene directed guerrilla actions throughout the area. Isolated British outposts were soon abandoned or fell to the Americans. By late May, even the substantial post at Georgetown was evacuated. By then, Greene had already set his sights on the remaining outpost at Ninety Six, South Carolina. Ninety Six was an important post; the garrison guarded trade and communication routes between the coast and Britain's Cherokee allies in the interior and between other British fortifications at Augusta, Georgia, and Charlotte.

As Greene marched toward Ninety Six, he sent Andrew Pickens and "Light Horse Harry" Lee to attack Augusta. On June 6, after a 15-day siege, the British surrendered to Pickens. In the meantime, Greene had reached Ninety Six on May 21. His 1,000-man force faced formidable obstacles. The fortification, large, well-constructed and well-provisioned, featured an enclosed stockade, deep ditch, and a spiked, wooden abatis barricade surrounding the entire structure. A large redoubt, the Star Fort, allowed protected fire from defenders along two walls. A similar, though smaller, structure covered the remaining walls and the fort's water supply.

The Americans immediately put the fort under siege and at one point succeeded in placing a trench within 30 yards of the Star Fort. The British commander, Lieutenant Colonel John Cruger, put up a superb defense and in several nighttime sorties disrupted the trench-building efforts directed by Greene's chief engineer, Thaddeus Kosciouszko. A series of innovative moves and countermoves followed: the Americans posted sharpshooters on a quickly-built siege tower and used the position to fire into the compound; the British responded by erecting tall sandbag barricades that sheltered their own riflemen. Use of fire was attempted, mostly without success, by both sides—the Americans against buildings in the compound and the British against the siege tower.

As the struggle wore on, Greene received word that Rawdon had left Charleston on June 7, bringing 2,000 men to break the siege. The news did not reach Greene until June 11, which made time a critical factor: Rawdon's 2,000 men plus the 500–600 Cruger had inside the fort would give the British more than a two to one advantage over the American attackers.

Rawdon's approach made it essential for Greene to attempt to take the fort quickly, before he was vastly outnumbered. Greene's plan was to send a force to capture the small redoubt while a second, larger, assault team went after the Star Fort. There, while the assault continued, the first group to reach the walls would pull down the sandbags, exposing the fort's defenders to sweeping fire from the siege tower.

Greene launched his attack on June 18. At first all went well: the smaller redoubt was captured and the group sent against the Star Fort penetrated the abatis and cleared the ditch, reaching the walls and pulling down the sandbags. Cruger counterattacked and in vicious, close-in fighting characterized by bayonets and muskets used as clubs, struck the flanks of the attacking force. As had happened at Hobkirk's Hill, in the midst of the melee officers leading the American assault were killed and the attackers withdrew to their trenches. Rawdon and his relief force were now only 30 miles away. Greene lifted the siege and moved into the countryside. Rawdon sent a large force after him, but short of supplies and exhausted by their long march from the coast, the chase failed.

Rawdon found himself in possession of an isolated post. With Augusta having fallen to the Americans, there was no other British outpost of any size within 200 miles. With no hope of relief and his long supply lines vulnerable to repeated cuts by Marion, Lee, Sumter, and other guerrilla bands, Rawdon abandoned and burned the fort. The Americans now controlled the entire interior.

When Rawdon left Ninety Six, Greene tried to quickly reassemble his forces and strike the British before they reached the coast. Some of his guerrilla units were late in arriving, however, and Greene abandoned plans for an immediate full offensive. While several guerrilla units harassed the British withdrawal, Greene rested his main body of troops for about two months before launching another attack. It would come outside of Charleston at Eutaw Springs and would be the last major battle in the South.

In early September, the British garrison near Charleston, now led by Colonel Alexander Stewart, was camped in cooler hills at Eutaw Springs, about six miles east of present-day Eutawville. Action began early in the morning of September 8 when an American scouting party decoyed a British cavalry unit into an ambush led by "Light Horse Harry" Lee. Some cavalrymen escaped to warn Stewart of the American's presence, after four or five were killed and another forty captured. Lee's work continued that morning when his unit surprised a party of foragers at some distance from the main British base, taking large numbers of them prisoner.

Stewart, warned by the cavalrymen who had escaped Lee's trap, readied his 2,000 men for battle. Greene, with a force of equal size, formed his units into two lines, militia in front and regulars from Virginia, North Carolina, and Maryland close behind. Stewart moved directly to the attack, temporarily breaking the American's first line with an initial charge. North Carolina regulars from the second line then moved forward to bolster the reeling militia. They succeeded for a time in halting the British advance but were subsequently pushed back by a charge from reinforced British forces. Greene met that thrust with a counterattack by Virginia and Maryland Continentals. The assault by American regulars first stopped the advance and then broke it, sending the British fleeing from the battlefield in disarray.

The Americans continued the chase through the nearby British camp. There, for some of the perpetually hungry, ill-clad American units, the temptation became too great: they stopped to plunder the ample quantities of food and supplies left behind by the British.

When the Americans' forward surge slowed, the momentum of the battle again began to change. Earlier in the fight a retreating British unit had fallen back into a strong brick house at the northeastern comer of the camp. After the Americans attacked the house but failed to take it, the British commander was able to stabilize the rest of the front. With the house as a strongpoint the British launched a counterattack that drove the Americans from the camp. In an effective rear guard action, an American battalion delayed the British advance, allowing American units to withdraw in good order.

Casualties were high on both sides. The British lost almost 45 percent of their total force: 85 killed, 297 wounded, 70 wounded prisoners and 430 captured. Greene's losses were variously reported as about 119 killed, 382 wounded, 18 missing and 60 captured.

The outcome of the battle continues to provoke discussion among historians. Greene may have intended to resume the fight the next day but was prevented from doing so by wet weather that dampened his powder supplies. Neither side immediately left the battlefield area. When Greene finally withdrew he left a sizable force to guard against any British advance. When Stewart left, however, he turned back to Charleston and remained there for the duration of the war.

When Cornwallis surrendered at Yorktown, the British forces that remained in the Carolinas and Georgia were penned inside the port cities of Wilmington, Charleston, and Savannah—far indeed from controlling the entire South, an objective that seemed within their grasp only a year before.

Greene's generalship in the South was of the highest caliber. Astutely dividing his forces, eluding his pursuers, tiring his opponents physically, stretching their resources, and inflicting disproportionate casualties in battles fought at places of his own choosing, Greene caused his adversaries to pay dearly for advantages that were always temporary. Cornwallis said of him: "Greene is as dangerous as Washington. I never feel secure when encamped in his neighborhood. He is vigilant, enterprising, and full of resources."

Greene's personal leadership was equally as commendable. He kept a hungry, ill-clad, poorly equipped army together despite repeated setbacks on the battlefield. Somehow, Greene's men grasped his vision and understood every part of "we fight, get beat, rise, and fight again."

America's southern campaign was a strategic victory on a scale not often matched. That it was won by a self-taught general who some thought too infirm for military service and who seldom prevailed on a battlefield made it all the more remarkable.

Before and After

Greene was an early advocate of American independence, and with war on the horizon after the clashes at Lexington and Concord, he helped raise a force from Rhode Island. Despite concerns about his health, armed with a musket purchased from a British deserter, he enlisted as a private. His abilities were quickly recognized and he was soon made a brigadier general, one of four initially in the fledgling army.

In 1775, Greene took his Rhode Island Army of Observation to join the American Army at Boston. Washington was immediately impressed by Greene's military knowledge, clear-headed practicality, and shrewdness. As Greene's "presence" and high moral character also became evident, the relationship between the two was cemented. Greene and Henry Knox would be the only senior officers to serve with Washington during the entire eight years of the conflict. When Greene's attractive and vivacious wife Catharine joined him at Boston, "Caty" Greene became one of Washington's favorite dancing partners and a friend and confidant of Martha Washington. Nathanael and Caty named their first son George Washington Greene and their first daughter Martha Washington Greene.

For the next few years, before his appointment in the South, Greene served in a variety of roles where he rendered solid, but not exceptional service. In March 1776, Washington gave him his first major assignment, command of the city of Boston, after British forces evacuated the city. His tenure there was short: he was soon called to New York and placed in command of 4,000 American troops on Long Island. Greene, whose health was always tenuous, was ill when the British launched a major attack in August. He missed the subsequent fight for the island and the desperate, narrow escape of the American forces. Soon after New York City fell, the Americans failed in an attempt to retain Fort Washington, a fortification overlooking the Hudson that Greene had intended to use to hamper the movement of British ships and troops on the river.

In December, Greene commanded one of two columns in the American victory at Trenton. At Brandywine in August of the following year, with the British threatening to trap and destroy Washington's army, Greene and Brigadier General Anthony Wayne rushed forces to points in peril along the front and held long enough for Washington to extract his army from the field. In October 1777 at Germantown, Greene led three divisions in a blundered, confused battle fought in heavy fog and rain. The British claimed the field at the end of the day but their victory was dearly won. Although Germantown was yet another in a string of American defeats, the battle provided evidence of a much-improved Continental Army.

When the Army went into winter quarters at Valley Forge, Washington prevailed upon Greene to take on the onerous duty of Quartermaster General. It was a thankless task. Congress was bankrupt and had no power to tax. The states could tax, but most of them had neither money nor supplies. Those that did often reserved their largesse for units from their own states; support for the Continental Army was typically lacking. In the absence of hard cash, merchants were disinclined to provision Washington's army. The near-impossible task was made even more difficult by the fact that only in the most dire circumstances did Washington and Greene seize supplies by requisition. Thus, in the midst of plenty, the American Army was almost always hungry, ill-clothed, and poorly supplied.

Greene accepted the position with reluctance and only with the proviso that he could continue to lead troops in the field. Once in the job, Greene rendered remarkable service in perhaps the most difficult staff position in the Continental Army.

In June 1778, the British decided to abandon Philadelphia and move back to New York City. Washington followed and caught them at Monmouth Court House. The results of the training regimen the troops had endured during the bitter winter at Valley Forge were now much in evidence. The Continentals, with Greene commanding the right flank, repelled repeated attacks on every part of the line by some of the most famous regiments in the British army. When the Continental Army prepared to fight again the following day, they discovered the British had resumed their march to New York City where they arrived safely a few days later.

Soon after, Greene, along with the Marquis de Lafayette, was dispatched to Rhode Island to supplement American forces led by John Sullivan. The expedition that followed, intended to be conducted in concert with French Admiral d'Estaing, was bungled from the outset and achieved very little.

In June 1780, Greene commanded American forces in the battle of Springfield, New Jersey. Greene's outnumbered forces turned back a combined British-Hessian expedition led by Lieutenant General Wilhelm, Baron von Knyphausen that was moving to attack Washington's army at Morristown. Sometimes called the "forgotten victory," Springfield was the last major battle fought in the North.

In August, after a series of contentious struggles with Congress over provisioning the Continental Army, Greene resigned the Quartermaster General position he had held since Valley Forge. Washington then named him Commander of West Point where he served only briefly before being appointed Commander of the Southern Army.

There, a month later, he began the campaign that saved the South for the Americans.

Greene remained in command of the Southern Army until the war ended. Soon after, he was awarded land in the South, a portion of which he immediately sold to pay for rations used by his troops, fulfilling his promise to personally guarantee payments for army provisions. Selling property and liquidating his personal finances left Greene financially strapped for a considerable time in the war's aftermath.

Greene declined offers of positions in the Articles of Confederation government and settled in Georgia where, without the use of slaves, he farmed an estate near Savannah. He died there of an apparent sunstroke on June 19, 1786, at age 44. He is buried in Johnson Square in Savannah.

DANIEL MORGAN

Subjected as a teenager to 500 lashes by a British official (Morgan said later that the British had miscounted; there were really only 499), Morgan's retribution came at Cowpens when his classic double envelopment utterly destroyed a famous British formation led by one of Britain's most feared commanders.

On January 17, 1781, in a remote region of South Carolina, a rough-hewn, self-taught American frontiersman named Daniel Morgan fought the most technically brilliant battle of the War of Independence.

Cowpens, as the place was named, was a military masterpiece: a classic, well-executed double envelopment that all but annihilated the larger opposing force.

The victory came at a crucial stage in the war—late in the conflict when the British were perilously close to attaining control of the southern colonies. Only a few weeks earlier, Nathanael Greene, newly appointed Commander of the Southern Army, had split his small force and sent Morgan to draw off a portion of Lord Charles Cornwallis' considerably larger army.

Morgan, a teamster by trade, was a veteran commander who had led American forces in Canada and at Saratoga. Forty-five years old, Morgan was a rugged six-footer with a leathery face notable for its prominent nose, high forehead, firm mouth and square chin. He carried a scar on his left cheek from a gunshot wound sustained during the French and Indian War.

When Morgan parted from his December meeting with Greene in North Carolina, he took with him about 600 men, 300 to 400 of whom were Continentals, the remainder experienced Virginia militia. Along the march and at the Cowpens site, he was joined by other militia units from Georgia and the Carolinas, eventually assembling a force numbering 1,000 or more.

Cornwallis, planning an invasion of North Carolina and fearing the potential threat posed to his left flank, obliged Greene by sending Lieutenant Colonel Banastre Tarleton after Morgan. Tarleton's youthful appearance belied his reputation as a tough, ruthless commander. Alleged by many to have committed atrocities against patriot Americans and Americans attempting to surrender—such as a massacre of American Continentals at Waxhaws, South Carolina, in May 1780—Tarleton set after Morgan leading 1,150 troops including the British Legion, an elite 450-man mixed force of infantry and cavalry, and veteran units such as the 71st Highlanders and the 17th Light Dragoons.

Morgan's trail was quickly picked up by Tarleton's scouts. As Morgan moved generally west, crossing into South Carolina, Tarleton's aggressive, fast-moving pursuit closed the gap between the armies. By the 16th of January Tarleton's chase brought him up against Morgan's force of Continentals and frontiersmen.

Morgan chose to make his stand at a place known locally as Cowpens, a well-known crossroads meeting place and pasturing ground for settlers' livestock. Morgan readied his force for battle in an area of about 500 yards on each side, sprinkled in places with trees but mostly cleared of underbrush by grazing cattle. A few evergreens interspersed among the red oak and hickory trees lent a hint of color to timbered areas otherwise made bare of foliage by the winter season. The ground sloped gradually to form a small rise that Morgan made the center of his position. A ravine on the right and a creek on the left shielded the field from British sweeps around the flanks. It was an ideal site for the sort of battle that Morgan envisioned, but his choice was controversial; a few miles to the rear, the Broad River, swollen in near flood stage, blocked the potential line of retreat. If Morgan lost the battle his army would be trapped.

By most reckoning, the choice was deliberate, a communication to his militia force some of whom were known to flee from battlefields after initial contact—that retreat was not an option. Alternately, others have suggested that perhaps Morgan simply did not want to risk being caught and attacked while attempting to cross a difficult river. Whatever his motivation, Morgan's exceptional use of his militia the following day demonstrated a sure understanding of their capabilities and limitations.

Morgan spent the night before the battle moving among his bivouacked troops, talking with them individually and in groups, spelling out his battle plan, encouraging them, laughing, and trading stories. To some of the companies who gathered around him that night, he showed the scars on his back from a lashing during the French and Indian War, received after he had flattened a British officer following an altercation. Morgan had been sentenced to 500 lashes, punishment that could kill a man. Morgan jokingly told his soldiers that he thought the person administering the lashes had miscounted and that he had really gotten only 499. To most, he spoke emotionally of past battles and the dream of American independence. He challenged his militia units to outdo one another during the coming battle. Even the most hardened veterans later recalled being drawn in by his words. Morning found Morgan's small army confident, well prepared, and ready to fight.

Sunrise at Cowpens on January 17, 1781, came crisp, clear, and very cold. Morgan was up early, if indeed he had slept at all, rallying his men. After spending considerable time questioning veterans in his army who had fought Tarleton in the past, Morgan understood his opponent: Tarleton would come fast and hard with a straight-ahead frontal assault.

Morgan chose to meet the attack with his army deployed in three lines. In front, hidden in the trees, he posted handpicked sharpshooters. Morgan's riflemen, with weapons that out-ranged the British muskets, were among the best in the Continental Army. He selected 150 from the elite group and used them to pick off the officers in Tarleton's dragoons who would lead the attack. After blunting the initial assault, the riflemen were to fall back 90 yards to join the second line composed of militia units of varying quality. Understanding the limitations of these mostly untrained troops, Morgan asked his militia units to get off two aimed shots before retreating and eventually join the third line held by Continental regulars another 150 yards to the rear. Morgan intended the militia units to withdraw to the left, move behind the third line, and then re-form and support the Continentals engaged there. Behind the third line farther to the rear, out of sight of the advancing British, Morgan posted his cavalry commanded by William Washington, a second cousin of George Washington.

Anxious to catch and destroy the Americans before additional militia reinforcements arrived, Tarleton had his soldiers up and on the march at 2 o'clock in the morning. Tarleton approached from the southeast along Green River Road, a trail that bisected the pastureland before shifting ever so slightly to the northwest at about the place where Andrew Pickens waited with his militia in the second American line. He reached Cowpens in the early morning hours, believing he had Morgan trapped in front of a swollen river on grounds well suited to his infamous dragoons. In fact, within the hour it was his own legendary unit that would face annihilation.

Tarleton paused only long enough to form his lines for battle. When his attack came soon after, it mirrored the plan anticipated by Morgan. After placing his two cannon in the center between units of British regulars and American loyalists, Tarleton launched a frontal assault led by dragoons on each flank. Posted in the trees, Morgan's sharpshooters in the first line took a horrific toll of dragoon officers, killing or wounding 15 in the initial minutes, blunting the attack of a force accustomed to acquiring quick supremacy over a battlefield.

The riflemen's deadly fire forced the dragoons, with many saddles now empty, to retreat and rejoin Tarleton. As the dragoons moved away, Morgan's riflemen moved back to join the second line held by militia units under the overall command of Andrew Pickens.

The dragoon's initial losses did not dissuade Tarleton. The British attack continued with infantry now moving up the rise towards Pickens' men in the second line. As Morgan had requested, most of the militia got off two aimed shots, knocking down more attackers perhaps as many as 40 percent of the British casualties were officers—before moving back toward the third line.

Interpreting the militia units' movement as a full retreat, Tarleton sent his mostly re-formed dragoons after them, intending to run them down. As the dragoons caught the Americans, Morgan sent William Washington's cavalry against them. Washington's fierce attack surprised and overwhelmed the dragoons who raced away from the battlefield in a headlong flight.

Despite the defeat of the dragoons, Tarleton continued to press his attack. The British infantry maintained its fast march up the slope, exchanging several rounds of fire with the Continentals and militia units assembled along the crest. At one point Morgan rode in front of the militia, rallying and steadying them, urging them to maintain their line.

With the initial assault units engaging the Americans and the infantry battle underway, Tarleton threw his reserve force, the 71st Highlanders, into the fight with orders to attack the American right flank. To the tumult and noise of the battle being waged higher on the hillside, the wail of bagpipes now added to the din as the Highlanders stepped quickly up the hill.

As the Highlanders approached, Colonel John Howard, commanding the American forces along the right flank, ordered his forces to face right to meet the British assault from that direction. Instead, Howard's men mistakenly began an orderly withdrawal. Seeing the Americans fall back, believing the battle to have been won, the British ranks broke into a wild charge. Morgan, noting the move of the American units and the developing charge of the British, raced to the scene slightly beyond the crest of the hill. Arriving as the oncoming British were drawing ever closer to the Americans, Morgan and Howard halted the militia, ordering them to face about and fire in unison.

They did so as the British were nearly upon them. The almost point-blank broadside devastated the British ranks. As the British attack first stopped and then fell apart, Howard ordered a bayonet charge that turned the battle into a rout. Pickens' militia force, having completed a full circuit behind the third line, re-emerged on the field, striking the British left flank. From the opposite side, Morgan sent William Washington's cavalry again into the battle, sweeping along the right and behind the British force, creating a double envelopment of Tarleton's army.

Engulfed and taking heavy casualties, the Highlanders and other British infantry units began surrendering en masse. With his cavalry already having fled the scene, for a time Tarleton and a few others fought on. Eventually, seeing the futility of continuing the fight, he and a small number of survivors raced away from the battlefield, barely escaping capture.

The battle of Cowpens lasted for about an hour. When it was over, Tarleton's army was shattered. Out of 1,150 in his attacking force, Tarleton lost 110 killed and 200 wounded, all the latter whom, along with 512 others, were made prisoners of the Americans. Morgan's men also captured hundreds of muskets as well as horses, cannons, and 35 wagons. American losses totaled 24 killed and 104 wounded.

The effect of the victory at Cowpens combined with Nathanael Greene's destruction of a large portion of Cornwallis' army at Guilford Court House two months later was to persuade Cornwallis to move into Virginia. There, at Yorktown, nine months after Cowpens and seven months after Guilford Court House, he surrendered his army.

While Cowpens was his magnum opus, earlier in the war Morgan had also played a notable role in another victory of enormous significance to the American cause. The surrender of General John Burgoyne's British army at Saratoga, New York—precipitated by battles fought at Freeman's Farm on September 19 and at Bemis Heights on October 7, 1777—induced France to enter the war as an ally of the United States.

In mid-summer 1777, Burgoyne moved south out of Quebec down the Hudson River Valley in an attempt to sever New England from the rest of the colonies. Two months into a slow moving campaign that began well but had more recently bogged down with difficulties, Burgoyne and his army of about 7,000 reached the Saratoga area. There, beset by supply and logistical problems, he faced the decision of whether to fall back (at least as far as Ticonderoga, captured early in the campaign) or press on in an attempt to reach Albany. He decided on the latter. At Albany he hoped to link up with forces he believed were being sent from New York City by General Henry Clinton.

Confronting him at Saratoga, and barring his way to Albany, was a sizable and growing American force under the nominal overall command of Horatio Gates. Included among Gates' troops was the newly formed Provisional Rifle Corps commanded by Daniel Morgan. Comprised of 500 specially selected marksmen, Morgan and his men were dispatched from Washington's army and arrived at Saratoga in mid-August. Gates placed his army about 10 miles south of Saratoga in ground suited for defense. The site held a commanding view of the surrounding area and controlled the only road to Albany, a track which ran nearby in a defile bounded by a steep ridge on one side and the Hudson River on the other.

The American left, commanded by Benedict Arnold and anchored on heights that dominated the battlefield, became the focal point for the first engagement. The importance of controlling that key terrain was obvious to both sides. Burgoyne sent three columns to take it. Arnold anticipated that one of the British wings would try to move around this flank by working through heavily forested ground that bordered the position on two sides. Arnold sent Morgan's frontiersmen and a light infantry company on a reconnaissance in force to identify and hold the attackers.

Morgan took his troops quickly through the woods. As they broke out of the trees they came upon a cleared field owned by a settler named John Freeman. From the open ground, Morgan's troops spotted an advance column of British troops that had moved ahead of the main force. Morgan's riflemen sighted quickly and killed or wounded nearly every officer in the advancing column. Stunned, the British troops began falling back. The Americans rushed the retreating troops further scattering them, but the charge brought them up against the main body of Burgoyne's army. Morgan then pulled his men back to the sheltering woods where they rested and re-formed during a lull in the action.

Both sides were reinforced and readied for fighting that erupted in spasms throughout the day. Posted in the woods, Morgan's sharpshooters exacted a fearful toll on British officers and artillerymen as the armies surged back and forth across the field. British artillery pieces were taken, lost, retaken, and lost again in the shifting fight. Finally, further reinforced late in the day, the British put enormous pressure on both American flanks, threatening to turn the right before darkness ended the fighting. The Americans returned to the defensive lines they had held at the start of the day. The British possessed the battlefield but had little else to show for 600 casualties. The American losses were about half that in killed and wounded.

What came next was an unanticipated interlude of two and a half weeks as Burgoyne decided to await possible word of Clinton moving towards him up the Hudson. The delay would prove costly. The size of the American force increased almost daily as militia units flooded into the area to join Gates' army. Already short of supplies and food, on October 3 Burgoyne placed his army on half rations. In the days ahead, his strength reduced by desertions, sickness, and casualties suffered at Freeman's farm and his patrols punished daily by Morgan's riflemen, Burgoyne's situation grew steadily more precarious. Finally, disregarding the advice of his senior commanders who counseled retreat, Burgoyne decided on another attempt to fight his way through the American lines.

In the early afternoon hours of October 7, Burgoyne launched 1,500 to 2,000 men, more than a third of his force, against the left wing of the American Army. Intended as a powerful reconnaissance in force that would either punch its way through or find soft spots for later exploitation, the British advanced against Americans deployed along the high ground known as Bemis Heights.

Gates, forewarned of Burgoyne's movement by American scouts, sent Morgan's riflemen to the far left and placed Morgan in command of the threatened flank. The British attack quickly ran into trouble up and down the entire line. In Morgan's sector, his marksmen pushed aside

Canadian and Indian allies of the British and moved forward to engage British regulars under the command of General Simon Fraser. Morgan's troops, although slightly outnumbered, broke up several British attempts to move west, eventually trapping Fraser's troops in a crossfire with another American unit.

As the struggle continued unabated, General Fraser was killed by rifle fire traditionally attributed to one of Morgan's sharpshooters. The loss of Fraser, the driving energy behind the British attack, and the arrival of American reinforcements soon after, forced the British into a disorganized retreat.

In about one hour the first phase of the battle cost Burgoyne another 400 men, six artillery pieces, and the loss by capture of almost an entire grenadier unit. Burgoyne himself was nearly killed by fire from Morgan's riflemen.

Fighting erupted again later in the day, initiated this time by an attack from the Americans. Although unauthorized by General Gates, Benedict Arnold led a furious assault against two key redoubts that defended the right side of the main British encampment. In desperate fighting the British managed to hold one of the strongpoints (named the Balcarres Redoubt after its commander). As other American forces were preparing to attack the second strongpoint, the Breymann Redoubt, Arnold shifted his focus to that sector, racing across the battlefield to lead a charge that forced its way through the gap between the two fortifications. The momentum of the assault carried Arnold's band around and to the rear of the position, there to connect with Morgan's riflemen circling in from the opposite side. The redoubt fell after a desperate fight in which the Hessian commander, Heinrich von Breymann, was killed, and Arnold was wounded. As darkness approached, an attempt by Hessian forces to retake the redoubt failed and led to the capture of most of the attacking force.

The battles at Freeman's Farm and Bemis Heights cost Burgoyne about 1,000 men killed and wounded. American losses approximated 500. Now, with the Americans in control of the Breymann Redoubt, Burgoyne's forward defensive line was breached, exposing the main British camp to attack. That night the British lit fires in their forward positions and withdrew under cover of darkness. For the next five days Burgoyne struggled unsuccessfully to extract his army and retreat to safety. Moving northwest with the British, Morgan's riflemen cut up Burgoyne's patrols along the intended escape route. By October 13, Burgoyne was surrounded by American forces that now outnumbered him by about three to one. On October 17, he surrendered his army.

The American victory at Saratoga changed the calculus of the war. Financial support for the impoverished Americans came more readily, from more donors and in larger amounts. Most importantly, France recognized American independence and entered into a formal alliance with the fledgling nation. Eventually the Spanish and Dutch also joined, in essence transforming the conflict into a world war.

Saratoga ranks as one of the most consequential battles in America's military history, and Daniel Morgan contributed significantly to the triumph. Like the lesser known battle at Cowpens with which his name is most associated, its reverberations echoed far beyond the immediate battlefield.

Before and After

Daniel Morgan was born in 1736 in Hunterdon County, New Jersey. A quarrelsome, cantankerous youth, he left home in his early teens after a fight with his father. Eventually settling on the Virginia frontier, he worked a variety of jobs clearing land, running a sawmill, and driving freight wagons. In a year he earned enough to buy his own team and began contracting out as a wagon master.

Morgan had little formal education. In his youth, his renown as a hard worker was matched by his reputation for general carousing: drinking, gambling, and brawling. The latter side of his character was in evidence when, at about age 18, he hired out to haul supplies for the British army during the French and Indian War. Sometime in 1854 he struck a British officer with his fists following an altercation. The 500 lashes he received as punishment left him with a lifelong enmity toward the British, a horrifically scarred back, and a visual aid that he used with good effect before Cowpens and other battles.

When the Continental Army was being formed after the battles of Lexington and Concord, the Virginia House of Burgesses chose Morgan to raise one of the colony's two rifle companies. In 10 days

Morgan recruited nearly 100 men—an elite group of snipers quickly named 'Morgan's Sharpshooters'—and in 21 days moved them all the way to Boston to support Washington's siege of the city.

Later in 1775, Morgan was chosen to lead three volunteer rifle companies in support of Benedict Arnold's wing in the invasion of eastern Canada. Arnold's expedition met with enormous difficulties in weather, terrain, and sickness on a grinding trek that lost or left behind 400 of the 1,000 or so who began the journey.

After an epic three-month march, Arnold's force crossed the St. Lawrence River and arrived before the walls of Quebec City. On December 31, 1775, the Americans attacked with Arnold and General Robert Montgomery each commanding a wing in a two-pronged assault. When, early in the fight, Montgomery was killed and Arnold wounded, the attack fell apart. Morgan took charge of Arnold's units and fought his way into the city, only to be surrounded when additional British forces came to the scene after Montgomery's units had withdrawn. Split up and under fire from all sides, Morgan's men surrendered piecemeal. Morgan refused to hand his sword to the British general, giving it instead to a local priest. Morgan was held captive until being released in an exchange of prisoners several months later.

Promoted in recognition of his service in Quebec, Morgan rejoined Washington's army as a colonel in early 1777. There he raised, and was given command of, a new infantry regiment. In mid-year, now also in command of the Provisional Rifle Corps, an elite unit of 500 hand-picked sharpshooters, Morgan was sent by Washington to harass the rear guard of General William Howe's army as Howe withdrew across New Jersey.

On August 30, Morgan joined Horatio Gates at Saratoga and played a consequential role in one of the most important victories of the war. After Saratoga, Morgan and his unit again rejoined Washington's army, then based near Philadelphia. Throughout 1778 Morgan's forces struck British outposts and supply lines in New Jersey, capturing prisoners and provisions.

In mid-1779 Morgan resigned from active service and returned to his home in Virginia.

Despite his robust outward appearance, Morgan was seldom in the best of health. The ordeal of the Quebec Expedition exacerbated long-prevalent problems with his legs and back. In addition to his physical circumstance, Morgan was frustrated by Congress' failure to promote him to brigadier general, believing that recent promotions favored officers better politically connected but with less experience and success on the battlefield.

Fifteen months later, after Gates' debacle at the battle of Camden threatened to cost the Americans the South and, perhaps, the war, Morgan put considerations of health and personal disappointment aside and returned to the Army. In October 1789, he was given command of a light infantry corps. Eleven days later he was promoted to brigadier general.

In December, at Charlotte, North Carolina, he met Nathanael Greene, the new commander of the Southern Army. As part of his unorthodox strategy, Greene sent Morgan on the journey that led to Cowpens. There, in mid-January just across the South Carolina border, Morgan won one of the most surprising, significant, and brilliantly handled battles of the war.

Aggravated by the Cowpens campaign, back problems again placed Morgan in constant pain. Less than three weeks after the battle, he returned to his Virginia farm. Five months later, in July, he briefly returned to active service, joining Lafayette in Virginia in an attempt to chase down Banastre Tarleton.

With a brief exception in 1794 when he was recalled to active service to help put down the Whisky Rebellion—the show of force resolved the issue with little turbulence—Morgan's life after the war was considerably more mellow. He built a new home, accumulated a considerable estate through investments in land, and joined the Presbyterian Church. After losing on his first attempt, Morgan was elected to the United States House of Representatives, serving a single term from 1797 to 1799.

Morgan died in 1802 on his 66th birthday. He is buried in Winchester, Virginia.

Deeper in the Shadows…

JOHN STARK

"The Hero of Bennington" was one of the most active of the American commanders in the northern war zone, serving from Bunker Hill through the end of the conflict. Stark's phrase "Live free or die," written in a letter to wartime colleagues, became New Hampshire's state motto.

Few American commanders in the northern war zone saw as much action or served so well as John Stark. Although his name is most often associated with one battle, in reality the 'Hero of Bennington,' as he became known, was a skillful combat commander who successfully led troops in several important engagements.

Stark was born in 1728 in Londonderry, New Hampshire, to Irish immigrant parents. The family moved to Derryfield (now Manchester) when Stark was eight years old. He lived in the Manchester area, where his childhood home still stands, for the remainder of his long life.

No absolutely reliable likeness of John Stark has survived. Existing depictions and contemporary accounts portray an angular face, prominent nose and deep-set blue eyes. Slightly above average in height, his physique was slender but muscular, reflecting a life of physical labor as a farmer and woodsman.

Stark received very little formal schooling. Self-possessed and confident to the point of occasional brusqueness, he was renowned for his capacity to command and for his exceptional personal courage.

Stark had led an adventurous life long before his service in the War of Independence. In 1752, at age 24, he was captured by Akenanki Indians and held for a year before being ransomed. By some accounts, he was befriended or adopted by a chief impressed with his bravery.

When the French and Indian War erupted in 1754, Stark was commissioned a second lieutenant in Rogers' Rangers, an early precursor of today's elite Ranger/Special Forces units. Stark campaigned with Rogers and his men in actions along the northern frontier before returning to Derryfield. It was a pattern he would follow for the rest of his life. When he was not called to arms he was at home on his farm with his family.

In 1758 Stark married Elizabeth "Molly" Page. Their marriage produced 11 children, even as their life together brought Molly her own notoriety. Before leading the attack at Bennington, Stark shouted to his men, "There are your enemies, the Red Coats and Tories. They are ours, or this night Molly Stark sleeps a widow!" Molly was known for opening her house as a hospital, nursing wounded soldiers, and on at least one occasion caring for them during a smallpox epidemic.

When the colonies' quarrel with Great Britain escalated into a shooting war, Stark's services were immediately called upon. Beginning at Bunker Hill, he saw action in some of the conflict's most notable campaigns and battles, leading troops in combat during the invasion of Canada and at Trenton, Princeton, Bennington, and Saratoga.

After the shooting began at Lexington and Concord on April 19, 1775, Boston became the immediate focus of the war. Stark accepted command of the 1st New Hampshire regiment on April 23 and marched his men to the Boston area. Pushed forward by Stark, the regiment was among the first of the units that arrived on the scene from outside Massachusetts.

Forewarned of a possible British pre-emptive attack, on the night of June 16, the Americans occupied high ground at Dorchester Heights, Breed's Hill, and Bunker Hill. Daybreak on June 17 revealed a hurriedly built American redoubt on the crest of Breed's Hill. With the Boston garrison now at risk, the British brought the redoubt and the American force—initially a few hundred untrained militia under the command of William Prescott—under intense fire from ships in the harbor and from positions around the city. Lacking both guns and men, and about to be confronted by a major attack, Prescott called for reinforcements. Although some units refused to risk running the Charleston Neck gauntlet, which was under bombardment, Stark responded immediately, leading his regiment across the narrow strip of land that connected the American camp with positions on the hill.

Given authority by Prescott to deploy his men where he saw the greatest need, Stark noted vulnerable areas below and to the left of Breed's Hill where the British might land troops and flank the Americans, as well as at an unfortified gap on a section of beach along the Mystic River.

To address the first threat, Stark's men, along with a Connecticut unit led by William Knowlton, added shelter to a two-rail fence that stretched down the left side of the hill toward the river. Perhaps even more serious at the outset was a gap area along the beach. There, an open, unobstructed space between the end of the fence line and the river had been left undefended. Stark's men hurriedly piled rocks to construct a rudimentary defensive wall that extended to the water's edge. When the barricades were completed, Stark deployed his men three-deep behind the wall, where they crouched and readied themselves for the British attack.

Stark's anticipation proved correct.

In the early afternoon a British force under the command of General Sir William Howe began landing in large numbers. Led by Royal Fusiliers, the attack came straight at Stark's position on the extreme left of the American line. Stark had his men wait until the British almost reached the wall, then stand and fire in unison. (By some accounts, he had placed a stake about 100 feet in front of the fence and ordered his men not to fire until the British moved past that marker.) The point-blank barrage, delivered literally in the faces of the Fusiliers, broke the assault, instantly felling as many as 90 of the attackers and sending the survivors into a panicked retreat.

The British tried Stark's defenses twice more with infantry charges carried out over bodies that now littered the ground. Each charge was blown apart with heavy losses to the British who then abandoned the effort in favor of assaults elsewhere along Breed's Hill.

As the battle continued, the British pressed attacks against fortifications held by Prescott, Stark, and others. Eventually, persistent thrusts, particularly against Prescott's redoubt, and a shortage of ammunition caused the Americans to retreat. Stark's men were on the field to the last, providing covering fire as Prescott's troops withdrew across Bunker Hill. The disciplined retreat conducted by Stark and Knowlton prevented the encirclement of the main body of American troops and drew praise even from British General John Burgoyne, who witnessed the battle.

The British paid a heavy price for their 'victory'. The assault units suffered more than 40 percent casualties—226 dead and 828 wounded (some historians place the figure as high as 1,150 total casualties)—out of the 2,500 or so who saw action that day. A disproportionate amount of the British casualties were officers: nearly 100 were killed or wounded. The largest portion of the 450 American casualties (out of perhaps 1,500 who were engaged at some time during the fight) came at the close of the battle when Prescott's men ran out of ammunition and fell back from the redoubt.

Later that year, Stark was again in the midst of heavy action leading troops during Washington's Christmas Day attack on Trenton, New Jersey.

Stark led a bayonet charge on a Hessian regiment that broke the unit's resistance, forcing it first into retreat and then into eventual surrender.

In mid-1777, Stark disregarded a request to move his troops directly to Saratoga to join other American forces preparing to receive British General John Burgoyne's attack coming down from Quebec. Instead, he took his New Hampshire units to the area of Willoomsac, New York, a few miles from Bennington, Vermont. There on August 16 he defeated a mixed force sent by Burgoyne to forage for food, horses, and draft animals. Burgoyne, his supply situation becoming more desperate each day, was not aware of Stark's presence, believing the area to be only lightly defended.

The initial force designated by Burgoyne consisted of about 800 dismounted Brunswick dragoons commanded by Lieutenant Colonel Frederick Baum. While on the march, Baum's column was joined by groups of Loyalists, Canadians, Indians, and a company of British riflemen.

Lead elements from each army collided on August 14. Stark's men, having identified the attackers, fell back after destroying a bridge and slowing down the advance of Baum's main force. Baum, realizing that he was confronted by larger than anticipated numbers of American defenders, sent a message to Burgoyne asking for reinforcements.

Though known to history as the Battle of Bennington, the fighting actually took place about 10 miles west, across the New York/Vermont border near Willoomsac in extreme east central New York. There, amid heavily timbered rolling hills cut by the Willoomsac River a short distance to the south, the two sides gathered their forces and prepared for combat.

For the next day and a half both armies waited through continuous heavy rains. Baum built a fortification on the crest of a hill, hoping the major battle would be delayed until additional units sent by Burgoyne reached him. Stark sent skirmishers to test the Brunswickers' defenses, killing about 30 of Baum's Indian allies in the firefight that developed.

On the 15th, reinforcements for both armies arrived, marching through downpours that made travel difficult. Burgoyne sent Baum 550 Hessians under the command of Heinrich von Breymann. Stark's original force of about 1,500 was joined by 350 of Vermont's Green Mountain Boys, some Massachusetts riflemen, and early the next day, by some Stockbridge Indian allies. Eventually, Stark's force numbered about 2,000 men.

At midday on August 16, the rains finally ceased and Stark prepared his force for battle, sending flanking units into the woods on either side of the German lines. For a time, the move caused Baum to believe the militiamen were falling back. In mid-afternoon Stark opened heavy fire on Baum's fortification, which was by then surrounded by American units. Several Loyalist companies and Baum's Indian allies fled or surrendered when their positions were overrun.

Baum's dragoons fought on, encircled and trapped in the redoubt at the top of the hill. Eventually, running low on ammunition, their supply wagon having been destroyed, Baum led a saber charge in a desperate attempt to break through the American lines. Baum was killed during the charge, and the dragoons surrendered

The battle then progressed to a second phase. As Stark's men were busy disarming their prisoners, von Breymann arrived with the reinforcements sent by Burgoyne. Seeing the Americans occupied, von Breymann ordered an immediate attack. As the Americans at first fell back, struggling to regroup under fire, Green Mountain Boys under the command of Seth Warren arrived to reinforce Stark. Heavy fighting erupted and persisted until dark, when both sides broke off the action. When the fighting ended, von Breymann had lost nearly a quarter of his men and all of his cannons. The next day, he began a rapid retreat that took him back to Saratoga where he rejoined Burgoyne's main force.

The battle cost the British and their Hessian, Canadian, and Indian allies 207 killed and wounded and another 700 captured, against American losses of 30 killed and 40 wounded. For the British, the consequences were devastating.

Stark's triumph at Bennington was preliminary to the American victory at Saratoga and contributed greatly to it. In addition to reducing the British force by nearly a thousand men, the loss cost Burgoyne the 'eyes and ears' of his most capable scouts, as his Indian allies drifted steadily away. Most directly, Bennington prevented Burgoyne from addressing his shortages of food, supplies, and transportation. Burgoyne's immobility and the general condition of his army led to the action that began the next month around Saratoga.

After Bennington, Stark took his force to Saratoga where, after the battle at Freeman's Farm, he contributed further to the ultimate victory by blocking Burgoyne's prospective escape route back toward Lake George and Lake Champlain. Foreclosed of any possibility of retreat and effectively surrounded by American forces, Burgoyne surrendered on October 17.

Later, Stark served as Commander of the Northern Department on three occasions between 1778 and 1781. After the war, as he always did, Stark returned to his farm in Derryfield.

In 1809, veterans of the Battle of Bennington held a reunion. Stark was ill at the time and could not attend, so instead he sent a letter which was read to the assembled veterans. Stark closed his note with "Live free or die. Death is not the worst enemy." Stark's phrase "Live free or die" became New Hampshire's motto.

Stark died in 1822 at age 94, the oldest surviving American general from the War of Independence. He is buried at Manchester, New Hampshire.

JOHN GLOVER

Glover was the only American officer to hold senior command of both infantry and naval forces. Glover's adroit handling of a flotilla at night in rain and fog rescued Washington's army from Long Island. Four months later in even worse conditions, his "amphibious regiment" ferried American forces across the Delaware River for a surprise attack on Trenton, New Jersey.

John Glover's contributions to the American cause were among the most exceptional of any participant. During the course of the conflict he commanded infantry forces as well as warships and transport flotillas: he was the only American officer who led both major land and naval forces.

Glover was born in 1732 in Danvers, Massachusetts. After his father died when he was four years old, his mother moved the family to Marblehead where Glover made his home for the rest of his life. Industrious and energetic, Glover worked a variety of jobs—shoemaker, sailor, merchant, fisherman—while growing up. He eventually acquired a fishing schooner and used the profits from that successful venture to purchase several additional vessels. By his late '20s, Glover was a pillar of the Marblehead community.

Not long after, he was chosen to command a militia unit formed from residents of the surrounding area. Initially known as the Marblehead Regiment, the unit was later redesignated the 14th Continental Regiment. Probably as a result both of the seafaring background of many of the regiment's members and Glover's leadership, the unit became known for its exceptional discipline.

At the outset of the war, Glover took his militia unit to Boston to join the siege of the city, although he was away building fortifications elsewhere along the coast when the clash occurred at Breed's Hill. In Cambridge a few weeks later, a chance meeting with Washington developed into a life-long friendship between the two men. Glover, like Washington, was known for his good taste and decorum. Dressed impeccably and equipped with two silver pistols and a broadsword, Glover was regarded as one of the best uniformed officers in the Continental Army.

As their relationship grew, Washington asked Glover to create a naval force that could disrupt the otherwise unfettered flow of supplies to the British forces. Glover was placed in charge of the entire operation—organizing the effort, acquiring the vessels, converting them to wartime use, and planning the campaign. Glover donated his own vessel, the *Hannah*, and six other ships to raid British supply vessels. Historically, that event has assumed considerable significance: many have called *Hannah* the first ship in the United States Navy.

The capture of a British ordnance brig, H.M.S. *Nancy*, by one of Glover's captains provided the supply-starved Continentals with 2,000 muskets, 100,000 flints, 30,000 rounds of artillery ammunition, 30 tons of musket balls, and a 13-inch mortar.

On two occasions in the early months of the war, Glover's nautical skills helped save the American cause.

In August 1776, American forces were trapped on Long Island. Washington, hemmed in on Brooklyn Heights and facing overwhelming numbers, asked Glover to organize the evacuation of the American Army. Glover delivered an operational masterpiece: 9,000 troops, horses, artillery, and supplies were ferried safely across the East River to Manhattan. The nighttime operation, skillfully conducted in rain and fog, saved Washington's army.

In December of the same year, the 'amphibious regiment,' as Glover's unit was nicknamed, saw its last, but most famous action. On Christmas Day it was Glover's unit that took Washington's army across the Delaware River for the surprise attack on Trenton, New Jersey. In bitterly cold weather that changed from rain to sleet to snow during the pre-dawn crossing, Glover's men navigated the ice floes and the tricky shallows, delivering Washington's force along with horses and 18 field guns to the New Jersey shore.

The operation started at sundown when Glover's men began moving the assault units through the ice-clogged current. Near midnight, a blinding snow storm decreased visibility to almost zero. Despite the obstacles, the operation was superbly handled—and then repeated, as Glover's men carried the army safely back across the Delaware to Pennsylvania when the day was over. The surprise victory provided the impoverished Americans with several cannons, a small mountain of supplies, and 918 Hessian prisoners. More importantly, after a series of dismal American defeats, the triumph at Trenton kept the Revolution alive.

In the interval between the two naval operations, Glover led a major force in land combat for the first time. Following the evacuation of Long Island, the British occupied New York City while Washington's army encamped on Manhattan Island. After a considerable delay, the British commander, General Sir William Howe, attempted to cut the American Army off by seaborne flanking moves that would close the Americans' remaining avenues of escape.

Howe's first move, landing troops at a narrow causeway called Throgs Neck, was rebuffed by a Pennsylvania rifle company. The second, six days later, came at Pell's Point against four Massachusetts infantry regiments commanded by Glover. As the British and Hessian troops landed, formed, and advanced, Glover arrayed his 750 men in successive lines, placing them, where possible, behind stone walls. Glover had his men hold their fire until the Hessians approached within a hundred feet before the first line rose from behind their sheltering wall and poured a withering fire into the attackers. The regiment holding the first line delivered seven volleys before falling back. The regiment in the second line held for seventeen more. As Glover's men moved to their third line, the British called off the attack.

The stands made by the Pennsylvanians at Throgs Neck and Glover's men at Pell's Point bought Washington sufficient time to extricate himself from Manhattan. By the time the British were ready to move again, Washington had taken his army to White Plains.

For a time soon after, Glover temporarily left active service to care for his sick wife. He rejoined the Army in February 1777 after a personal appeal from George Washington. Promoted to brigadier general, Glover saw service in the Saratoga campaign in 1777 and in Rhode Island in 1778.

The significance of Glover's role at Saratoga is evidenced by his presence in the famous painting by John Trumble depicting British General John Burgoyne's surrender to the American commander, Horatio Gates. After the American victory, Glover was assigned to escort the defeated army—2,139 British, 2,022 Hessians, and 850 Canadians—to Cambridge, Massachusetts, a task that he accomplished with his usual proficiency. For the remainder of his time in uniform, his skills were employed guarding the Hudson River to prevent British forces from moving north along the waterway from their main base in New York City.

For Glover, as with many American leaders, victory came at a cost. He suffered for a time financially as the shipping industry faltered. His first wife, Hannah, died during the war and his oldest son was lost at sea while being sent to England as a prisoner of war.

In poor health, Glover retired from the Army in 1782. He returned to Marblehead, where he served in several local offices until his death, from hepatitis, in 1797 at age 64. He is buried in Marblehead.

"LIGHT HORSE HARRY" LEE

Along with Nathanael Greene, Lee was one of a small number of senior leaders who saw extensive service in both the northern and southern theaters of war. His success as a raider led Washington to award him an independent command. Later, "Lee's Legion" supported Greene's successful campaign in the South.

Few leaders in any of the nation's conflicts have fought in as many battles in such varied terrain as Henry Lee. Along with Nathanael Greene and Daniel Morgan, Lee was one of a small number of American commanders who saw extensive service in both the northern and southern theaters of operation.

Lee, a Virginian, was posted with Washington's forces in the north from late 1776 until early 1780 and saw action in many of the major engagements fought throughout the northeast during that time. "An active and daring officer, high-spirited and meticulous," his abilities first attracted attention in the fall of 1776 when, on his own initiative, the 20-year-old commander led his cavalry unit on raids that helped provision Washington's supply-starved army. In December of that year, Lee and his troopers provided reconnaissance that supported Washington's successful attack on Trenton.

With most of the Army in winter garrison, Lee remained active during the bitter early months of 1777, attacking supply lines and harassing British forces in a series of raids that captured desperately needed provisions and enhanced the morale of the impoverished American forces. On one occasion he returned with 20 wagons full of supplies and on another with a small herd of well-fed livestock taken from the British. His achievements prompted several senior commanders, Henry Knox and Daniel Morgan among them, to successfully prevail upon Washington to deploy Lee and his horsemen as a detached, independent command.

Lee's repeated forays against supply depots and outposts earned him the sobriquet "Light Horse Harry" and provoked frequent clashes as the British tried repeatedly, without success, to run him down. Later that year, Lee's forces drew first blood when the British army moved across the Delaware toward Philadelphia. In a surprise attack against a larger force, Lee's raiders killed and captured sizable numbers of a British cavalry unit while sustaining only one casualty, a cavalryman slightly wounded.

Lee's strike against the invading British was a precursor to a series of actions over the next several months. In September, Lee and his men fought alongside Nathanael Greene defending the center of the American line at Brandywine, Pennsylvania. As the British push toward Philadelphia continued, Lee resumed attacks on their supply lines. A month later, Lee and his men served as Washington's personal bodyguard during the battle of Germantown. In December, Lee's performance in an action commanded by Greene was lauded in communications to Washington.

That winter, with the British encamped in Philadelphia and the Americans freezing at Valley Forge, Lee and his cavalry, now joined by a small number of Iroquois warriors, returned repeatedly from successful raids with vital stores for Washington's beleaguered troops. Frustrated by Lee's success, the British dispatched a full regiment of cavalry with orders to pursue Lee and capture or kill him. The effort nearly succeeded, but in a remarkable encounter at Scot's Farm, Lee repulsed the attempt and inflicted casualties on the attackers.

Washington's high regard for Lee was made apparent by the offer, in March 1778, of a position on Washington's staff. Lee declined, preferring to command troops in the field. Soon after, he was assigned as commander of a newly formed unit, composed of cavalry and Iroquois Indian allies, responsible directly to Washington.

May 1778 saw a change of command in British forces from William Howe to Henry Clinton, and with it a repositioning of British forces out of Philadelphia and back to New York City. Clinton's decision to return to New York was precipitated in part by Lee's continued success in interrupting the extended supply lines necessary to sustain his army in Philadelphia. In large measure, however, the effect of the move was to exchange one difficulty for another. Rather quickly the British found themselves bottled up in New York City. Blocked by Washington, the British supply routes to and from the interior were repeatedly slashed by Lee's fast-moving horsemen.

The spring and summer of 1779 brought reconnaissance duty along the Hudson River. At Washington's request, Lee's troopers gathered the intelligence information that led to General Anthony Wayne's successful July 16 attack on Stony Point, a key garrison situated on the river not far from New York City.

Held in reserve at Stony Point, a month later Lee's unit formed the main striking force in an equally audacious assault on the British fortification at Paulus Hook in present-day New Jersey. Located across the Hudson from New York City, Paulus Hook was a small, thumb-like projection that jutted out into the river. After careful reconnaissance of a fortress considered virtually impregnable by the British, Lee developed a detailed plan of attack. Provided with several hundred additional infantrymen by Washington, Lee's assault on August 18, 1779 killed or wounded 50 British soldiers and led to the capture of 150 more. Not a shot was fired during the initial attack as Lee's forces burst through the abatis that ringed the fort. Striking with bayonets in the pre-dawn hours, Lee's men scaled parapets and battered their way into a blockhouse. In a few minutes, it was over. Lee lost two killed and three wounded.

On September 22, the Continental Congress presented Lee with a gold medal for his actions at Paulus Hook. During the entire course of the war, Lee was the only officer below the rank of general to receive a similar award.

As Lee's cavalry continued to probe and reconnoiter British forces, Washington added to Lee's duties by directing him to build and operate an extensive spy ring inside New York City, the headquarters of British forces in America.

Four years into the war, Lee's service in the North ended and he was ordered to join American forces operating in the South under the command of General Nathanael Greene. As the months ahead would reveal, it was an assignment that would further burnish his already extraordinary reputation.

Lee, promoted to lieutenant colonel, was assigned to work independently under Greene's overall command. He took with him a newly formed unit, an elite force of cavalry and hand-picked infantry. By the standards of the American Army, "Lee's Legion", as the unit quickly became known, was well supplied and equipped. The Legion's distinctive green and white uniforms were personally designed by Lee.

In Carolina, Greene had met with the South's guerrilla leaders, Francis Marion, Andrew Pickens, Thomas Sumter, and Elijah Clarke to outline his concept of operations for the theater. Indeed, Greene intended to use the irregular forces as an integral part of his scheme. Henry Lee arrived not long after, on January 13, 1781, with about 100 cavalrymen and 180 infantry. As Greene assembled and trained his force, major roles were initially given to Lee and Marion. After a brief period of friction between the two, they came to respect each other's abilities and developed close bonds that led to a number of well-planned and executed joint operations.

The first, at Georgetown, South Carolina, met with only partial success but paved the way for the several more promising outcomes that rather quickly followed.

In the coming weeks, Lee, sometimes alone, sometimes in concert with Marion, took Fort Watson, Fort Motte, Fort Granby and Fort Galphin. With Andrew Pickens, he captured Forts Grierson and Cornwallis, dual bastions that guarded Albany, Georgia. At Fort Watson, Lee and Marion, without artillery and lacking time for a protracted siege, erected overnight a rectangular structure tall enough to overlook the formidable stockade. From a platform at the top, American sharpshooters poured fire into the fort, every part of which was now visible to them, while two assault teams moved through the surrounding abatis, forcing the post's surrender. At a cost of two killed and six wounded, Lee and Marion inflicted losses on the British units and their Hessian allies and captured 114 prisoners. It was a precursor of things to come.

As he moved through the vast distances of the Carolina-Georgia countryside, Lee became renowned for his rapid movements—an advantage gained by periodically dismounting his cavalrymen and mounting his foot-weary infantry on their horses.

In February 1781, Lee's Legion shielded Greene's masterful retreat to the Dan River—the historic "race to the Dan"—while pursued by the full might of Cornwallis' army. During this epic campaign, Lee's unit faced the British cavalry in the South, led by Lieutenant Colonel Banastre Tarleton, for the first time. Enraged when Tarleton's unit killed an unarmed American bugle boy, Lee led a charge that shattered the larger British force and captured 40 prisoners.

As Greene readied his forces for the forthcoming battle at Guilford Court House, he sent Lee and militia commander Andrew Pickens to harass Cornwallis and Tarleton. After re-crossing the Dan on February 25, Lee and Pickens intercepted a contingent of 400 Loyalist recruits on the way to join Tarleton who was operating nearby. Lee, whose men wore uniforms similar to Tarleton's dragoons, tricked the Loyalists into an engagement. In a controversial battle, soon known as Pyle's Massacre after the Tory commander John Pyle, Lee and Pickens' combined force killed more than one hundred Loyalists, wounded others, and sent the remainder fleeing into the surrounding forests.

Meanwhile, Greene was maneuvering Cornwallis into battle at a site carefully selected near the remnants of an abandoned public building called Guilford's Court House. As the armies closed on each other, Lee's forces collided again with Tarleton's cavalry. In a bitter clash preliminary to the main engagement Lee's force clearly bested Tarleton's vaunted dragoons, killing several and forcing Tarleton's horsemen to retreat from the field. During the encounter, Lee had a horse shot from under him but caught a riderless British mount and continued to lead the battle. When the major fight between the two armies occurred soon after, Lee's Legion was active at several points on the battlefield, inflicting losses on the British and Hessian units that marched against Greene's three defensive lines.

Though Cornwallis possessed the field at the end of a bloody day, for the British Guilford Court House was a pyrrhic victory. Cornwallis' heavy losses and the exhausted condition of his troops prompted him to retreat to the coast. Guilford Court House was a turning point for Greene and for American prospects in the South.

Greene subsequently moved into South Carolina with the bulk of the American forces. Lee and Francis Marion were sent to attack British posts in North Carolina. They did so successfully, reducing and confining the major British presence in the South to the port cities of Savannah and Charleston. Scattered outposts also remained on the Georgia coast, but were soon overcome, some by Lee's Legion and militia forces commanded by Pickens. By mid-June, the British had abandoned or been driven from the interior of the Carolinas and Georgia. Cornwallis moved his major combat units into Virginia where fate and George Washington awaited him.

Later in the summer of 1781, Greene sent Lee to harass British units in and around Charleston. On September 8, the British attempted to break the American ring that enclosed them by initiating battle at Eutaw Springs. With Lee's troops seeing major action, the British were initially driven from the field. When the desperately hungry, ill-clad American troops slowed to loot the main British camp, the tide of battle turned and the struggle transformed into a bitter, close-in fight in which both sides were heavily battered. While the British again claimed victory, heavy casualties—almost twice as many as sustained by the Americans—forced them to fall back to Charleston. They remained there for the duration of the war, having been drained so severely they could no longer undertake major offensive operations. Greene, aided superbly by Morgan, Lee, Marion, Pickens and other militia leaders, had won the war in the South.

Still, though confined to Savannah and Charleston, some British forces remained intact.

Greene chafed at the stalemate and sent Lee to Virginia to solicit reinforcements from Washington. Lee reached Washington at Yorktown and was on hand to observe Cornwallis' surrender on October 19. The British capitulation freed Washington to send brigades commanded by Anthony Wayne and Arthur St. Clair, as Lee hurried back to provide the details to Greene. For the remaining weeks of 1781, Greene tightened the ring around Charleston. Lee led his Legion on a series of raids and maneuvers that kept the British penned inside the city.

Late in January 1782, with the end of the war clearly in sight, Lee received approval to resign his commission and return home to marry Matilda Lee, a second cousin. George Washington and several other notables attended the March wedding ceremony. (Matilda died in 1790. Three years later, Lee married Anne Hill Carter, a union that produced six children.)

Lee's remarkable service during the nation's War of Independence was over. As the future would reveal, he was destined to lead a particularly eventful life. Unlike his military career, however, not all would be crowned with success or glory.

Lee was born January 29, 1756, near Dumfries, Virginia. He graduated from what is now Princeton University in 1773, intent on pursuing a legal career. Those plans were discarded when the war broke out two years later. Lee was offered, and immediately accepted, a commission as a captain in a Virginia dragoon unit. His remarkable service in the field followed; he remained a commander of combat troops until the fighting subsided.

Lee's life after the war was a mixture of politics, periodically renewed military service, failed business ventures, and financial hardship.

Elected to the Congress of the Confederation in 1785, Lee was a proponent for a strong federal government, a view not universally held by several other of his Virginia colleagues including Patrick Henry,

Richard Henry Lee, Edmund Randolph, and George Mason. By a narrow margin Lee and his friend James Madison, both delegates to the Virginia Constitutional Convention, secured Virginia's vote in favor of ratification.

Other public offices followed. In 1790, he was elected to the Virginia House of Burgesses. A year later he became Governor of Virginia. As governor, he introduced a form of taxation based on income rather than property, a forerunner of the graduated income tax aimed in part at easing some of the tax burden for property owners. In 1799, with George Washington's vote publically cast in his favor, Lee won a close election to the United States House of Representatives. He served one term before retiring from politics.

Lee's ventures into public life were interspersed with renewed periods of military service. In 1794, he was commissioned a major general and recalled to duty to help put down the so-called Whiskey Rebellion. Centered in Pennsylvania, the rebellion was an armed uprising in protest of the government's tax on distilled spirits. Although Lee personally opposed the tax, he believed the rebellion was unlawful. He served as one of the key leaders in a force of nearly 13,000 militiamen that put down the insurrection without bloodshed.

In 1798, when war threatened with France, Lee was one of four officers designated to serve as major generals under Washington, who was called out of retirement to serve if the need arose.

In 1808, with a new war with England seemingly imminent, he was again commissioned as a major general. Lee actively recruited and trained troops for the fledgling army, but returned to civilian life when the threat receded. Ironically, when war with Britain did erupt four years later, Lee's poor health prevented him from accepting command of the United States Army—an honor he had sought for much of his adult life—when it was offered by President Madison.

For several years Lee had been chronically ill. As his condition worsened he was prevented from moving to a more favorable climate by travel restrictions imposed early in the war. His health further deteriorated when he was beaten by a mob in Baltimore after defending a newspaper editor friend who wrote in opposition to the war. Nearly killed by the savage pummeling, he was hospitalized for an extended period before being allowed to travel.

Lee's physical condition was but one of the difficulties that confronted him in his later years. Beginning in the mid to late 1790s, Lee began turning to land speculation and various money-making schemes. All of them failed. Over the coming years, he lost the plantation and other businesses inherited from his wife, and sank further into debt.

Unable to pay his mounting bills, in April 1809 he was forced into debtor's prison. He was incarcerated for a year before being released after declaring bankruptcy. It was an ignominious episode in the life of a man who 20 years earlier had been rightfully hailed as one of the infant nation's greatest heroes.

In 1811, Lee finished a book of memoirs that was well received and again made him a national figure. Living frugally, he was a sometime White House guest of his friend and admirer James Madison. The health issues that prevented him from accepting Madison's offer of military service did not diminish a friendship that remained steadfast throughout the remainder of Lee's life.

Eventually, seeking a climate more conducive to his health, and perhaps trying to avoid lingering problems associated with indebtedness, Lee was able to move to the West Indies. He remained in the islands until February 1818, and had reached Georgia on his journey home when his health took a precipitous downturn. He died March 25 while staying at the residence of Nathanael Greene's daughter. He was buried with full military honors at Dungeness, Georgia, alongside Greene. In 1913, his remains were reinterred at Lee Chapel on the campus of Washington and Lee University in Lexington, Virginia.

Today, Lee's name is primarily recalled for two reasons. The first is the remarkable "first in war, first in peace, first in the hearts of his countrymen" eulogy he delivered at George Washington's funeral on December 26, 1799. Indeed, it is a mark of the great respect with which he was held at the time that Congress asked him to give the funeral oration for America's greatest citizen.

The second is that he bequeathed to the nation a son, who would go on to achieve a military reputation of his own, named Robert E. Lee.

The Guerrilla Leaders

Favored by circumstances of topography, thin populations scattered at great distances, and the usual absence of large numbers of Continental soldiers deployed in the area, the southern theater of operations proved fruitful ground for the emergence of irregular forces. Several such units were formed throughout Georgia and the Carolinas, and all at times operated independently. On occasion most assisted or served under regular forces, standing side by side with Continentals in battle or functioning as extensions of primary campaigns by scouting, gathering intelligence, or raising havoc with British supply lines and outlying fortifications.

For the most part, the men in the guerrilla bands served without pay and supplied their own horses, weapons, and food. Leadership demanded special qualities. Fortunately for the American cause, several exceptional commanders of irregular forces emerged during the war. Most notable among them were Francis Marion and Andrew Pickens.

FRANCIS MARION

A master of terrain and a superb leader of irregular forces, the "Swamp Fox" led guerilla units in the Carolinas and Georgia. Initially operating almost alone after a series of catastrophic American defeats, Marion later teamed with other partisan leaders in removing British presence from the interior of the Southern colonies.

Thanks to a Walt Disney television series, Francis Marion, "The Swamp Fox," is probably the best known of the American guerrilla leaders.

Marion came to the fore after American forces sustained a series of near-catastrophic losses in the South: defeats at Monck's Corner, South Carolina, on April 14, 1780, and at Waxhaws, near Lancaster, South Carolina, on May 29, bracketed the loss of an entire American army at Charleston on May 12. After the rout at Waxhaws, Marion raised a small troop, less than 75 men at the outset, that for a time was almost the only American force opposing the British in all of South Carolina.

Partisan leaders like Marion found the interior of South Carolina particularly well suited to guerrilla operations. In that region a spider web network of rivers and creeks slices through miles of marshes creating a maze of secluded hideaways. In the east, the coastal zone rises gradually to a plateau that in the northwest gives way to forests and the mountains that form the Blue Ridge. Along the coast a remarkable number of bays, inlets, and small islands add further numbers of prospective safe havens and ambush sites.

Marion and his colleagues were intimately familiar with the landscape and adept at exploiting the advantages it afforded them. Indeed, for considerable periods during the war small bands of partisans striking suddenly and then disappearing into the vastness of the interior were almost all that kept the rebellion alive in the South.

The American Revolution was not Francis Marion's first acquaintance with guerrilla warfare. As a junior officer during the French and Indian War, he fought against the Cherokees in campaigns that were notable for the brutalities inflicted by both sides. Marion was a keen observer of the Indians' fighting style and incorporated their tactics—knowledge of the terrain, ambushes, and fast-moving raids—into his own operations.

Forty-three years old when the war began, Marion was described as notably handsome, soft spoken, frugal in his habits, and a strict disciplinarian. He was small in stature and walked with a limp because of slightly malformed legs.

For Marion, the War of Independence began at Charleston in 1776 when he commanded a battery that helped repel an attempted British invasion. The Americans' early success was short-lived, however. On October 9, 1779, Marion was in the field at Savannah during the Patriots' failed attempt to take the city. Savannah was but one of an entire series of calamities that befell the Americans during this time, culminating with General Benjamin Lincoln's surrender of an entire American army at Charleston on May 12, 1780, followed a short time later by Horatio Gates' horrific defeat at Camden on August 16.

Through a combination of circumstances, Marion was not present at either debacle. For the next many months his command would operate almost alone, setting ambushes, raiding supply caravans, and striking isolated columns. Marion and his men became a persistent thorn in the side of British authorities. His "Swamp Fox" nickname came from an episode in November 1780. After British dragoon commander Banastre Tarleton and his elite unit failed to catch Marion after a tortuous seven hour, 26-mile chase, Tarleton was alleged to have said "As for this damned old fox, the Devil himself could not catch him."

Before the battle at Camden, Horatio Gates—not trusting Marion and his irregulars—had sent Marion off on a scouting mission. Marion thus missed the battle, but four days later, on August 20, intercepted and defeated a British detachment, releasing 160 American prisoners taken during the Camden fight and capturing 20 British guards.

For a time after Camden the British and their Loyalist allies had almost free rein in the Carolinas and Georgia. Their efforts to establish a string of linked posts met with general success except at Willtown, where their force was driven off by Marion at the battle of Black Mingo on September 28.

Marion's successes after Camden and Black Mingo were represented in a series of strikes, supply raids, ambushes, and intelligence gathering reconnaissance missions conducted throughout large portions of the Carolinas. British commander Lord Charles Cornwallis later said that "Marion had so wrought the minds of the people, partly by the terror of his threats and cruelty of his punishments and partly by the promise of plunder, that there was scarcely an inhabitant that was not in arms against us." Dissenters would reply that the depredations committed by Cornwallis' own forces and his Loyalist allies were perhaps even more consequential.

Marion's days of operating almost in isolation against the British ended when Nathanael Greene took command in the South in late 1780. There were at the time about 8,000 British and Loyalist troops based in the Carolinas and Georgia. Greene's notion was to go after them using the South's partisan forces in concert with his Continental Army regiments and other militia units. In the months ahead, Marion would often be teamed with "Light Horse Harry" Lee in clearing the British from the interior. In rapid succession, Fort Watson (April 13, 1781) and Fort Motte (May 8) fell to their forces. After Fort Motte, Greene sent Lee against Fort Granby while Marion struck against Georgetown. On May 21, they recombined to reduce Fort Galphin.

Marion was present at Greene's attempted siege at Ninety Six in mid-June and led the right wing of Greene's 2,200-man force at Eutaw Springs on September 8. After that stalemated battle, the beleaguered British fell back to Charleston, cut off from food and forage by Marion and other partisan formations.

In January 1782, with the war winding down, Marion left the unit when elected to the new state assembly. He returned to uniform temporarily in June to help quell a last gasp Loyalist uprising along the banks of the Pee Dee River. The battle against the Tories was Marion's last substantive military duty during the war.

There is some uncertainty about Francis Marion's birthdate, but he is generally thought to have been born in 1732 in Berkeley County, South Carolina. After an early misadventure as a sailor during which his ship was wrecked, he returned to South Carolina to manage his family's plantation. In 1773 he purchased his own plantation which he named Pine Bluff. Over time he became a superb horseman, a skill that would serve him well during the French and Indian War and as he raised and led units during the Revolution.

After the war Marion rebuilt his war-ravaged plantation and spent a considerable career serving in the South Carolina Senate. He retired from those duties in 1790 after helping write the state's constitution.

Opinions differ regarding aspects of Marion's life and his actions during the war. As many have noted, he was clearly a man of his times—he owned slaves and participated in a notably brutal war against the Cherokee tribe. The War of Independence as fought in the South was at times virtually a civil war between Loyalists and American patriots. It was by nature a vicious conflict in which little quarter was asked or given by either side. Marion, along with other leaders, has sometimes been criticized for the harshness of his measures. Others, however, have written of his conduct as being chivalrous: "void of ruthlessness and cruelty to his victims." There is a persisting belief that his unit may have contained both black and white volunteers. As a member of the South Carolina legislature after the war, Marion championed amnesty for Loyalists.

Marion's tactics and employment of irregular forces are credited in the direct lineage of American Army Rangers and Special Forces.

Marion died on his plantation in 1795. He is buried at Belle Isle Plantation Cemetery in Berkeley County, South Carolina.

ANDREW PICKENS

One of America's foremost militia leaders, the dour Scotsman was successful both as a senior commander on the field (Kettle Creek) and as a key subordinate (Cowpens). He led the campaign to capture Augusta, Georgia, and with other guerilla leaders conducted operations that cleared the Southern interior of British and Loyalist forces.

Andrew Pickens was a dour, pinched-face Scots-Irishman who seldom smiled and was never known to laugh out loud—a demeanor perhaps befitting his ancestry and his strict Presbyterian faith. The latter earned him the nickname "the Fighting Elder." A second nickname, "Wizard Owl," accorded him by Cherokee Indian tribesmen, was a reflection on both his sagacity and his appearance: a long, narrow face with strongly marked features.

Along with Francis Marion, Pickens was an accomplished leader of irregular forces in the Georgia–South Carolina region. In a conflict in which the population was sharply divided in its sympathies, Pickens declared for independence at the immediate outset of the war.

As would be the case with other leaders of partisan units, the numbers and types of troops under Pickens' command varied greatly during the course of the war. At times he led hundreds, on other occasions only a few dozen. The composition of his forces changed as well, with multiple, fluctuating combinations of infantry and cavalry. There was also great variety in the numbers and quality of weapons and uniforms, or lack of them. At times, especially after Nathanael Greene assumed command in the South, Pickens' men acted in concert with Continental regulars; at other times they attacked and raided independently. If defeated they scattered, taking refuge in nearby swamps and forests only to later reassemble and fight again.

Pickens' name first surfaced in a major way when as commander of a 300-man militia unit he defeated a force more than twice as large at Kettle Creek in north Georgia. Sent by British commander Henry Clinton to rally support for the crown, the Loyalists plundered their way across Carolina into Georgia. On February 14, 1779, Pickens caught up with them at Kettle Creek while many were busy slaughtering a herd of stolen cattle. Pickens, seeing that the Loyalist's horses were turned out to graze and their camp was in disarray, formed his unit for attack. Simultaneous assaults from Pickens in the center and two wings which swept around the sides of the bivouac struck the encampment. After an hour of combat, 40 Tories were killed and dozens more wounded. Most of the rest fled into the countryside. Pickens lost nine killed and 23 wounded.

Kettle Creek was but a momentary bright spot for the patriot cause. By the summer of 1780, British forces dominated the interior and on May 12, took the surrender of an American army at Charleston. Pickens and his militia, assigned to General Benjamin Lincoln's forces, were in the city when Lincoln relinquished his sword to the British commander. Pickens was paroled and returned to his home. After informing the British, he renounced his parole a few months later after Tory raiders destroyed much of his property and threatened his family.

Pickens' return to the American forces was timely; Nathanael Greene, newly named commander in the southern theater, would make masterful use of guerrilla forces. Pickens' value to the American cause was then demonstrated anew at Cowpens on January 17, 1781. Pickens had hurried his militia unit to join forces under General Daniel Morgan, and by some accounts was among those who urged Morgan to make a stand at that location.

Morgan placed Pickens in command of the second line of battle. Posted about 150 yards in front of the third and final line, Pickens' unit consisted of 300 North and South Carolina militiamen placed in open order in a line about 300 yards long. Pickens superbly executed Morgan's instructions to get off aimed shots firing "low and deliberately" until pressed. They were then to fall back to the left and reform behind the third line. British forces led by Lieutenant Colonel Banastre Tarleton mistook Pickens' movement as a retreat. Their subsequent all-out charge was struck by Morgan's double envelopment. Nearly all of Tarleton's 1,100-man force was killed, wounded, or taken prisoner. A substantial portion of the British casualties occurred when their attacking infantry was blown apart by Pickens' riflemen in the second line. After the battle, Pickens was promoted to brigadier general in the South Carolina militia and was awarded a ceremonial sword by the Continental Congress.

After Cowpens, Pickens aided Greene's retreat across the Dan River, intercepting British foragers and disrupting intelligence gathering activities. With a newly raised 700-man militia force, Pickens threatened Cornwallis' left flank, slowing his advance as he moved after Greene. On February 18, Pickens, in command of a force consisting of South Carolina militia, Lee's Legion, and two companies from Maryland, intercepted 400 Loyalist mounted infantry under Colonel John Pyle on their way to join Banastre Tarleton. Tricked into a fight, the Tory force was essentially annihilated in an encounter that became known as Pyle's Massacre.

Called home soon after to deal with local threats, Pickens missed the March 15 battle waged by Greene at Guilford Court House. Returning quickly to the main army, he was dispatched by Greene to help 'Light Horse Harry' Lee and Francis Marion in clearing South Carolina's interior of British and Loyalist forces. Combining with Lee and assisted by Elijah Clarke, Pickens led the campaign against Augusta, Georgia. In a well-executed operation the Americans maneuvered skillfully, cut off British reinforcements and captured two forts—Cornwallis with a garrison of 250 Tory militia and 300 Creek Indian allies, and Fort Grierson with 80 militia and two cannons—that formed the city's defenses. Augusta itself fell to Pickens and the Americans in the first days of June.

After taking the British surrender, Pickens and Lee hurried to Ninety Six, South Carolina, a strong fortification which Greene had placed under siege. Pickens and other forces were sent to join other partisans under Thomas Sumter in blocking a large British relief column. Sumter, though, as was his frequent inclination, chose not to assist. On June 19, Greene lifted the siege and moved further into the interior. Soon after, the British abandoned the post, now isolated and cut off from provisions and communications by American units that controlled the countryside.

With the abandonment of the post at Ninety Six, major British forces in South Carolina were effectively bottled up at Charleston. In early September they brought Greene's army to battle, aiming for a victory that would restore their freedom of movement. When the two armies came together at Eutaw Springs on September 8, Pickens commanded the American left wing, leading 307 South Carolinians in an attacking force that numbered about 2,400. In the prolonged and ultimately stalemated battle that followed, both sides sustained heavy casualties. British losses, though, were more severe and caused them to fall back to Charleston. There, other than for occasional minor skirmishes, they remained quiescent for the rest of the war.

Late in the conflict, Pickens led a campaign in north Georgia against Britain's Cherokee Indian allies. The Cherokees had entered the war in 1776, siding with the British because of longstanding disputes with the colonists. Their several attacks, however, while damaging, were not conducted in concert with British maneuvers and had little ultimate effect on the war. When Virginia, Georgia, and Carolina militia forces were sent against them, their crops and villages were destroyed. A subsequent uprising in 1779 also resulted in the burning of their principal villages. When yet another outbreak erupted in 1782, Pickens, though considerably outnumbered, directed a successful expedition that led to the Long Swamp Treaty and the tribe's ceding a considerable amount of territory.

Despite being a sometime opponent on the battlefield, the Cherokees apparently held Pickens in high regard. His farm adjoined Cherokee land and he traded extensively with them. He was respected by the Cherokees not only for his military acumen but also for his fair treatment, honesty, and wise counsel. After the war, he served as a liaison between the Cherokee nation and the new American republic, often lending his support to Native issues. His home, called Hopewell Plantation, was the scene of several treaties with the tribe.

The expedition against the Cherokees in the latter days of the war brought Pickens' military service to a close. Through the long years of conflict, his guerrilla units had performed admirable service attacking isolated outposts and detachments, interrupting communications, capturing baggage trains, disrupting foraging parties and harassing British forces on the move. For a considerable period of time, Pickens and partisan leaders like him represented the only effective opposition to British pressure in the region. As one historian noted, even during the darkest times, "little bands of outraged patriots were roaming all over the territory, sniping at redcoats, cutting off couriers, and making nuisances of themselves."

The arrival of Greene, who understood and exploited the abilities of irregular forces when led by commanders like Pickens, changed all that. In 1780, all had seemed lost for the American cause. Within a year, the Americans controlled the South.

Andrew Pickens was born in Bucks County, Pennsylvania, on September 13, 1739. When he was 13 his family, along with many other Scots-Irish, moved south, eventually settling in Waxhaws on the South Carolina frontier. In 1764, Pickens moved to Abbeville County, buying land along the Seneca River that would eventually form Hopewell

Plantation. Of medium height, he grew to manhood lean and healthy. His strong religious faith was manifested in his service as an elder in the Presbyterian Church. Pickens' first experience under fire occurred as a 21-year-old during a conflict with the Cherokees in 1760–1761. Like Francis Marion, he would adopt many of the Indians' tactics and employ them against the British a decade and a half later.

Pickens maintained an active public life following his wartime service. For 13 years, beginning in 1781, he was a member of the South Carolina legislature. From 1793–1795, he served a term in the United States House of Representatives. An unsuccessful attempt at a United States Senate seat in 1797 was followed by six consecutive elections (1800–1812) to the South Carolina House of Representatives. Nominated for governor in 1812, he declined to run.

Pickens died at age 78 in Tomassee, South Carolina, on August 11, 1817. He is buried in Old Stone Churchyard, Clemson, South Carolina.

CHAPTER 2
THE BARBARY WARS

STEPHEN DECATUR

The youngest officer to achieve the grade of captain in U.S. naval history, Decatur was the foremost American hero during both the First and the Second Barbary Wars.

The Barbary Wars are perhaps the most forgotten of America's "forgotten wars". And, except among military historians, Stephen Decatur is one of the nation's most forgotten military leaders, despite the fact that he was the young country's most successful commander during the two conflicts waged in the Mediterranean and along the North African littoral.

The wars pitted the United States against pirates operating along the Barbary Coast (present-day Morocco, Algeria, Tunisia, and Libya) of North Africa. The raiders functioned under the auspices of the Sultan of Morocco, an independent nation, and three pseudo-states loosely tied to the Ottoman Empire: Algiers, Tunis, and Tripoli. The direct involvement of the four "states" varied in intensity from time to time. Morocco, having signed a treaty with the United States in 1777, was not actively embroiled in the conflicts. The "Barbary Pirates" ranged the Mediterranean, looting and capturing ships, most often holding crews and passengers for ransom. Over the course of three centuries the pirates made the Barbary rulers wealthy, and collectively made the Barbary States a considerable naval power.

Before the Revolutionary War, American shipping in the Mediterranean was protected by Great Britain. During that conflict, American vessels were safeguarded by France. After achieving independence the United States initially lacked sufficient military power of its own to guard American ships sailing in troubled waters. Initial attempts to negotiate a treaty failed, and for the next decade and a half the United States paid a million dollars a year to assure the safe passage of American vessels and the safe return of American hostages. By some reckonings, the amount paid for ransom and tribute may have absorbed as much as one-fifth of the infant republic's revenues.

When Thomas Jefferson, long opposed to paying tribute to the Barbary States, became President in 1801, he refused a demand from the Pasha of Tripoli to continue the payments. After the Pasha responded by cutting down the flagpole in front of the U.S. Consulate, Jefferson sent warships to the Mediterranean. The resulting hostility, known as the First Barbary War (1801–1805), was among the earliest of America's undeclared conflicts. Although Congress appropriated money and authorized the President's actions, there was never a formal declaration of war.

Eventually, an American fleet under the command of Commodore Edward Preble blockaded ports and with mixed results conducted a series of raids along the coasts and against the naval forces of the Barbary States. Three significant encounters highlighted fighting that occurred in spasms during the conflict. The first, in February 1804, involved an extraordinary act of leadership and daring by Stephen Decatur. The previous October, Tripoli had captured the frigate U.S.S. *Philadelphia* after the mishandled vessel ran aground in Tripoli's harbor. The ship's entire crew was taken prisoner and the vessel was anchored in place and used as a gun platform by the Tripolitans. On the night of February 16, using a captured native ketch (renamed the *Intrepid*) to fool the Tripolitan sailors, Lieutenant Decatur led a small force of Marines that stormed the *Philadelphia* and burned it to prevent its further use by the enemy. Decatur became an instant hero, one of the nation's first after the War of Independence.

Six months later Decatur added further to his renown. During the navy's bombardment of Tripoli on August 3, 1804, Decatur's men boarded a Tripolitan gunboat and after an intense hand-to-hand engagement, succeeded in capturing the enemy vessel.

The final major encounter of the war, the Battle of Derna, led to the eventual winding down of the conflict. In November 1804, a contingent of U.S. Marines along with a mixed-nationality force of mercenaries began a 600-mile march from Alexandria, Egypt to the city of Derna in present-day Libya. Aided by a naval bombardment, the American-led force stormed and captured the city on April 26, 1805, and then held it for several weeks in the face of repeated counterattacks. Historians recall the Derna episode as being the first time the American flag was raised on a foreign shore after a military triumph.

The victory at Derna helped persuade Tripoli's ruler—already pressed by raids, punished increasingly by Preble's blockade, and anxious about threats to his throne—to agree to the treaty that ended the war. Signed on June 4, 1805, the pact gave only temporary respite.

Within two years some of the Barbary States, Algiers predominate among them, resumed attacks on American shipping. Vessels and crews were again captured and held for ransom.

For several years the renewed piracy posed a problem that the United States, which was faced with an imminent war with Great Britain, could not address. When the War of 1812 was eventually declared, the British navy swept American forces from the Mediterranean, thus removing any remaining inhibitions the pirates might have had about attacking American merchant shipping. Sensing no threat, the Dey of Algiers expelled the American Consul General and demanded tribute. For a time the United States quietly resumed the payments. Finally, at the close of the War of 1812, the United States again sent forces into the Mediterranean to deal with provocations from the Barbary States.

America's principal involvement in what became known as the Second Barbary War took place entirely within a few active months in mid-1815. In March, Congress authorized President Madison's request to send American warships to the Mediterranean and to deploy them against forces of the Dey of Algiers. On May 20, Stephen Decatur, now a commodore, led the first American flotilla to depart for the Mediterranean. Decatur's squadron consisted of 10 ships: the frigates *Guerriere* (his flagship), *Macedonia*, and *Constellation*, the sloop of war *Ontario*, and the brigs *Epervier, Flambeau, Spark*, and *Firefly*. By early July he had defeated the Dey and negotiated a treaty.

Decatur brought the squadron into Gibraltar on June 15. Learning that several Algerian warships had recently passed through the strait, he immediately gave chase, intending to destroy the Algerian vessels or, at the minimum, prevent them from reaching their base at Algiers.

On June 17, off Cape Gata, Spain, Decatur's squadron caught up with the Algerian flagship *Meshuda*. The encounter began with an attempt by *Meshuda* to break free and race to the safety of Algiers. Those plans changed after an exchange of fire with *Constellation*, one of the first American vessels to close on her. *Constellation's* barrage damaged *Meshuda* and wounded her admiral, causing the Algerians to change course and seek sanctuary in a neutral port along the Spanish coast.

Other U.S. ships then joined the fight, and began pouring shells into *Meshuda*. Eventually, Decatur brought his flagship *Guerriere* directly alongside and unleashed a full broadside severely damaging *Meshuda* and killing the admiral. Decatur then ordered a momentary ceasefire, anticipating an Algerian surrender. For a time, however, the Algerians continued to resist. Decatur then directed *Epervier* to fire a series of close-in broadsides at *Meshuda*. Suffering heavy casualties and with their ship being destroyed around them, the Algerians surrendered. After taking control of the vessel, Decatur sent the captured ship under escort to Cartagena, Spain.

Decatur lost four sailors killed and 10 wounded in the sea battle. Algerian casualties are less certain, but in addition to the loss of the ship, more than 400 of the crew were taken prisoner, 30 or so were killed, and several score wounded.

On June 19, two days after the clash with *Meshuda*, Decatur's squadron chased down another Algerian warship, the brig *Estedio*. The engagement, fought off Cape Palos in proximity to Cartagena, was the last naval battle of the war.

Sighting the *Estedio* in open sea, the American squadron pursued the brig into waters along the coastline near Cape Palos. Wary that his larger, deeper draft ships might face difficulties in the shallower water, Decatur sent four of his smaller vessels to deal with *Estedia*. The vessels exchanged fire in a short, sharp encounter that damaged the Algerian craft. After several minutes, some of *Estedio*'s crew began leaving the vessel, attempting to reach Cape Palos in smaller, open boats. Decatur's crews fired on the fleeing craft, sinking one, dissuading others from further attempts at escape, and inducing the crew members remaining on the *Estedio* to surrender.

Decatur reported no losses from the engagement. Algerian losses are usually estimated as 80 captured, more than 20 killed, and many others wounded. *Estedio* was taken under escort to Cartagena to be interred with *Meshuda* until the conclusion of hostilities.

Two substantial Algerian warships, including the fleet's flagship, now having been dispatched, Decatur sailed his entire squadron into the harbor at Algiers at the end of June. Threatening destruction of the city, Decatur demanded restitution for American shipping seized by the Algerians. On July 3, the Dey surrendered. All American hostages plus several hundred European captives were released. The Dey paid $10,000 in compensation for ships captured by Algiers. The treaty, signed aboard *Guerriere*, ended payments of tribute and granted full, unfettered rights of transit to the United States.

After settling with Algiers, Decatur sailed to Tunis and Tripoli to ensure compliance with prior agreements made by leaders of those two states. Though the Dey of Algiers rather quickly repudiated his pact with Decatur, the United States' involvement in the Second Barbary War was essentially over. The following year a day-long bombardment by a combined British-Dutch flotilla forced the Dey to capitulate a second, final, time.

Before and After

Decatur was born in Berlin, Maryland, on January 5, 1779. After attending the University of Pennsylvania and working as a supervisor for a ship building contractor, he accepted an officer's commission in the navy in 1798. During the undeclared naval war with France, Decatur served mostly aboard the *United States*. Decatur's abilities were immediately apparent. When the navy demobilized after the war, he was one of only a handful of officers retained by the service.

Decatur was in command of the *Argus* when the First Barbary War began. In the combat zone he was given command of the *Enterprise* and was in that billet at the time of his fabled capture and destruction of the *Philadelphia*.

Having been promoted to captain as a result of his actions against the *Philadelphia* and during the battle of Tripoli, Decatur spent several years immediately following the war in a series of command billets, skippering some of the young navy's most renowned warships.

Decatur was in command of the *United States* when war was declared on Great Britain in June 1812. In early October, the *United States* was part of a three-ship squadron that captured the British warship *Mandarin*. Sailing alone, Decatur then took the *United States* far to the east where on October 25, several hundred miles south of the Azores, he met H.M.S. *Macedonian*. In the battle that followed, Decatur and the *United States* battered the *Macedonian* into submission.

Decatur had the *Macedonian* refitted after the battle and brought her back to New York.

Eventually, a large British squadron forced that ship, along with the *United States* and another U.S. vessel, the *Hornet*, into port at New London, Connecticut. The *Macedonian* and the *United States* remained blockaded at New London for the rest of the war.

In the spring of 1814, Decatur, now aboard the flagship *President*, took command of a five-ship squadron home-ported in New York City's harbor. As at New London, a formidable British blockade prevented transit from the port. In January 1815, seeking to carry out a mission to Tristan da Cunha in the East Indies, Decatur attempted to fight through the blockade with his flagship *President*, a vessel of 44 guns. A day after setting sail, the *President* was intercepted by four

British warships numbering among them 56, 40, 36, and 38 guns. Decatur managed at first to evade the pursuers and then in a savage encounter disabled the first British ship to reach him, the 40-gun H.M.S. *Endymion*. However, damage sustained to the *President* during the fight with the *Endymion* allowed two other British warships to close on Decatur's flagship. His ship crippled, with no chance of evading or outrunning the British vessels, Decatur surrendered his ship. Decatur was himself wounded during the course of the running battle that cost the crew of the *President* 24 dead and 55 wounded.

Decatur and the crew of the *President* were taken first to Bermuda and then later repatriated at New London, Connecticut, when hostilities ended.

Two months later Decatur sailed with his squadron of 10 ships to the Mediterranean where he swiftly and effectively dealt with the Barbary States that had threatened American interests in the region. Sent to Algiers to put an end to the practice of paying tribute, free Americans held hostage, and receive reimbursement for ships taken by the pirates, Decatur accomplished it all in a flurry of action that lasted only a few days. Soon after, at Tripoli and Tunis, he demanded, and received, reimbursements owed the United States by those governments.

After returning from the Mediterranean, Decatur served four years in Washington, D.C., as navy commissioner. On March 22, 1820, he was killed in a duel by a disaffected officer on whose court-martial board Decatur had sat more than a decade earlier. He was only 41 years old at the time of his death. President Monroe, his cabinet, justices of the Supreme Court, members of Congress, and several thousand citizens of Washington, D.C., attended his funeral. Decatur is buried at St. Peter's Church in Philadelphia.

During his relatively brief but notable career, Decatur's shipboard commands included some of the most illustrious warships in the American fleet. He received a ceremonial sword from Congress for his achievements in the Barbary Wars and a gold medal for his service in the War of 1812.

Decatur remains the youngest officer to achieve the rank of captain in the history of the U.S. Navy.

CHAPTER 3
THE WAR OF 1812

JACOB BROWN

Though personally opposed to the war and almost completely lacking in formal military training, during the War of 1812 Brown became one of America's few outstanding and consistently successful military leaders.

The War of 1812 was the least popular of America's declared wars. The Declaration of War sent by Congress to President Madison in June passed by the narrowest margin in the nation's history. The vote in the House of Representatives was 79–49. On June 12 the first vote in the Senate ended in a deadlock. The second vote on June 17 was 19–13. President Madison signed the declaration the following day.

Ironically, two days prior to the United States declaring war (unknown, of course, to Congress) the British rescinded Orders in Council that would have ameliorated several of the American concerns.

The declaration cited America's grievances against Great Britain: impressment, boarding, and searching American vessels in American waters, detrimental trade embargoes that violated international conventions regarding neutrality, and inciting violence from Native tribes along the frontier. These allegations did not prevail without protest, but only a few expressed misgivings about the state of the nation's armed forces.

America was, in fact, woefully unprepared.

The nation's military establishment consisted of a tiny army augmented by militia forces that were often ill-trained, ill-equipped, and poorly led; and by an almost nonexistent navy dwarfed in size by that of Great Britain, the world's preeminent naval power.

Internally, divisions within the nation were extreme. Sustenance, both material and emotional, from one entire region of the country—the Northeast—was lacking throughout the war. Marginal in the best of times, New England's sympathies seldom tilted in favor of active support for the war effort.

The war on the American continent was fought concurrently with a wider conflict that raged in Europe between France and Great Britain and its allies. When the Treaty of Ghent eventually ended the American-British war, natural boundaries were essentially left unchanged. Both sides were ready for peace after an exhausting conflict that saw few notable triumphs by either side. From three years of sometimes difficult fighting, the victories by William Henry Harrison at Tippecanoe and Andrew Jackson at New Orleans (fought, ironically, three weeks after the Treaty of Ghent was signed ending the war) are typically the most often—or indeed, perhaps the *only* ones—recalled by most Americans.

Thus, there is some special added irony in the fact that an individual who was personally opposed to the nation's entry into the war, who had little formal military training, and whose name today is generally unknown, was, in fact, one of America's few outstanding and consistently successful military leaders.

Few things in Jacob Brown's past would have foretold his success as a combat commander. A Quaker, he was opposed to the war. The sum total of his pre-war military experience consisted of occasional, some-times casual, duty as an officer in the New York State militia. Yet it was Brown who won a major victory at Sackets Harbor; captured Fort Erie; won the Battle of Chippawa; fought, along with Winfield Scott, one of the largest battles of the war at Lundy's Lane, and then prevailed at the siege of Fort Erie.

Thirty-seven years old when the war began, Brown was a briga-dier general in the New York state militia. He had almost no military background, having only joined the militia as a captain in 1807. He was appointed to the rank of brigadier general in 1811, and when war was declared was given responsibility for organizing American defenses over an extensive portion of the New York frontier bordering the Great Lakes region.

Brown's name first surfaced in the nation's consciousness with his success at the Battle of Sackets Harbor in May 1813. Sackets Harbor, on the eastern shore of Lake Ontario, was an American base and principal dockyard for the U.S. naval squadron operating on the lake.

Attacking at a time when most of the American fleet was away from the base and several infantry units were deployed elsewhere, British com-mander Lieutenant General Sir George Prevost saw an opportunity for a decisive strike that would capture the American post and ensure British naval supremacy on the lake.

The British opened the battle on May 28. As they and their Indian allies were engaged in landing operations, a flotilla of 12 small American ships carrying recruits to the harbor area was intercepted. Although the ensuing encounter resulted in the destruction or capture of much of the American contingent, initial uncertainty about the size and nature of the approaching forces caused the British to momentarily call off the attack. The delay allowed the Americans to reinforce the defenses, which consisted of two forts at the harbor entrance, and several blockhouses and partially completed earthworks that shielded the town and dockyard. Two American schooners were in port.

The next morning, May 29, the British resumed their attack in full force, making a successful opposed landing on Horse Island south of the town. After sustaining several casualties and securing the beachhead, follow-on landing parties charged across a causeway leading to the mainland. The British attack put to flight the American militia units posted there. Some of the fleeing militiamen were rallied by General Brown and would return at a decisive moment to play an important part in the fight.

Once on shore in force, the British pivoted left, swinging northeast toward the town and the dockyard, attempting to take both in a sustained attack. They were engaged by American regulars with artillery who fell back slowly to prepared defenses. Posted in blockhouses and behind earthworks, Brown's troops beat back repeated British attacks that lasted throughout the day.

While the struggle ashore was ongoing, the naval component of the battle evolved into a confused sideshow. The small British gunboats were generally ineffective, remaining too far offshore for their limited-range weapons to be useful. But when shells from a ship that had worked itself close to shore fell nearby, a young American naval officer, mistakenly thinking that a U.S. fort had fallen, burned large quantities of supplies and a ship under construction.

Meanwhile, the militia forces that had initially fled and were subsequently rallied by Brown launched attacks on the British right flank and rear. The British could not bring their field guns into action and by late in the day it was clear to General Prevost that success was unattainable. Under difficult circumstances the British retreated and re-embarked, saved, perhaps, by the fact that after a long march to the battlefield the U.S. 9th Infantry arrived too late to intervene in the battle. Of the 870 British combatants, 30 were killed, 200 wounded and 35 additional wounded were taken prisoner. Among the 500 American regulars and perhaps 900 assorted militiamen, casualties numbered 307, many of whom were the recruits killed or captured when intercepted on the way to the harbor on the first day.

Coming as it did after a string of American defeats in the northeast, Brown's victory at Sackets Harbor was welcome news to the nation. Brown was promoted to brigadier general in the regular army. The following spring he was appointed overall commander of the regulars, replacing General James Wilkinson after Wilkinson's most recent embarrassing loss to a much smaller force in an encounter along the Richelieu River.

Brown immediately set out to properly train his army. Camps of Instruction were established at Buffalo and Plattsburgh, New York. Primarily under the auspices of Brown's chief subordinate, Winfield Scott, Brown's army was shaped into a solid fighting force. Brown and Scott drilled their units tirelessly, instilled discipline, standardized orders and maneuvers, improved camp routine and sanitation, and stripped incompetent officers of command. Standardized uniforms were also provided: blue for the American regulars, although an initial shortage caused Scott's brigade to be clad in gray—a circumstance that would have a bearing on the outcome of a forthcoming battle.

Brown's initial intention was to move against a major British base at Kingston, Ontario, a plan that required support from the American flotilla on Lake Ontario. When the American naval commander, Commodore Isaac Chauncey—ill, timid, and reluctant to move pending construction of additional ships—declined to cooperate, Brown elected to make an attack across the Niagara River as his main effort.

By mid-summer 1814, Brown was ready to move. Leading an army made up of 2,400 regular infantry, 300 artillerymen, 600 Pennsylvania militia and 600 mostly Iroquois Indian allies, Brown crossed the Niagara and moved against British forces in Canada. In a three-week period he would fight three engagements: July 1814 would turn out to be one of the most active, and bloodiest, months of the war.

Action began on July 3 when Brown's army captured the small British garrison at Fort Erie, a post on Canadian soil directly across from Buffalo. Led by Scott's brigade of regulars, Brown's forces hurried north, where after 16 miles they collided with the advance guard of a British army led by General Phineas Riall. Riall's force was headed south to relieve Fort Erie in the mistaken belief that the post remained in British possession.

Scott's scouts found Riall's army, about 1,700 British regulars plus 400 or so Canadian militia and Indian allies, massed on the north bank of the Chippawa River. Scott pulled back momentarily, awaiting Brown and the remainder of the army encamped to the south near Street's Creek. Brown first took his force west, intending to cross the Chippawa farther upstream.

Skirmishing began on the morning of July 5 when Riall's scouts and Indian warriors engaged American outposts north and west of Street's Creek. General Brown sent troops under the command of Brigadier General Peter Porter to drive back the British skirmishers. As Porter's troops advanced against the British, they saw Riall's main column moving to attack. Pulling back, Porter informed Brown that the British were in motion moving south toward Scott. Learning of the move through Brown, Scott advanced his four regiments, quickly deploying his artillery along the river, using the Niagara as his eastern flank, while extending his line west of the river.

Riall, leading the massed British advance, saw the gray uniforms, and judging them to be militia anticipated an easy victory. His initial rapid assault met with no success. In fact, the Americans formed a precise line under fire and moved toward him with fixed bayonets. Surprised by their staying power, Riall is alleged to have said, "Those are regulars, by God," or words to that effect.

Still, Riall continued to push forward, his lines losing continuity as his troops moved across rough and uneven ground. As his advancing troops neared the American lines, Riall ordered a volley followed by a quick charge seeking to shock and overwhelm the American ranks. The Americans did not break, and Riall's move opened a gap in the British lines between the right flank and a heavily wooded area nearby.

Scott saw the opportunity presented by the fractured line and sent a regiment (the 215th) to take the British in the flank. They did so, pouring a devastating fire into the enemy ranks.

Meanwhile, seeking to further entrap the British, Scott sent the 11th Regiment to the right and the 9th and 72nd to the left, striking the British force from three sides. After about 25 minutes of deadly fire, absorbing heavy losses, Riall ordered a retreat. Harassed by American troops led by Porter, the British made a fighting withdrawal toward the Chippawa.

The Battle of Chippawa was a difficult encounter. Brown and Scott lost 61 killed and 255 wounded. British losses were more severe: 236 killed, 322 wounded, and 46 captured. Far more importantly, the battle was a turning point for the U.S. Army, showing that American troops properly trained and led could defeat veteran British regiments. Chippawa was the first time that regular forces from both sides met in close combat on even terms—and an American army under Jacob Brown had prevailed.

Brown continued north after the battle, outflanking British forces posted along the river. Their defenses having been turned, the British fell back to Fort George, on Lake Ontario near the mouth of the Niagara River. The continued lack of support from the U.S. naval commander, Commodore Chauncey, now ill with a fever, and the American naval squadron precluded Brown from transporting the additional troops and artillery necessary to attack the fort. Chauncey's actions, or lack thereof, in effect conceded control of Lake Ontario to the British, freeing them to move additional forces across the lake to reinforce the Fort George garrison.

Brown initially posted his army a few miles south of the fort, then on July 24 moved back to the Chippawa River. There he intended to resupply, secure his base, and then move east toward Burlington, Vermont. As Brown shifted his army, the British under Riall sought to maintain contact by moving forces to Lundy's Lane, about four miles north of the Chippawa. Riall's move set the stage for a major battle the following day.

On July 25th, Lieutenant General Gordon Drummond arrived at Fort George to take personal command of British forces on the Niagara peninsula. Drummond immediately ordered a force under Lieutenant Colonel John Tucker to move from Fort Niagara down the east side of the Niagara River. Drummond intended that the move by Tucker would cause Brown and the Americans to evacuate the west bank of the river. Instead, Brown responded immediately by ordering an advance north, an action that might cause Drummond to recall Tucker's column to protect Fort George while at the same time curtailing threats to Fort Schlosser, the nearest American supply base.

While Riall, at Lundy's Lane, learned that Brown was advancing, he ordered his troops to fall back to Fort George. The order was countermanded by Drummond who had fast-marched from Fort George with large numbers of reinforcements.

Lundy's Lane was a trail leading west from the main north–south road that ran close to the Niagara River. As the path moved west the ground rose and afforded a commanding view over the area nearby. The British reached the high ground first and Drummond placed his massed artillery at a small church and cemetery at the highest point of the lane.

Emerging from a forested area, the first American unit on the field was a brigade led by Winfield Scott. Although outnumbered, Scott chose to attack the left and center of the British line, which extended generally on a west to east direction along the trail. Scott's initial assaults, moving from the south to the north and northwest across mostly open ground, were beaten back. Failing in his first attempts, Scott then sent the 25th U.S. Infantry to outflank the British on the left (west). The Americans found an abandoned track, moved around the British and Canadian units, and drove them back in confusion. Further attacks secured the road junction and netted large numbers of prisoners, including General Riall himself. As the fighting moved back and forth, several of the captured British (but not Riall) escaped when the Americans were in turn attacked while attempting to return to their own lines.

The intensity of the initial American assault and the steady fire from Scott's brigade caused Drummond to pull back forces from his center in order to maintain contact with his units on the left and preserve the general alignment of his defensive front. The withdrawal of units from the center of the line left the British artillery in front of the infantry, open to direct attack.

As night approached, Brown arrived on the field with the main body of American troops.

Brown shifted units to relieve Scott's exhausted regiments and ordered the 21st U.S. Infantry to capture the exposed British guns. Aided by a distracting attack by the 1st U.S. Infantry on the British right flank, the 21st Infantry moved against the British artillery, firing a volley that killed most of the gunners and following up with a bayonet charge that captured the guns and cleared the remaining British forces from the hilltop.

British infantry behind the guns counterattacked immediately but were driven back as other Americans reached the crest near the church and cemetery. As the struggle around the guns was raging, a newly arrived British force blundered into an American unit and lost control of additional guns that remained out of action for the rest of the fight.

After taking the high ground and the British guns, the Americans deployed their own artillery in the same area. Desperate to recover his guns, Drummond launched three costly, head-on attacks, the last occurring near midnight. All were beaten back after intense, short-range infantry duels that resulted in heavy casualties on both sides.

While the second of Drummond's three assaults was underway, Scott led the remainder of his brigade against the British center. Ground changed hands as the lines surged back and forth and Scott was severely wounded while moving units to a trouble spot.

By midnight, after more than five hours of furious combat, both armies were exhausted. On the American side, Brown and Scott were both wounded. Among the British officers, Drummond was wounded and Riall, also wounded, was a prisoner of the Americans. Brown was left with only 700 combatants on the line. Supplies and water were running short.

The U.S. artillerymen had suffered particularly as fighting raged around their position; artillery officers had difficulty finding enough draught horses to pull guns away. Eventually, two pieces, one damaged, had to be abandoned but another was recovered after it was extracted from a difficult position near the British center. An abortive attempt to recover the abandoned British guns was made the following morning, when outnumbered American units observed British forces reoccupying the field.

Both sides retreated in the immediate aftermath. Brown moved the Americans back to Fort Erie. Drummond pulled a portion of his forces away, then later returned to the area.

The fight at Lundy's Lane began with about 1,500 British combatants facing 1,000 Americans. As the struggle progressed, reinforcements totaled about 1,500 Americans and 1,700 British. The battle's inconclusive outcome could not mask the fact that Lundy's Lane was one of the bloodiest engagements of the war. Of the nearly 6,000 who participated in the fight, total casualties killed, wounded, missing, or taken prisoner approximated 1,700, almost evenly divided between the two sides. Even British veterans of the Napoleonic wars were aghast at the carnage.

As with the Battle of Chippawa, the strong showing of the outnumbered Americans evidenced the success of the hard training and discipline initiated by Brown and Scott. Losses during the fight, lack of supplies, and continued British supremacy on Lake Ontario dissuaded Brown from considering a push farther north. In the days following the battle he shifted the bulk of his army back to Fort Erie.

The Fort Erie chapter would close Jacob Brown's major participation in the war. As with most other of his endeavors, it met with success.

Stung by his own losses, after several days Drummond, the British commander, cautiously followed the American Army toward Fort Erie. There, the British engaged in what turned out to be a disastrous siege, first sustaining heavy losses in a failed attempt to take the fort by storm, then suffering from sickness and lack of supplies along the siege line. In September, Brown ordered an American sortie that broke the deadlock and caused the British to raise the siege. Total casualties numbered 609 British and 511 American.

At that point Brown was posted to other duties and General George Izard took over command of the front. Izard followed up Brown's victory at Fort Erie in a lethargic manner, and with the war winding down, the northeastern theater saw little major action after Fort Erie. The British did not attempt further offensive operations and the Americans, also desperate for supplies, eventually burned the fort and set aside thoughts of invading Canada.

Before and After

Jacob Brown was born on May 9, 1775, in Bucks County, Pennsylvania, the son of Pennsylvania Quakers. After graduating in 1790 at age 15 from the University of Pennsylvania he taught school before moving to upstate New York in 1798. There, as settler and landowner, he helped open the Black River region to settlement, establishing mills, opening a store, and improving roads and river navigation.

Brown was commissioned a captain in the New York state militia in 1807, promoted to colonel in 1809, and advanced to brigadier general in 1811, the rank he held when the war began. Officer positions in local militia were not unusual for leading citizens, but Brown's advancement most surely recognized obvious leadership and organizational abilities.

The battles of Sackets Harbor, Chippawa, Lundy's Lane, and Fort Erie made Brown a national hero. On November 3, 1814, he was awarded a Congressional Gold Medal for his success during the war.

Brown remained in the army after the war ended. By 1821, he was the only major general in an army greatly reduced in size, and he was named Commanding General that same year. Brown was well regarded in that post, running the day-to-day operations of the army and advising national administrations on military affairs. During his seven-year tenure, he reorganized the headquarters staff, established the precursors of present-day service colleges, and installed the first army recruiting organization.

Brown died in Washington, D.C., in 1828 while still on active duty. His funeral procession down Pennsylvania Avenue was a mile in length, and the entire government stood down for the funeral, which was attended by major dignitaries. President John Quincy Adams remarked that "...in the late war [Brown] contributed perhaps more than any man to redeem and establish the military character of the country."

THOMAS MACDONOUGH

MacDonough's decisive victory in the waters off Plattsburgh, New York, forced invading British forces back to Canada and preserved the northern border of the United States.

Thomas MacDonough's career as a combat leader began inauspiciously. Posted to billets that saw little action at the outset of the war, MacDonough quickly requested reassignment. In October 1812, he was given command of the U.S. naval forces on Lake Champlain, headquartered at Burlington, Vermont. In his first action he lost two ships.

MacDonough's fleet initially consisted of only two gunboats and three sloops. Despite lacking experienced sailors, guns, and supplies, in June 1813, he sent two of his sloops, *Growler* and *Eagle*, in pursuit of enemy vessels that had established a presence nearby and might threaten his base. In the action that followed, both ships were captured and the British gained naval superiority on the lake.

MacDonough worked tirelessly to rebuild his flotilla, constructing in short order three additional sloops and four gunboats. Later that fall his force was sufficient to drive the British across the lake and into Canadian waters.

The following year, 1814, would prove decisive for operations in MacDonough's theater. On August 31, General Sir George Prevost—in a reprise of General John Burgoyne's campaign in the Revolutionary War—launched a major British offensive aimed at taking control of the lake and invading the Hudson River Valley, thus potentially severing the northern portion of the United States from the remainder of the country. Newly reinforced by sizable numbers of Wellington's veterans just arrived from Europe, Prevost moved into upstate New York, opposed on the American side by only 1,500 mostly untried regular forces and 3,000 militia. Prevost intended to make a frontal assault on American fortifications at Plattsburgh while the British naval squadron swept MacDonough's flotilla, guarding the American flank, from the lake.

While Prevost made good progress on the ground, the British naval forces under Commodore George Downie set sail to meet MacDonough's fleet. Anticipating the attack, MacDonough anchored his ships in the waters off Plattsburgh. Downie's opening sally on September 11 met with initial success due mainly to the firepower of his 36-gun flagship, the H.M.S. *Confiance*. In subsequent close-in fighting, however, the British suffered heavy losses that included Downie himself, killed when an American shell shattered a nearby cannon. As the fighting continued, MacDonough skillfully manipulated cables to swing the undamaged side of his own flagship, the 26-gun *Saratoga*, around to bear on the British ships. When *Confiance* attempted the same maneuver, MacDonough delivered withering fire that severely damaged the British vessel. With *Confiance* out of the fight, the Americans sank or captured the remaining major British warships. The defeat was total and the British were forced to surrender.

The consequences of MacDonough's victory were significant. Realizing that further operations were futile without control of the lake, Prevost broke off his invasion of New York. After Prevost abandoned considerable quantities of supplies and retreated back to Canada, the front remained quiet for the rest of the war.

The triumph was of abiding importance in another way as well. By forcing Prevost to return across the border, the British were left with no grounds to make territorial claims in the region when peace negotiations resumed at Ghent. Thus, MacDonough's victory on that other, almost forgotten, September 11 date in American history preserved the northern border, and perhaps the entire northern portion, of the United States.

Before and After

Thomas MacDonough was born December 21, 1783, in New Castle County, Delaware. As a lad he clerked in a nearby town before receiving, in February 1800, an appointment as a 16-year-old midshipman in the U.S. Navy. Within two months of his appointment he was aboard the U.S.S. *Ganges* in the West Indies when that ship captured the first of three French vessels during the undeclared naval war with that country.

Late in the following year he was assigned to the U.S.S. *Constellation* and fought with distinction in early engagements with Tripoli in the First Barbary War. In 1803, MacDonough was transferred to the U.S.S. *Philadelphia* but was on shore leave when the ship was captured by the Tripolitans. Reassigned to the U.S.S. *Enterprise* under the command of Stephen Decatur, MacDonough volunteered for Decatur's raid on the harbor in Tripoli that succeeded in destroying the *Philadelphia*.

Promoted to lieutenant for participation in that action, MacDonough then served in a succession of increasingly responsible billets, first on board the U.S.S. *Syren*, then as Isaac Hull's assistant overseeing ship construction, and finally as commanding officer of the U.S.S. *Wasp*.

When his tour with the *Wasp* was completed, MacDonough took a two-year leave of absence as captain of a merchantman plying the trade routes to India. With war looming on the horizon he returned to active duty before the conflict with Britain began in 1812.

Following the war, MacDonough's career was marked by a series of prestigious assignments. He commanded the Portsmouth Navy Yard before taking command of the Mediterranean Squadron where he was diagnosed with tuberculosis. MacDonough returned to the United States and was given command of the U.S.S. *Ohio*, at 76 guns one of the navy's largest ships, which was then under construction. Five years later, in 1824, he returned to the Mediterranean as captain of the U.S.S. *Constitution*. Late the following year he removed himself from command because of failing health, and on November 10, 1825, on his way home to the United States, MacDonough died at sea near Gibraltar. He was buried at Middletown, Connecticut.

Deeper in the Shadows...

ISAAC HULL

Hull's legendary exploits as captain of the U.S.S. Constellation *provided a beacon of hope to the beleaguered American war effort in the early months of the war.*

On August 19, 1812, Isaac Hull, commanding the U.S.S. *Constitution*, battered the British frigate H.M.S. *Guerriere* into submission. Coming as it did early in the conflict (President Madison had signed the Declaration of War on June 18), Hull's victory electrified the nation. *Constitution's* triumph also showed that ships from the tiny American fleet could match those of the British navy, the world's most formidable naval power.

At one time during the fight the *Constellation* and *Guerriere* became entangled. While they rotated counterclockwise, Hull fired continuous broadsides, making the *Guerriere* a shattered wreck before she struck her colors. Although the *Constitution* (nicknamed 'Old Ironsides' after the battle) would, under other captains, go on to further victories over H.M.S. *Java, Pictou, Cyane,* and *Levant,* Hull's decisive win provided a beacon of hope for the American cause during the many dark days that followed.

Hull's exploits with the *Constitution* had actually begun before the war's first shots were fired. After taking command in June 1810, he refitted the ship and the following August delivered the American ambassador to France, returning safely after being shadowed by British frigates. When war was declared, Hull took the *Constitution* to sea. Sailing off the New Jersey coast on July 17, the vessel was sighted by a flotilla of five British ships. After a legendary chase that lasted two and a half days, Hull evaded the British squadron which eventually gave up pursuit.

After replenishing supplies, Hull quickly took the *Constitution* to sea again, burning three British merchantmen near Halifax in the Gulf of St. Lawrence. In mid-August, Hull learned of the presence of a British warship to his south. He sailed immediately to meet her, setting up the confrontation with H.M.S. *Guerriere* that made him famous and his ship immortal.

Hull rendered further service during the war as commander of the Portsmouth Navy Yard.

Complemented by outstanding seamanship, the well-designed and superbly constructed vessels delivered by Hull's and other American shipyards proved worthy adversaries for their far more numerous British opponents.

After the war Hull remained on active duty with the navy until 1841. He died in Philadelphia on February 13, 1843.

A FAMILIAR NAME IN A LESSER KNOWN ROLE:
WINFIELD SCOTT

Thirty years before his towering performance during America's war with Mexico, Scott's remarkable training and leadership skills helped shape American units into disciplined, effective fighting forces.

Winfield Scott's towering status in American military history is most closely associated with his triumph as commanding general during the war with Mexico (1846–1848). The audacity, generalship, and extraordinary competence demonstrated in every phase of that campaign prompted even the Duke of Wellington to remark upon its brilliance.

Scott's contributions during the War of 1812 were also quite exceptional although not nearly as well known. At age 26, he was the youngest brigadier general in the U.S. Army. His leadership on the battlefields at Chippawa and Lundy's Lane was superb. Equally as important for the American cause was the training regimen he devised and installed while serving as Jacob Brown's subordinate. Using the 1791 drill manual from the French Revolutionary Army, Scott trained his regiments intensely, building a responsive and disciplined organization. He standardized orders and maneuver schemes, upgraded camp operations and hygiene, and weeded his units of incompetent officers. Perhaps more than any other individual, Scott helped build the American Army into an effective, disciplined fighting force.

CHAPTER 4
THE SEMINOLE WARS

WILLIAM WORTH

A senior commander in two of America's wars, Worth's masterful counterinsurgency campaign against the Seminoles brought closure to the nation's longest war until Vietnam.

The name William Jenkins Worth is little known to most present-day Americans. Military historians, however, recall Worth as an officer who left a formidable legacy as a combat leader not just in one, but *two*, of the nation's wars. Worth's achievements during the War with Mexico are chronicled in the following chapter.

Worth's initial fame came during one of America's least known conflicts. Known collectively as the Seminole Wars, three difficult, extended, expensive struggles were waged in Florida during the early- to mid-19th century. Each tied up a significant portion of the nation's small army establishment. The starting and ending dates ascribed to each conflict vary somewhat by source, but generally accepted timelines are 1817–1818 for the First Seminole War, 1835–1842 for the Second, and 1855–1858 for the Third.

Sometimes labeled *The* Seminole War, the second conflict was the most consequential of the three. Waged over a period of more than seven years, it was the most expensive Indian war and, between the War of Independence and Vietnam, the nation's longest lasting conflict.

Indeed, the similarities with the conflict in Vietnam well over a century later are rather striking: it was an increasingly unpopular war whose mounting costs were a drain on the nation's resources. What would now be called 'search and destroy' missions became a common feature of the army's counterinsurgency operations. Negotiations to conclude the conflict were prolonged, and the ending itself was clouded with ambiguity. Like Vietnam, the army's eventual withdrawal involved a phased drawdown of forces.

Provisions of the 1832 Treaty of Payne's Landing required the Seminoles to move west of the Mississippi within three years. Many did, but the largest faction, led at the time by Chief Osceola, refused to go. Hostilities commenced in December 1835 with the murder of the government's agent and the ambush of a contingent of soldiers led by Major Francis Dade near present-day Bushnell. The loss of perhaps as many as 100 soldiers prompted the full intervention of United States military forces.

Over the next several years of inconclusive combat, intensity levels waxed and waned as clashes erupted up and down the Florida peninsula. Casualties, many of them resulting from disease, mounted, as did frustrations and costs. Eventually, by some estimates, the government spent as much as $40 million on the war, an enormous outlay in 1830s-40s dollars. Fueling the war's increased unpopularity were allegations of graft on the part of government contractors and questionable prices for military goods paid by purchasing agents.

In 1841, after six years of war with no end in sight, General William J. Worth took command of U.S. forces. Worth was the eighth commander in a conflict that disrupted careers as well as taking lives.

Worth took over at a time when the Indians had evolved a form of warfare that employed small, fast moving groups that would attack, disperse, and evade pursuit by finding concealment and sustenance in their familiar terrain of unexplored swamps and islands hidden in the Everglades. Florida's extreme temperatures dissuaded American commanders from conducting campaigns during the heat of summer months, a respite the Seminoles used to plant crops and replenish supplies.

Worth changed all that. The Seminoles would be given no sanctuary during the summer or at any other time. Worth reshaped his army, structuring it to wage a campaign of continuous pressure, pursuing the Seminoles, destroying or capturing them when possible, but always keeping them on the move and under duress. Employing a strategic concept that involved simultaneous movements in every military district, Worth's soldiers broke up Seminole camps and destroyed fields, crops, and food stores. Using innovative boat detachments, Worth sent troops down rivers and into swamps and parts of the Everglades never before touched by white soldiers. His troops burned weapons caches, corncribs, huts, and fields wherever they went. Worth mapped large parts of the peninsula for the first time as every swamp and Indian habitat between the Atlantic Coast and the Gulf of Mexico witnessed the appearance of his wide-ranging forces.

In one of the few large-scale encounters of the war, the Battle of Palaklaklaha, fought on April 19, 1842, Worth personally led U.S. forces into battle. After wading a great distance through swamps and underbrush, Worth's soldiers inflicted a disastrous defeat on the Seminoles, capturing several chiefs during the fight.

Foreshadowing techniques employed in 20th and 21st century conflicts, throughout the war Worth used captured Seminole leaders to persuade still-warring chiefs to surrender, sometimes adding monetary awards as inducements. Preferring negotiations to combat wherever possible, but by a judicious combination of both force and diplomacy, Worth used techniques that by the autumn of 1842 had substantially reduced the Seminole threat. Many had moved west and those who remained were generally quiescent, clustered mainly in a portion of southwest Florida.

In August, Worth met with the remaining chiefs. Each was offered weapons, money, and food supplies in return for moving west of the Mississippi. Some did so but others, with Worth's concurrence, chose to remain in place on an informal reservation. Believing the remaining small numbers of Seminoles to no longer be belligerent, Worth declared an end to hostilities on August 14, 1842. No formal peace treaty was signed.

After an extended leave, Worth returned to attend to two small bands that had not declared their intentions. One came in when ordered to do so; the second was captured and sent west. By the end of the following year, only one regiment of the U.S. Army remained in Florida.

The rapid drawdown of forces was yet another similarity between Worth's situation and that which confronted General Creighton Abrams in Vietnam nearly a century and a half later. Like Abrams, Worth understood the nature of the conflict he was fighting as well as the political environment in which he operated. The war was costly and highly unpopular—the American public's patience was exhausted. Casualties were mounting. U.S. Army dead numbered nearly 1,500, mostly from disease, although Worth instituted hygiene and sanitation measures that greatly improved camp conditions. Even while the fighting continued, the army cut back on costs, reducing the number of military personnel and civilian employees while consolidating several small commands to conserve funds and people.

Few commanders have succeeded so well under such unpromising circumstances.

Before and After

William Jenkins Worth was born at Hudson, Columbia County, New York on March 1, 1794. As an 18-year-old, he applied for, and received, a commission at the outset of the War of 1812. Worth served as aide-de-camp to General Winfield Scott and saw heavy action at the battles of Chippawa and Lundy's Lane, being severely wounded in the latter encounter. Lauded for his bravery, he received a brevet promotion for his conduct under fire. Scott befriended Worth and they remained close acquaintances for more than three decades until an incident in the Mexican War—a disagreement over Scott's tactical decisions at Molina del Rey—ruptured their friendship.

In 1820, Worth began a notable eight-year assignment as Commandant of Cadets at the United States Military Academy. While in those duties, Robert E. Lee was one of his students. Lee also served under him for a time during the war with Mexico. Lee later said of Worth that he was "a splendid horseman; he was physically the ideal soldier." Command slots and other key billets followed and led to his appointment in 1841 as commander of forces in Florida. Three years after the end of the conflict in Florida, hostilities with Mexico began. One of the few major commanders to lead forces in key battles in both the northern and southern theaters of operations, Worth would play an important role in the American victory.

After the Mexican War, Worth was assigned as commander of the Department of Texas. While posted to those duties he died of cholera in San Antonio in 1849. Several years later, after an elaborate ceremony, he was interred in Worth Square at the intersection of Broadway, Fifth Avenue, and 25th Street in Manhattan.

CHAPTER 5
THE MEXICAN WAR

WILLIAM WORTH

To most Americans, the transcendent figures of America's war with Mexico are Zachary Taylor and Winfield Scott. Taylor led an American army into northern Mexico, and four months after the war was officially over he was elected President of the United States. Scott conceived and conducted the greatest amphibious assault the world had seen since William the Conqueror invaded England, and then led a campaign that drew the admiration of even the Duke of Wellington. Scott, too, later ran for President.

Far less recalled now, though widely renowned immediately after the war, was the service of General William Worth. In 1857, when a 51-foot-tall obelisk was erected over his monument tomb in New York City, a speaker prophesied that "His fame will endure when his monument shall have crumbled."

That has not proven to be the case.

Today, as with his exemplary service during the Second Seminole War, described in the preceding chapter, Worth's achievements during the Mexican War are often overlooked.

Worth was seen by some as having a propensity for publicity or glory-seeking. He led the first army across the Rio Grande; he was the first to plant the American flag on Mexican soil; he personally raised the Stars and Stripes over the Bishop's Palace in Monterrey; he was the first American on shore at Veracruz; he personally lowered the enemy's flag atop Mexico's National Palace and raised the American flag in its place. Although critics would, with some justification, cast him as a vain and ambitious officer, Worth was one of the finest combat commanders of the war—and there could be little questioning of his personal courage under fire. Beginning with his serious wound at Lundy's Lane during the War of 1812, many of Worth's accomplishments came while directly under the guns of the enemy.

Worth was one of the few senior American commanders who saw service both in the north under Taylor and in the south and interior with Scott. Of those who did, he was by far the most effective.

Worth began the war as a brigadier general, having been brevetted to that rank for his service in the Second Seminole War. Posted initially to the Texas border, he was assigned to Zachary Taylor's army at the outbreak of hostilities. To admirers, his abilities were quickly evident and played an instrumental part in the American victory. To critics, many of his actions seemed intended to draw attention to himself. In any event, Taylor called on him to negotiate the capitulation of Matamoros (across the Rio Grande from Brownsville, Texas), the first city in Mexico to fall to American forces.

From Matamoros, Taylor pushed south toward Monterrey. There, he faced a formidable Mexican force positioned in a series of natural strongpoints and well-conceived fortifications. One hundred miles deep in hostile territory and at the end of a tenuous supply line, Taylor felt compelled to attack, although considerably outnumbered. The resulting battle would rage over parts of three days, much of it in bitterly contested street-by-street and house-to-house combat.

On September 20, 1846, Taylor sent Worth with 2,000 troops on a sweep around the city. The battle's opening move was intended first to block the Mexicans' prospective escape route while skirting two major fortifications. Then, after closing the exit road at Saltillo, Worth was to position his men on the west side of Monterrey and attack from there while the remainder of Taylor's army stormed the city from the north and east.

Worth's contingent was designed as a quick-striking, highly mobile force. One unit, the First Texas Mounted Rifles, was unique: trained and equipped as infantry, all of its members were mounted on horseback giving the force unusual flexibility and lethality. Worth also carried with him two companies of lightweight, 'flying' artillery capable of rapid movement and repositioning on a battlefield.

After a night spent in the open under a driving rain, in the early morning of September 21 Worth's men were attacked by a force of 2,000 Mexican cavalry. Led by Lieutenant James Longstreet, the Americans launched a spoiling counterattack that bought sufficient time for Worth's riflemen to position themselves behind a wooden fence and pour aimed fire into the charging cavalrymen. As the Mexicans regrouped, Worth brought up his mobile artillery. When the Mexicans charged again, the cannons, loaded with canister, fired repeatedly into the massed cavalry, blowing apart the attack and leaving the field a scene of carnage.

The Saltillo Road was secured soon after, but as his force continued its western loop it became obvious to Worth that the two strongpoints he and Taylor had hoped to bypass would have to be taken. Without possession of the high ground, works, and batteries that made up the two fortifications—called La Independencia and La Federacion—the city could not be secured.

In the meantime, Taylor's attacks in the north and east were repeatedly thrown back with horrendous losses. Some units that managed for a time to get into the city at first moved down its streets in straight, orderly lines, only to be shot to pieces from houses, rooftops, and hidden gun emplacements.

One triumph eventually came at a fort called La Teneria, on the east side of the city. After initially being pinned down, Americans finally took the fortification with a bloody charge assisted in considerable measure by the leadership of Colonel Jefferson Davis, commander of the Mississippi Rifles, later Secretary of War of the United States, and later still President of the Confederate States of America. Elsewhere, however, the Americans continued to be repulsed. Nearly half of one attacking force led by John Garland was killed in Monterrey's deadly streets.

To the west, Worth's forces succeeded in storming the redoubts and the high points that comprised the La Federacion fortification. Their hard-won respite was short-lived, as they were soon placed under heavy fire from La Federacion's companion stronghold. Indeed, the La Independencia fortification posed an even more difficult obstacle. Crowned by a substantial building called the Bishop's Palace, the elevation teemed with Mexican troops and artillery.

At sunset, Worth made preparations to attack La Independencia and the Bishop's Palace the following morning. For the Americans the first full day of battle had been especially costly. From a beginning force only half the size of the one it was attacking, Taylor's army had lost nearly 400 killed and wounded—almost a tenth of the total number that saw action.

By far the heaviest casualties came from street fighting and ill-advised frontal assaults led by John Quitman and John Garland across town from Worth in the northern and eastern sections of the city.

Worth's actions in the early morning of September 22 began to turn the tide of battle.

Stealthily moving 500 troops forward under the cover of three o'clock in the morning darkness and later, heavy fog in the pre-dawn hours, Worth's men moved within 50 yards of the redoubt known as Fort Libertad. Pausing only a moment, they stormed it with a bayonet charge.

About 350 yards away, the Bishop's Palace, the second major fortification that made up La Independencia, posed a more ominous challenge. Two initial attempts to take it with light weapons were thrown back. Worth then ordered a 12-pounder howitzer dismantled and hauled piece by piece up the mountain. Reassembled on the hilltop, the howitzer began hammering away at the Palace.

Worth had positioned his men so that only a few in advance of the main line were visible to the Mexicans; the remaining 1,200 were sheltered out of sight behind a small ridge near the howitzer. As Worth anticipated, the thin infantry screen induced the Mexicans to attack. Mexican lancers, followed by infantry, charged from the Palace, intending to overrun the apparently few defenders and capture the 12-pounder that was raining destruction on them. As the Mexican attack closed on the American position, the lancers were stunned to see three full regiments rise from behind the rocks and fire into their ranks. The lancers' attack broke, as did that of the Mexican infantry. Both groups began a pell-mell rush back to the Palace. The Americans raced close behind, some of them reaching the Palace before the gates could be closed. By mid-afternoon, the fortification was cleared of defenders and the battle for La Independencia was won. Contemporary accounts credit Worth with raising the flag over the Bishop's Palace. The several Mexican cannon captured on La Independencia were quickly turned and began to fire down on Mexican positions inside the city.

Worth's were the only forces engaged in a substantial way on the 22nd, and his victories at La Federacion and La Independencia gave Taylor control of the western side of the city. That, with the Americans' substantial toehold at La Teneria in the east, pinned the Mexican force into the interior of the city. Ironically, that was a battle anticipated—and indeed welcomed—by the Mexican commander, General Pedro de Ampudia.

Ampudia pulled his entire force into the center of the city. Around the main plaza the Mexicans had constructed a carefully designed defensive stronghold. Anchored by the massive cathedral, fortified buildings surrounded the open square. Almost all were continuous one-story structures with window barricades and shutters suitable for firing platforms. Flat roofs facilitated sniper nests and gun emplacements, and the cathedral's bell tower allowed unobstructed views of the prospective battle zone. Ampudia intended to bleed the American Army into submission by turning the streets into killing fields even more deadly than those that had decimated Quitman's and Garland's forces on the first day of the battle.

Worth, however, had no intention of fighting that kind of battle. One of the qualities that distinguished him as an exceptional commander was an ability to observe, adapt, and innovate. Having learned through couriers of the disastrous street fighting earlier in the fight, Worth chose not to put his men in column order on city streets. In fact, in large measure he kept them off the streets. Instead, when fighting began on the 23rd, his men moved in small teams from house to house, battering down conjoining walls with sledge hammers, axes, and picks, clearing each dwelling and then moving on, sometimes using his 'flying' artillery to blow apart walls or strongpoints that interfered with his advancing forces. Worth equipped his troops with ladders to scale the flat roofs of Monterrey's buildings and remove them as vantage points for the enemy. Amidst the carnage of the house-to-house onslaught, some of the bitterest fighting took place on the city's rooftops.

Later in the day Worth introduced into his attack a 10-inch mortar that he used to place the main plaza under fire. After advancing into the interior of the city in assault teams that moved down several different streets as opposed to converging on a single avenue, Worth's units fought house to house, often room to room, tearing down common walls while his heavy weapons cleared paths that led to a plaza called the Capella. The Capella, smaller than the main plaza but in close proximity to it, provided a site for Worth to set up his biggest mortar and begin shelling the central square.

By mid-afternoon, firmly in control of the Capella, Worth began launching enormous shells into the main plaza at 20-minute intervals. Packed with explosives, each round created carnage, wreaking havoc on defenders and tearing gouges in strongpoints. Worth intended the shells and their timing, precisely 20 minutes apart, as a message to Ampudia that his forces were trapped, vulnerable to fire at times and places of the Americans' choosing.

Meanwhile, American units under the overall command of General David Twiggs launched attacks from the eastern side of Monterrey. Fighting quickly escalated as the troops moved through the streets into the heart of the city. Both sides took casualties in combat that was some-times hand-to-hand and flowed back and forth in repeated attacks and counterattacks. Eventually, Twiggs' forces also penetrated to the vicinity of the main square.

At 11 p.m. Taylor ordered Worth and Twiggs to cease fire until the following morning.

Before sunrise a messenger carrying a white flag made his way through the streets to Taylor's headquarters. Ampudia was willing to surrender the city if the remnants of his army, minus artillery, munitions stores, and other military property, were allowed to leave. Outnumbered two to one, having sustained heavy casualties, and lacking both manpower and heavy weapons to conduct an extended siege, Taylor accepted the terms. The Battle of Monterrey was over.

For William Worth, however, Monterrey was only the beginning of his war. Brevetted to major general for his sterling performance during the battle, he soon was called upon by General Winfield Scott. After Monterrey, Scott had Worth transferred from Taylor's army to his own, where he would play an instrumental role in Scott's forthcoming inva-sion. Indeed, as events unfolded, Worth would lead troops from the first wave to touch the beach at Veracruz all the way through to the capitu-lation of Mexico City.

For its time, Veracruz was an enormous undertaking: it would remain the largest landing of American troops on foreign soil until D-Day, June 6, 1944, and the largest joint amphibious operation. The assault force consisted of 13,000 troops, all of whom had to be housed on ships, fed, transported, put ashore, and provisioned. Artillery, munitions, horses, and other implements of war had to be landed on hostile ground in sufficient quantities to sustain an army severed from other means of support.

On March 6, 1847, Worth led the first American division ashore. Sixty large barges, each carrying 50 to 60 soldiers, were rowed in line toward the landing zone along Collado Beach. As the barges neared the shore, Worth was the first one over the side and the first to plant an American flag on the shore. With the landing zone at Veracruz secured and his entire force ashore without incident, Scott chose to take the city by siege, using Worth to seal the southern edge of the American encirclement. On March 29, with their water cut off and after days of bombardment, the Mexicans surrendered the city.

The road ahead would be increasingly more difficult. The 300 or so miles between Veracruz and Mexico City followed a twisting path that rose from sea level and wound through a series of narrow passes and defiles—all of them along a route the Mexicans knew Scott must travel.

Cerro Gordo was the first test. The mountain pass was ringed with strongpoints and cannon sited on a mountaintop. The Mexican commander, Antonio Lopez de Santa Anna, had arrayed his 12,000-man army in seemingly impenetrable positions along a narrow defile squeezed by steep walls on each side. However, in one of the many feats that would earn him his initial notoriety, Robert E. Lee, a captain at the time, found a small, little-used path that skirted Santa Anna's emplacements. Scott used it to facilitate a turning movement, sending units into the flank and rear of Santa Anna's position. In a battle fought over parts of two days, April 17–18, 1847, Scott trapped and nearly destroyed Santa Anna's army.

Worth, who much to his displeasure had been temporarily left in Veracruz with duties as military governor, was positioned east of the pass where his division served as a reserve force in support of the attack. The victory at Cerro Gordo opened the way for Scott's continued drive into the interior. On May 14, Worth's and other American forces brushed aside Mexican units positioned along the road at Amazoque as Scott continued his offensive through the spring and summer months. By mid-August he had brought his army within a few miles of Mexico City. Finding the main road blocked by Santa Anna's army, Scott sent units over an arduous path through lava fields to flank a 5,000-man Mexican force commanded by General Gabriel Valencia. The battle at Contreras began on August 19 and continued until sunrise the following day. The main encounter, fought on the 19th, was relatively brief. Valencia's army was routed. Survivors from his 'Army of the North' fled from Contreras to Churubusco, setting up the penultimate clash of the war. At Contreras, Franklin Pierce, another future President, was wounded leading troops in battle.

The Mexicans' loss of Contreras made a nearby major position at San Antonio untenable. Mexican commanders responded by shifting the San Antonio garrison to the village of Churubusco, only five miles from Mexico City. There, they gathered additional forces from surrounding areas and awaited Scott's onslaught. It was not long in coming. Even before the bulk of the Mexican forces reached Churubusco, they were struck in the flank by one of Worth's brigades in an attack that captured numerous prisoners and five artillery pieces.

At Churubusco the Mexicans fortified a large Franciscan convent, entrenching along stone walls and placing strongpoints in and around the convent building. Access to the structure and to the heart of the Mexican defenses was possible only after crossing a river or the bridge that spanned it while exposed to fire from the garrison and its seven cannon.

Initial American attacks on August 20 were thrown back in heavy fighting that lasted for several hours. Eventually, while other units broke through on the right of the Mexican fortifications, Worth's units drove to the left, made a successful river crossing, and began attacking along the left flank and rear. Resistance outside the convent collapsed but concentrated fire from defenders inside the building persisted. Concerted attacks, with Worth's forces coming together with those of Persifor Smith and Daniel Twiggs, were then launched against the fortification. As in previous engagements, Worth's unique positioning of cannon inflicted severe and unexpected damage on the stronghold and contributed to its surrender later that day.

After Churubusco, Scott made an attempt to end hostilities. On August 23, Nicholas P. Trist, representing President James K. Polk and the U.S. government, negotiated an armistice. On September 3, Santa Anna rejected provisions related to boundaries and the ceding of Mexican territories and again called his forces to arms.

The American Army was now bivouacked on the doorstep of Mexico City. When Santa Anna refortified the city, Scott resolved to first attack a nearby foundry called Molina del Rey (King's Mill). Scott believed, erroneously, that the foundry was casting weapons for the Mexican army. Possibly the victim of faulty intelligence, he assessed the works as being lightly held. In fact, Molina del Rey would be one of the most intensely fortified positions confronted by the Americans during the entire war. For Winfield Scott, Molina del Rey was a rare tactical misstep. It was also the battle that would shatter his long, though already strained, friendship with William Worth.

Worth apparently objected to the attack as unnecessary, or believed if one was conducted that it should be carried out in concert with an attack on Chapultepec Castle, only a thousand yards to the west. Chapultepec was the key bastion guarding the approach to Mexico City, and enfilading fire from the castle could support the Mexican defenders at Molina del Rey. Nonetheless, Scott directed Worth to attack the position, blow up the foundry, and destroy any munitions he found there.

Awaiting Worth was a lethal hornet's nest. The Mexicans had converted the entire complex of stone buildings—the main grouping was nearly 1,500 feet long—into an immense fortification. As at Monterrey, flat roofs, heavily sandbagged, provided excellent firing positions. Five hundred yards north of those structures was another strongpoint, a massive stone building ringed with earthworks called Casa Mata. Three hundred yards west was a sheltering ravine backed by high ground, ideal for concealing infantry and cavalry. The Mexicans had ample numbers of both: several thousand infantry and another four thousand cavalry. Seven artillery pieces were positioned throughout the grounds.

At three o'clock in the morning of September 8, Worth advanced into the cauldron. Using a new tactic, Mexican commanders initially withheld their fire. Then, as the American units drew near, devastating barrages were launched from concealed gun emplacements carefully sited throughout the fortification. Radically outnumbered, Worth's force totaled only about 3,000 including cavalry. Possibly to compensate for the thinness of his numbers, Worth placed his mobile artillery on each wing to add punch to the assault. Worth's heavy ordnance was assigned to support the attack in the center.

As the Americans advanced, fire from the heavy weapons weakened the Mexicans' center, situated along the extended row of stone buildings. Led by an elite 500-man unit, the position was eventually taken by storm. Initially tom apart and repeatedly driven back, reinforced units finally fought their way into the buildings and cleared them under intense fire. The breakthrough came from the right, where Worth's men found an opening. Operating in small groups, one of them led by Lieutenant Ulysses S. Grant, the assault teams fought from building to building. Success was achieved at a very high cost: 11 of the 14 officers in the attacking force were killed while securing the center of the line.

In the midst of the fight, a Mexican attempt to flank American units who were falling back at the time was shattered by Worth's mobile artillery led by Lieutenant Thomas (later 'Stonewall') Jackson and was further routed by American dragoons who chased down the survivors. Fighting was equally desperate elsewhere on the battlefield. As an American brigade advanced on Casa Mata the unit was raked by artillery and small arms fire. Pushed back at first with heavy losses, a renewed attack supported by Worth's 'flying' artillery ultimately forced the Mexican defenders, who had been reinforced during the fight, to abandon the Casa Mata strongpoint. The fortification was then blown up and molds, machinery, and other materials inside the mills were destroyed.

Mexican losses at Molina del Rey totaled about 2,000 killed or wounded and another 700 taken prisoner. Three cannon and large quantities of weapons and ammunition were also captured.

Worth's victory came against a much larger, entrenched force that awaited his attack on a prepared killing field. It cost him more than 700 men killed or wounded—almost a quarter of his force. It was also a triumph for which he never forgave Winfield Scott. And even after the enormous effusion of blood, Chapultepec remained to be taken.

A quarter mile wide and three quarters of a mile long, Chapultepec was a massive fortification richly garrisoned with nearly a thousand Mexican infantry and ten cannon. Inside seven-foot-high stone walls that ringed the site, behind a copse of trees and a second set of high walls, stood a castle-like structure at the summit of a hill. The wreckage of Molina del Rey lay burning and shattered to the west. Between those ruins and the west-facing wall of Chapultepec was a mined ditch that further strengthened the fortress' defenses. To the east not much more than a mile away stood Mexico City, the ultimate objective.

In the capital city and on the narrow approaches to it, Santa Anna, drawing on a military establishment with three times the numerical strength of the attacking Americans, placed blocking forces along Scott's potential routes of attack. Rumors had it that a second Mexican army of 8,000 men—a force larger by a thousand or more than Scott's entire army—was moving into the area behind the American position. Scott realized that Chapultepec would have to be taken quickly, lest Santa Anna move large forces to its defense or trap him between it and the city or the converging army.

Scott began with a feint to the south in the general direction of the capital. The move was successfully aimed at holding Santa Anna's army in place or perhaps even inducing their reinforcement. That night under the cover of darkness, Scott moved his troops back to positions around Chapultepec. Lee was charged with selecting sites for Scott's artillery batteries. He chose four locations, placing 8-inch howitzers and a 10-inch mortar in positions around the fortification. Meanwhile, the enormous 24-pounder would ravage the castle from a position near the ruins of Molina del Rey.

The Americans opened fire on the morning of September 12 and shelled the Chapultepec complex throughout the day and into the evening. The barrage resumed at 5:30 the next morning. At 8 o'clock, the American infantry attacked, moving toward the fortress from all four sides.

Despite the preparatory shelling, intense fire from the walls, grounds, and castle building greeted the American advance. Indeed, the battle at Chapultepec would live on in Mexican lore as well, particularly the heroic defense by young military cadets at the crest of the hill. As the fighting raged, Jackson's gallantry again drew notice as he moved his artillery from place to place on the battlefield. Constantly exposed to fire, he personally manhandled one of the pieces and demolished Mexican cannon that blocked an access to the fortress.

Worth's division was held in reserve during the initial phase of the battle. As the assault reached the castle walls, Worth's men moved forward with ladders that allowed 50 or more men at a time to scale the walls.

Once inside, the fighting was savage, at close-quarters, as Scott's soldiers sought vengeance for Molina del Rey.

As Worth's men reached the fortress, James Longstreet was shot in the thigh as he carried the American flag near the castle wall. Before the colors could touch the ground, Longstreet handed them to Lieutenant George Pickett who took the Stars and Stripes over the wall. Under heavy fire, Pickett raced to the flagpole, lowered the Mexican tricolor, and raised the American flag in its place. Years afterward, long after the Civil War ended, one of the most vivid recollections of both Federal and Confederate veterans was not of the 'charge' at Gettysburg that came to bear his name, but of Pickett carrying the flag over the wall at Chapultepec.

The Stars and Stripes flying high above Chapultepec were visible for miles around, easily seen by Santa Anna and the Mexican army on the approaches to Mexico City. The flag's presence over the castle portended the end of the battle. Soon after, the few Mexican survivors fled down the causeway toward Mexico City.

A mile or so from Chapultepec, the spires of Mexico City loomed in the near distance. But for the American invaders few things came easily during this war. Mexico City was a defensive tactician's dream come true. Access to the city was confined to narrow causeways spanning salt marshes. Along the major southern approaches, Santa Anna had entrenched his army across three parallel crossings. The city itself was walled and at every city gate stood fortified customs houses that would channel assault teams down narrow passages.

The Americans had hoped to capture the city in one continuous rolling attack after Chapultepec fell. Although some American units, notably those of John Quitman and, once again, Jackson's mobile artillery, struck immediately towards the capital, it was late afternoon before most American forces were extracted from Chapultepec, replenished, and the major assault was formed and underway. The delay allowed Santa Anna to rush troops to the San Cosme city gate, which by then had become the obvious focus of the attack. By the time Worth's units reached the gate, three cannon including a huge 24-pounder and three fresh battalions blocked their way.

At the front of Worth's assault, Ulysses Grant saw a nearby church belfry that overlooked the San Cosme customs house and commanded the ground behind it. Grant had some nearby artillerymen dismantle a mountain howitzer and follow him toward the church. After gaining access to the city by wading through chest-deep swamps, Grant and his team reassembled the howitzer in the church steeple. Grant then began pouring fire on unsuspecting Mexican defenders at the customs house. As Grant's men shelled the chokepoint, other forces under Worth's command outflanked Mexican positions at and around the gate. After about an hour the 24-pounder was destroyed and a group of Marines gained access to a tall house overlooking the main enemy position. From that vantage point the Marines shot apart Mexican infantry and baggage trains that supported the San Cosme fortification. Having gained tenuous access to the city, Worth's men and American attackers at other gates settled in for the night.

The early hours of the next morning heralded unexpected, but welcome, events. At one o'clock in the morning, at the request of magistrates who did not want to see destruction inflicted on Mexico City similar to that visited upon Veracruz, Santa Anna and his army abandoned the city. At four o'clock a delegation of city officials journeyed to Scott's headquarters requesting terms for surrender. At sunup, the Stars and Stripes were raised over Mexico's National Palace. Most contemporary accounts identify Worth as the flag-raiser.

On June 12, 1848, Worth marched his division out of the city, ending America's occupation of Mexico's capital. In later days, he would identify himself as the first American ashore at Veracruz and the last to leave Mexico City. For William Worth the war was over. Few had fought it so long or so well.

Deeper in the Shadows…

JOHN E. WOOL

Wool's actions at Buena Vista and in other encounters played an important role in securing Zachary Taylor's triumphs in Northern Mexico.

General John E. Wool served under Zachary Taylor in the northern theater of operations. Wool, posted in San Antonio, Texas at the outset of hostilities, was given command of the Army's Central Division with orders to march his force into northern Mexico. Taylor, stripped after his victory at Monterrey of a large portion of his army that was sent to assist Winfield Scott's campaign in the south, nonetheless decided to move farther into the interior. In an impressive display of leadership, Wool took his units 200 miles deep into Mexico, 600 miles from San Antonio, and participated in the Battle of Saltillo. At Saltillo, Wool combined forces with Taylor to bring the small army to about 4,500 men, mostly volunteers and many of whom had only recently arrived.

Meanwhile, after his defeat at Monterrey, Santa Anna reconstituted a large army. Having learned from an intercepted letter that many of Taylor's veterans were being sent to Scott, the Mexican dictator determined to move quickly north and destroy Taylor's small and relatively untrained army. Then, having knocked Taylor out of the war, the entire Mexican force could be focused on stopping Scott before he reached Mexico City.

On February 21, 1847, Taylor learned from Texas Ranger scouts that Santa Anna was on the move toward him with an army 10,000 to 15,000 strong. Taylor moved his much smaller force from its temporary bivouac at Agua Nueva, 12 miles north, into a defensive position—a narrow mountain pass at the village of Buena Vista. Wool was charged with planning and organizing the defenses and was left temporarily in command while Taylor, greatly worried about the security of the army's provisions, went back to Saltillo to ensure supplies were adequately protected.

On the morning of February 23, while Taylor was away, the Mexicans launched a heavy attack against the Americans' left flank, manned by Indiana volunteers. Supported by an artillery battery, the outnumbered volunteers fought well but were steadily driven back, as was a second line of Illinois volunteers. Wool sent word to the Illinois commanders to hold at all costs. The unit was conducting a fighting withdrawal under great pressure when Taylor, just back on the field, struck the attacking Mexicans with the Mississippi Rifles, a volunteer unit led by Jefferson Davis.

As the Mississippians slammed into the flank of the Mexican army, Wool rallied the American units that had fallen back, using the walls of the hacienda at Buena Vista as a defensive strongpoint. Along the hacienda barricades Wool reformed his units and drew on additional support from an artillery battery and two regiments of dragoons. Another regiment of Indiana volunteers was then sent to aid the Mississippi Rifles, the two units forming an inverted V shape as they came together on the battlefield. The Mexicans attacked the new alignment, but were pinned down in the crossfire before managing to escape.

As the fight continued, Santa Anna launched another attack on the main American position. Amidst desperate fighting, Taylor ordered a nearby artillery battery commanded by Captain Braxton Bragg to double-shot his guns and rake the advancing Mexicans. Eventually, in the middle of a torrential downpour, the Mexican attack came apart. Santa Anna broke off the assault and hurried back to Mexico City to put down an attempted coup. Buena Vista was a closely fought battle, costly to both sides. The Mexicans lost an estimated 500 killed and 1,000 wounded. American casualties amounted to 267 dead, 456 wounded, 23 missing, and two guns captured. Wool later commanded the occupation force in northern Mexico. For his leadership at Buena Vista, he was brevetted to major general and awarded a Congressional Sword.

In later years, Wool helped resolve Indian wars in Oregon. When the Civil War began he was Commander of the Department of the East. Before retiring in 1863 at age 79, Wool was the oldest general to see active service in the war. He spent the remaining years of his life at Troy, New York, where he died in 1869.

The Naval Commanders

The conflict with Mexico was primarily a war of land combat. Because of that, American history deservedly recalls the two army commanders, Zachary Taylor and Winfield Scott, as the war's major heroes. However, U.S. naval forces played an important, but much less remembered, role in the American victory. Indeed, in the case of Scott's invasion, the navy's contribution was essential to the campaign's success.

In particular, two naval officers warrant recognition beyond the footnotes history has thus far accorded them.

DAVID CONNOR

Connor commanded naval forces during the amphibious assault on Veracruz, personally leading the landing craft ashore without the loss of a single American life.

Commodore David Connor commanded U.S. Navy forces during the brilliant amphibious assault on Veracruz. Leading an armada of 200 ships that carried Winfield Scott's 13,000-man invading force, Connor was renowned for his professional handling of the fleet and for his unselfish support for Scott's campaign. Connor personally led the flotilla of landing craft that carried the army ashore, accomplishing that mission without the loss of a single U.S. soldier.

During the siege of Veracruz, Connor lent Scott several heavy cannon and navy gun crews. Fire from the navy's heavy ordnance helped end the siege and induce the Mexicans to surrender the city. In the initial stages of the conflict Connor commanded the Home Squadron that operated in the Gulf of Mexico, blockading ports and transporting supplies and reinforcements to the army.

Ill health forced Connor from active service. A native Pennsylvanian, he died in Philadelphia in 1856 at age 64.

MATTHEW PERRY

Perry's operations along Mexico's east coast captured key facilities and shut down traffic in and out of Mexico's gulf ports.

In late March, with Scott still at Veracruz, Matthew Perry succeeded David Connor as Commander of the Home Squadron. Perry continued Connor's and the navy's superb support for the land campaign by transporting follow-on forces, horses, artillery, munitions, and other supplies as Scott's army moved inland.

After the surrender of Veracruz, Perry moved against remaining port cities in the Gulf of Mexico. Commanding what became known as the 'Mosquito Fleet,' Perry captured Tuxpan and Carmen in 1847. In the weeks ahead, Perry received news of a reported buildup of Mexican forces on and along the Tabasco (present-day Grijalva) River. Perry responded by leading an 1,100-man landing force transported in 47 boats towed behind his larger ships. On June 15, Perry began moving up the river. Running through ambushes and obstacles, he pressed upstream until major obstructions placed in a bend in the river caused him to move his force ashore and march overland toward his objective, the city of San Juan Bautista (now called Villa Hermosa). On June 16, the landing force encountered strong Mexican defenses at Fort Acachapan. Perry bombarded the fortification with four artillery pieces and then led a charge that overran the garrison's defenders.

In the meantime, Lieutenant David Porter (who in the Civil War would contribute greatly to Ulysses S. Grant's success at Vicksburg), in command of the ships in the river, destroyed the obstacles that had blocked the vessels and moved to join Perry. After taking a fort guarding San Juan Bautista, Porter linked up with Perry and the combined force took control of the city.

Perry's actions effectively shut down traffic in and out of the Mexico's gulf ports.

Perry went on to greater fame as commander of the American fleet on the two expeditions that opened Japan to Western trade. He died in New York City in 1858 and is buried at Newport, Rhode Island.

Familiar Names in Lesser Known Roles

Fast forward 13 years and the names of the lieutenants and captains who fought in the War with Mexico read like a litany of the senior commanders who led Union and Confederate armies during America's Civil War.

It was in Mexico that Robert E. Lee gained initial notoriety as Winfield Scott's indispensable assistant, and the qualities that marked him for later greatness first became apparent. Thomas Jackson—forever, after First Bull Run, known as 'Stonewall'—was brevetted three times for bravery under fire and displayed an almost other-worldly tenacity and aggressiveness. Ulysses Grant, whose actions at San Cosme gate were recalled long afterwards, was brevetted on two occasions. Others including James Longstreet, P.G.T. Beauregard, George Thomas, and Joseph Johnston were also brevetted or directly promoted twice. Prominent also, appearing in the pages of history for the first time, were Joseph Hooker, Irvin McDowell, George McClellan, John Pope, Richard Ewell, A.P. Hill, John Sedgwick, Edward Ord, Braxton Bragg, Ambrose Burnside, Winfield Hancock, George Pickett, George Meade, and numerous others.

The names of several commanders who primarily led volunteer units would also become familiar, permanent parts of the national fabric, including Jefferson Davis, Jubal Early, and Franklin Pierce. Pierce, along with Zachary Taylor and Ulysses Grant, would become one of three veterans of the Mexican War to be elected President of the United States. Two others, Winfield Scott and Winfield Scott Hancock, also ran for that office. After the war, Jefferson Davis represented Mississippi in the United States Senate, served as Secretary of War for the United States, and, when the South seceded from the Union, was elected President of the Confederacy.

Some historians have assessed the army that fought the war with Mexico as perhaps being the most able and professional ever fielded by the United States. Many others observe that the conflict served as America's training ground for the Civil War.

CHAPTER 6
THE CIVIL WAR

GEORGE H. THOMAS

Bruce Catton, America's great Civil War historian, concluded that Thomas "may have been the best of all" commanders on either side. Along with Napoleon's victory at Austerlitz, some military historians pronounce Thomas's victory at Nashville as one of the two most perfect battles ever planned or fought.

History, it has often been said, is written by the winners. It can also be argued that sometimes it is written by those who live longest or who write from the most exalted platforms.

George Thomas died in 1870, five years after the Civil War ended. Grant, Sherman, and almost all other notables who survived that conflict outlived him by several years and wrote extensively (and, as historians frequently discover, often self-servingly) about their wartime exploits. Thomas, an inordinately modest individual, left no such paean to his own virtues. Nor did he have any intention of ever doing so. In fact, he ordered his personal papers destroyed, not wishing to engage in the accusation/counter-accusation spectacle that consumed so many senior leaders on both sides for years after the last shots were fired.

Of all the leaders in the nation's conflicts, George H. Thomas has been most often identified by military scholars as being the most deserving of greater recognition. Bruce Catton, one of America's greatest Civil War historians, came to believe that Thomas "may have been the best of them all," and that histories of the conflict needed to be "upgraded" to properly assign him the credit he was due.

"Time and history," Thomas said, "will do me justice."

Perhaps so, but it is taking a very long time.

It is difficult to understand why recognition so richly merited has been so long in coming. Although Thomas fought mainly in the West, a theater less prominent in the public's attention, his achievements were transcendent, not only during the course of the Civil War but also as measured against accomplishments by leaders in any of America's armed conflicts.

Some have suggested that Thomas is sometimes overlooked because his triumphs did not come with horrific numbers of killed and wounded. If so, it is indeed unfortunate scholarship that credits superb generalship less than frontal assaults and casualty counts.

Thomas won every battle in which he was in overall command. In those engagements where he was a principal subordinate, he contributed immeasurably to eventual victories: Corinth, Stones River, the Tullahoma Campaign, Hoover's Gap, Missionary Ridge, Chattanooga, and Peach Tree Creek, among others. At Chickamauga his stand at Horseshoe Ridge saved an entire Union army.

At Mill Springs, Kentucky, on January 19, 1862, Thomas gave the Union its first major triumph, helping save Kentucky for the Union cause. At Nashville on December 15–16, 1864, he gave the Union one of its final and most decisive victories, wrecking a Confederate army in an encounter that some military experts proclaim as one of the two most perfect battles ever planned or fought. (The other was Napoleon's victory at Austerlitz.)

During the run-up to Fort Sumter, Thomas was a major, soon to be lieutenant colonel, assigned to the U.S 2nd Cavalry in Texas. Ironically, during the unit's posting in the southwest, one of Thomas' closest colleagues was his fellow Virginian, Robert E. Lee.

Recalled to the north, Thomas for a short time trained troops at Carlisle, Pennsylvania, before reporting to General Robert Patterson. At Chambersburg, Thomas, by then a colonel, assumed command of the 1st Pennsylvania Brigade.

On July 2, 1861, Patterson's force crossed the Potomac into Virginia. Near Falling Waters, Thomas' troops clashed with forces under the command of Stonewall Jackson in one of the war's early skirmishes. It would be the only time they met during the war. Thomas prevailed.

For several months thereafter, Thomas' small triumph along with minor victories won by George McClellan at Rich Mountain and Corrick's Ford in present-day West Virginia would rank among the Union's very few successes. Elsewhere, all was disaster. A series of defeats that began at Bull Run on July 21 extended through Wilson's Creek, Missouri (August 10); Lexington, Missouri (September 20); Balls' Bluff, Virginia (October 21), all the way to Grant's stalemated struggle at Belmont, Missouri on November 7. Finally, in January 1862, it was Thomas who would give the Union its first major victory.

Thomas had been promoted to brigadier general and sent to the Western Theater in mid-August of the preceding year. He would remain there for the duration of the war. After first positioning his regiment to prevent Confederate forces from seizing an arsenal at Frankfurt, Kentucky, Thomas was put in charge of a major troop training center near Lexington.

There, he brought order out of chaos. Finding thousands of new recruits milling around a 3,000-acre encampment mostly devoid of weapons, ammunition, uniforms, shoes, food, and shelter, Thomas quickly created the core of what would become the Union's Army of the Cumberland. When Thomas finished, the force was complete with formed brigades accompanied by trained and provisioned cavalry and artillery components. He put his force on the march soon after, unveiling a sophisticated new picket system that incorporated cavalry patrols along with infantry posts. The concept was intended to identify and delay advancing enemy forces while at the same time covering sentries as they pulled back to their own lines.

In the early morning hours of January 19, 1862, the system worked as planned, detecting a Confederate advance and giving Thomas time to form his own forces and move them into position. Thomas spoke calmly to each unit, steadying them as they moved into line. The battle, joined at Mill Springs, Kentucky, was fiercely contested through the morning hours. Fought over an expanse a mile long with terrain channelized by broken ground, scrub timber, and brambles interspersed with corn fields, the lines surged back and forth in close combat until about 11 a.m. Thomas then made a decisive move. Using two regiments recently arrived on the scene, he sent one against the Confederate right flank and used the other in a wheeling maneuver, launching a bayonet charge against the left side of the enemy's line. The Confederate front came apart; panic spread along the entire line as troops broke and ran. Thomas pressed the Confederates to their base camp where during the night they fled across a river then scattered through the countryside. Thomas' men occupied the camp the next morning, collecting 150 wagons, 1,000 horses and mules, an entire artillery train of 12 guns, and an extensive cache of small arms and assorted provisions.

Thomas with about 4,500 men had thoroughly beaten an attacking force of 6,500. Mill Springs was the Union's first significant triumph. After months of repeated setbacks, the victory did much to restore morale in the North. Strategically, it saved Kentucky for the Union.

The victory at Mill Springs came at the cost of only 262 casualties. That was a pattern that would repeat itself, as Thomas was a commander who carefully shepherded the lives of his men.

Thomas' name next surfaces, briefly, at Nashville when he and General Don Carlos Buell occupied the city and organized a supply base to sustain Federal armies in the Western Theater.

In April 1862, General Henry Halleck, commander of Union forces in the West, dispatched Buell from Nashville to join Grant's army at Pittsburgh Landing, Tennessee. Grant had not entrenched his army and handled its disposition rather casually around a country church called Shiloh. As Buell's force, which included Thomas' division, was on the march, Grant was surprised and nearly overwhelmed by a Confederate attack that began on April 6. Union forces fought desperately through the day and were driven back to within a stone's throw of the Tennessee River, in danger of being overrun. Buell's forces began arriving that evening. In concert with two Union gunboats on the river that pounded the Confederate positions, they stabilized the Union line. At dawn the next day, 25,000 fresh troops brought by Buell joined Grant's forces in a combined assault. After eight hours of hard fighting Confederate commander P.G.T. Beauregard, with no remaining reserves of his own, ordered a retreat.

Thomas' position on the order of march from Nashville was last in line, thus preventing his unit from participating in the fight. For Thomas and other Federal commanders, though, Shiloh was an object lesson on the need for entrenching, scouting, and having an army ready to fight. As events would show, it was a lesson that Thomas would apply with remarkable thoroughness and efficiency.

After Shiloh, Halleck reorganized Union forces in the Western Theater. Taking personal command of Don Carlos Buell's Army of the Ohio, John Pope's Army of the Mississippi, and Grant's Army of the Tennessee, Halleck began a ponderous, three-pronged move toward Corinth, Mississippi. As part of the reorganization, Halleck removed Grant from direct command and placed him in a deputy commander role for the entire force. On April 25, Thomas was promoted to major general of volunteers and given command of the right wing of the combined force, which included four divisions from Grant's Army of the Tennessee as well as his own division from the Army of the Ohio.

Grant was technically superior in rank to Thomas and apparently chafed at the decision which removed him from command. Though the decision was not of Thomas' making, or liking, by some accounts Grant perceived the reorganization and removal of his divisions as a personal slight and never forgot it.

In late May, Halleck's 120,000-man force reached and occupied Corinth after finding it abandoned by the Confederates. Thomas was placed in charge of the city and the surrounding area. In June, as a second reorganization took Halleck to Washington as General-in-Chief, Thomas asked to be transferred with his division back to Buell's Army of the Ohio. The change restored Grant to direct command and returned his divisions to him. Thomas apparently proposed the change out of deference to Grant, thinking it was proper to cede to Grant's seniority. It would not be the last time Thomas would make such a gesture, even though it personally disadvantaged him in terms of authority and rank.

He did it again later that same year. Buell had taken the Army of the Ohio on a several months' long series of unproductive marches and countermarches in an attempt to strike the Confederate army now led by Braxton Bragg. In late September, with a new campaign underway and the contending armies in close proximity, the War Department lost patience with Buell's leadership. Buell was removed from command and Thomas was named to replace him. Thomas immediately asked that the order be rescinded believing it was unwise and unfair to remove a commander 'on the eve of battle.' While Halleck acceded to Thomas and revoked the order, this second episode of Thomas' willingness to decline an opportunity, although for commendable motives, likely made the War Department less sure of Thomas' prospects.

On October 1, 1862, Buell, with Thomas second in command, moved his force of 60,000 against Bragg. A week later at Perryville, Kentucky, Union forces prevailed in a mismanaged battle. Moving with his separate columns widely dispersed, Buell fought with only a portion of his force. Along with other major elements of the Union Army, Thomas, five miles away, received no instructions and was not made aware that a battle was taking place. Perryville became a battle fought with little or no central direction on either side. To Buell's surprise, Bragg initiated the engagement with a full attack at mid-day. The struggle lasted for several hours. Casualties were high on both sides, although Buell's partially committed force suffered most heavily. Bragg eventually realized that the main portion of Buell's army was in the vicinity, and that night he withdrew under cover of darkness. Buell chose not to actively pursue.

Although Perrysville was seen as a quasi-victory for the North because Bragg had withdrawn, the Lincoln administration had by then lost confidence in Don Carlos Buell. On October 23, Buell was replaced by William S. Rosecrans. The troops operating in the department were brought together and redesignated the 14th Corps. Soon after, the full army would be renamed the Army of the Cumberland and would fight under that name for the first time at the battle of Murfreesboro. Later, the Army of the Cumberland would reach its greatest renown under the generalship of George Thomas.

Before launching an offensive, Rosecrans labored to re-equip and restructure his army, subdividing it into three grand divisions and assigning Thomas to command the center.

Rosecrans came quickly to rely on Thomas as an indispensable right hand and unselfishly made full use of Thomas' many talents.

Working in concert with Rosecrans, Thomas' wide-ranging professionalism came to the fore. Together, they organized an elite engineering 'Pioneer' brigade that excelled in vital tasks such as building and repairing roads and bridges, constructing fortifications, assembling pontoons, and a myriad of other essential tasks. Thomas devised a rapid strike force that exploited the power of the new repeating carbine and combined it with mounted infantry. He developed a signal telegraph train that was the most sophisticated in either army, radically speeding the process of stringing wire and transmitting information. The strike force and signal train foreshadowed other major innovations that would follow in areas such as medical care, food service, and the use of simulated battles as a training technique.

As Rosecrans labored to reconstruct his army, Thomas, encamped near Gallatin, Tennessee, kept supply lines open, trained and equipped new units, gathered 5,000 mules to sustain the pack trains of a mobile army, and with his Pioneer brigades repaired and reopened a vital railroad line, miles of which had been destroyed by Confederate raiders.

On the day after Christmas 1862, Rosecrans began his pursuit of Bragg's army. In miserable weather conditions he found the Confederates entrenched and waiting at Stones River adjacent to Murfreesboro, Tennessee. Ironically, both Rosecrans and Bragg proposed the same plan of attack—an envelopment of his opponent's right flank—at the same time. The dual assaults came on the morning of December 31. Bragg's was by far the more successful. The Union right, struck in the flank and rear by overwhelming numbers, was completely turned. The entire Union line was exposed as divisions under the command of Alexander McCook collapsed.

In the center, Thomas' division, flanked and nearly surrounded by onrushing Confederates coming from the right, fought their way out of a cauldron. As Bragg's wheeling movement threatened to over-whelm much of the Union army, Thomas regrouped Federal forces on a wooded knoll that would forever after be known as "Hell's Half Acre." On the hillock near a bend in Stones River, Thomas drew every available brigade to him and put six batteries on the crest

Through the day Bragg launched furious attacks, sometimes sending as many as 10 brigades in frantic attempts to overrun the hill. In mortal danger of being flanked and engulfed, Thomas stemmed the onrushing tide. Contemporary accounts mark his presence, always where the fight was most fierce, calmly directing actions and steadying his men. Four times through the long day, Thomas, joined later by Rosecrans, threw back attacks that sometimes came in waves four deep.

Darkness fell with the opposing armies still in close contact. The day had not gone well for the Union. Casualties were high and ground had been lost as well as artillery and wagons. At a late night conference, Rosecrans polled his generals. Many counseled retreat; Thomas preferred to stay and fight. Rosecrans agreed.

Cold rain lashed the battlefield as fighting barely sputtered through New Year's Day. That night Rosecrans sent a division across Stones River to occupy an area of high ground on the far side. Positioned on the height, fire from Union guns could enfilade the right side of the Confederate line. On January 2, Bragg tried desperately to retake the hill, once almost forcing the Federal forces back into the river. As the Confederates pressed their attack, however, they were devastated by massed batteries from across the river and then pushed back by a bayonet charge from fresh Union forces sent by Thomas.

Bragg retreated the following morning. Thomas moved his division into Murfreesboro the same day and drove the Confederate rear guard from the immediate area. The Battle of Murfreesboro, or Stones River, was a desperate battle, with both sides losing almost a quarter of their armies. Thomas' stand at "Hell's Half Acre" would presage his gallantry nine months later at Chickamauga.

After Murfreesboro, Rosecrans remained idle for almost half a year. Finally, at the prodding of the Lincoln administration, he launched a well-conceived, near-bloodless campaign that maneuvered Bragg out of his base at Tullahoma, Tennessee, and forced his withdrawal to Chattanooga. After another month and a half delay Rosecrans moved again, this time threatening Bragg's line of communications with Atlanta. On September 7, the Confederates abandoned Chattanooga. Then, after conducting one of the war's most masterful campaigns, Rosecrans made a disastrous decision.

Mistaking Bragg's orderly withdrawal from Chattanooga as a head-long retreat, Rosecrans split his army. Against Thomas' cautionary advice, Rosecrans divided his force into three widely separated columns and set out after the Confederate army. Thomas, commanding the center column, believed Bragg would use favorable terrain below Chattanooga to secure his communications and wait for reinforcements. Indeed, reinforcements numbering in the thousands were on their way. In addition to local militia levies, Jefferson Davis had sent James Longstreet with 14,000 men and an artillery battalion of 26 guns. The infusion of new manpower increased the size of Bragg's army to about 70,000 in a few days' time.

Probes by Thomas and other corps commanders revealed the depth of the peril as Bragg consolidated his army and moved to attack the Union columns before they could unite. As Rosecrans worked desperately to bring his forces together, Bragg moved past the Federal line on the north and prepared to engulf the Union left flank. Bragg's move, made in the early hours of September 19, would have separated Rosecrans' army from Chattanooga and foreclosed the possibility of seeking refuge there.

Thomas, however, by an exhaustive night march, passed his corps behind the army and extended to its left (to the north), interposing between Bragg and Chattanooga. At daybreak, Thomas had his corps in place. His move was timely: two hours later the first Confederates came up the road that Thomas now occupied. As Bragg readied the assault on the Union left, Thomas launched a spoiling attack on the Confederate right, driving back Nathan Bedford Forrest's cavalry and engaging with several infantry brigades before falling back to prepared positions. The encounter ignited combat on a wide scale, drawing units from both sides into the fray. Bragg abandoned his intended attack on the Union left, instead funneling troops into the burgeoning fight which spread along both lines to the south. Furious combat, sometimes waged with bayonets, lasted through the day. Nightfall found the armies still in contact on a nightmarish battlefield strewn with dead and wounded.

Morning brought repeated assaults on Thomas' position. The attacks were thrown back with heavy casualties. At about one o'clock, however, the entire complexion of the battle changed. A misguided order from Rosecrans inadvertently uncovered a portion of the center of the Union line just as Longstreet attacked the same sector. Longstreet poured enormous numbers into the gap, destroying divisions commanded by George Crittenden and striking those of McCook and Thomas in the flank. Masses of Confederates, sometimes six lines across stacked three deep, advanced almost unchecked, brushing aside all opposition. To no avail, Rosecrans hurried a reserve division, John Wilder's Mounted Infantry, and then Philip Sheridan with two brigades into the breach.

Amidst wild disorder, Crittenden and McCook, commanding two corps of the Union army, tried unsuccessfully to avert disaster. Neither could halt the rush of their divisions back to Chattanooga. Eventually, Rosecrans too, thinking all was lost, joined the flight over roads clogged with fleeing soldiers, walking wounded, ambulances, supply wagons and artillery caissons—the shattered remnants of an apparently defeated army.

In Chattanooga, Rosecrans organized the defense of the city in anticipation of an immediate attack, and wired the War Department to report what he thought was a complete and utter defeat: "My army is whipped and dispersed."

That proved not entirely to be the case.

In one of the most extraordinary episodes of the war, Thomas remained on the battlefield and with about 25,000 men made a stand that ranks among the greatest in the annals of warfare. Taking possession of high ground that after the battle came to be known as Horseshoe Ridge (after the horseshoe-shaped configuration Thomas employed to defend the position), Thomas and his men held off the combined weight of Bragg's entire army. Positioning his artillery superbly, adroitly shifting his outnumbered units from one threatened spot to another, Thomas fought off repeated attacks that came in multi-division strength and from all directions.

The fighting at Chickamauga was among the war's most fierce. Thomas' men at times used bayonets and clubbed muskets to beat back waves of attackers. As the battle raged on, ammunition began to run low as Bragg hurled his army against the ridge.

Late in the afternoon, three fresh Union brigades—two under the command of General James B. Steedman—reached the crest and joined Thomas. Thomas immediately sent Steedman to attack a nearby ridge. Steedman's assault came as a total surprise, clearing the hill of Longstreet's men and easing the pressure on one of Thomas' flanks, both of which were in danger of being overrun.

Early in the afternoon Rosecrans, not aware of Thomas' stand, sent word to Thomas to retreat at his discretion. Thomas declined. Indeed, so completely had Bragg been stopped and so high were the Confederate casualties that a Union victory was a possibility had fresh units been available to support his defense.

After sunset, Thomas received an order from Rosecrans directing a retreat. With some reluctance, Thomas complied, forming a new line at Rossville, Georgia, to cover his move. During the night of September 20, Thomas extracted his troops, conducting a withdrawal that was near-perfect in its execution. Thomas brought off his wounded from the battlefield and saved his artillery pieces.

In proportion to the numbers engaged, Chickamauga was one of the bloodiest battles of the war. Union forces lost 16,179 killed, wounded, or captured; Confederate losses numbered 18,454. Casualty rates exceeded those of more noted battles in the East. With other Union forces driven from the field, only Thomas and his men remained, and at Horseshoe Ridge they held until the rest of the army reached safety. Within days Thomas became known as the "Rock of the Chickamauga." Seldom has a label been so well earned.

By almost all accounts, Rosecrans was a shattered man for a time after Chickamauga, even as it was necessary to ready Chattanooga for defense. Command decisions drifted in uncertainty. Against the advice of his subordinate commanders, Rosecrans abandoned the high ground at

Lookout Mountain and Missionary Ridge, allowing Bragg to invest the city. Two Tennessee River ferries important to Union supply lines were also conceded to Bragg's forces. The Confederates chose not to storm the city, but with control of the heights, Bragg decided on a siege.

Meanwhile, events far from Chattanooga overtook Rosecrans and the Army of the Cumberland. In October, dissatisfaction within the War Department and Lincoln administration led to a major reorganization of the Western Theater. The armies of Ohio, Tennessee, and Cumberland were assigned to the Military Division of the Mississippi, and all were placed under Ulysses S. Grant as theater commander. Ambrose Burnside remained as Commander of the Army of the Ohio while William T. Sherman replaced Grant as commander of the Army of the Tennessee. Grant was given the option of retaining Rosecrans as commander of the Army of the Cumberland or appointing Thomas in his place. Although their relationship was not close, Grant chose Thomas.

Thomas quickly took action to secure additional supply routes, one on land and another by river, to better provision the Union forces. Although Bragg still held the high ground, the new routes made Thomas' army self-sustaining. It was increasingly evident that the siege was not going to starve out the Union force. Momentum was beginning to shift away from the Confederates.

Grant arrived in Chattanooga on October 23, later to be joined by Sherman from the west with six divisions and Joseph Hooker from the east with two corps. Sherman's arrival was delayed, but when all were finally in place, Hooker's force was assigned to the right and Thomas' the center. Sherman, whom Grant intended to make the main attack, was posted on the left of the Federal line.

Facing Thomas in the center was the looming presence of Missionary Ridge, a commanding height laced with rifle pits and well manned by Confederate troops. Between Thomas' line and the base of the ridge stood Orchard Knob, a rebel strongpoint that guarded the approach to the heights.

As the days wore on, Grant came to believe that Bragg was preparing to withdraw from the Chattanooga area. On November 23, Thomas sent five divisions against Orchard Knob to check the accuracy of Grant's information.

The Confederates had not withdrawn, but what followed was totally unexpected and, in the recollections of many Union officers who observed it: "magnificent." Thomas' troops struck the Confederate position with such speed and force that the strongpoint was completely overrun. Rather than a reconnaissance and withdrawal, Thomas' force took and held the key location in the Union center.

In dense fog the following day Joe Hooker fought and won 'the Battle above the Clouds,' sweeping Confederate troops off Lookout Mountain, and then he descended into Chattanooga Valley to take up position on the Union right.

On November 25 the Federals lined up with Sherman's Army of the Tennessee on the left, Thomas' Army of the Cumberland in the center, and Hooker's divisions from the Army of the Potomac coming up on the right. Grant intended his former command, now led by his friend Sherman, to make the main thrust. However, Sherman's attack toward Tunnel Hill at the north end of Missionary Ridge was stopped completely. Repulsed repeatedly with heavy losses by Confederate forces under Patrick Cleburne, Sherman dug in and called for reinforcements.

With Sherman unable to move, Grant eventually ordered attacks elsewhere along the line in an attempt to regain the initiative. At 3:40 in the afternoon, Thomas' troops moved from Orchard Knob toward Missionary Ridge, which was 600 yards away and covered by 42 cannon and a spider web of Confederate rifle pits. His two corps across a two-mile front advanced over open ground against defenders barricaded along and atop the 400-foot elevation.

Although Grant had ordered Thomas to simply attack and hold the rifle pits at the base of the ridge, as at Orchard Knob, the seemingly miraculous happened. Thomas' troops not only swept through the rifle pits but continued on, moving inexorably up the slope of the hill. Battling their way to the crest, they fanned out north and south capturing Confederate artillery and clearing the ridge of Bragg's troops. It was perhaps the most spectacular assault of the war.

In the aftermath, Bragg's troops fled the hill, routed and for a time out of control. On the left, the Confederate troops facing Sherman made a controlled withdrawal under Cleburne, saving guns and materiel. Altogether, though, the Confederate losses were devastating: 6,000 were made prisoner and numerous artillery pieces were lost, as were thousands of small arms and tons of supplies.

In addition to the victory at Chattanooga, the nation came to owe Thomas another debt of gratitude in its aftermath. While bivouacked in the city, he conceived the idea of a national cemetery for veterans.

Thomas had created a small cemetery at Mill Springs after the battle there in January 1862. Now, in the winter of 1863, he oversaw the laying out of another, much larger one on the slopes of Orchard Knob, on the soil where his troops had fought so gallantly. It became a model for an eventual national system of military cemeteries.

After Chattanooga, the next logical move for the Union army was Atlanta. Both sides knew it. At Dalton, Georgia, where he had withdrawn his forces, Bragg was replaced by General Joseph E. Johnston, who quickly established a series of fortified strongpoints and entrenchments.

Guarding the approach to Dalton was a narrow, heavily defended defile called Buzzard Roost Gap. Thomas, having made a personal reconnaissance, proposed to demonstrate against Buzzard's Roost to hold Johnston in place, while swinging his main force through Snake Creek Gap 10 miles to the south, which he found to be unprotected. If undertaken at the time and in the manner that Thomas proposed, it is likely that the flanking movement would have levered Johnston out of his defense of Atlanta, sparing the losses and the travails associated with the difficult, months-long campaign that followed.

Thomas' plan was overtaken by events. Grant was made General-in-Chief of the Armies of the United States and moved east to confront Lee. Sherman was named to replace Grant, and he declined Thomas' plan, deciding instead to send James McPherson's Army of the Tennessee against one rim of the Buzzard Roost defile and John Schofield's Army of the Ohio against the other, while holding Thomas' Army of the Cumberland in reserve.

With 61,000 men and 130 guns, Thomas' force was the most powerful of the three armies under Sherman and, as Sherman acknowledged, the best provisioned with equipment, engineers, and repair parties.

Sherman's attack failed. Three days of bloody fighting could not dislodge the Confederates. Eventually, Sherman tried to move through Snake Creek Gap but the moment had passed, as Johnston held the insufficient force initially dispatched by Sherman and then shifted his army to meet the larger, later threat.

Sherman's setbacks at Buzzard Roost and Resaca, and near Snake Creek Gap, shaped the campaign in the manner Johnston intended: punishing stands followed by slow withdrawals from one fortified position to another.

Thomas' Army of the Cumberland formed the center of the Union advance toward Atlanta, a march that would consume more than 100 days. Under fire all but three of those days, Thomas' force hammered Johnston's center every day, allowing Schofield and McPherson to turn the Confederate flanks. And thus it went through the summer of 1864 as Sherman's turning movements were countered by Johnston moving slowly back from strongpoint to strongpoint while keeping Atlanta safe in the rear.

Sherman was an impetuous man, and at Kennesaw Mountain his patience ran out. In late June, though Johnston's engineers had turned the mountain into a death trap, Sherman decided on a direct, frontal assault. Thomas and McPherson protested. Thomas suggested instead that McPherson be allowed to sweep around the mountain and attack Marietta. That move, Thomas believed, would at the minimum cause Johnston to dispatch forces from the mountain to counter it and might even cause him to abandon the position completely.

Sherman would not be dissuaded. Some, including General John Logan, have suggested that Sherman was distressed that back east the frontal assaults of the Army of the Potomac—Grant lost 50,000 men in one month—were drawing all the headlines. Logan's conjecture was that Sherman intended the attack to draw attention to the western theater.

Sherman launched his initial attack on the morning of June 27. Two more were attempted during the day. All were costly: Sherman's losses were quadruple Johnston's. In late afternoon, Sherman proposed a fourth assault. When Thomas protested its futility, Sherman mercifully agreed. Finally, at about 9 p.m. Sherman asked Thomas his opinion of a flanking movement. This having been Thomas' proposal from the outset, he readily agreed and suggested it be made with the entire army.

Sherman's movements were still parried by Johnston, who eventually withdrew to prepared defenses near Atlanta. Although Johnston had punished Sherman and had skillfully kept his army intact in the face of superior numbers, Confederate President Jefferson Davis wearied of his strategy. On July 18, Davis replaced Johnston with General John Bell Hood, a less cautious commander.

Hood immediately built on a plan formulated by Johnston to attack Federal forces as they were split while crossing Peachtree Creek. Anticipating little resistance, Sherman had momentarily separated his columns at distances that prevented mutual support. It fell to Thomas' army, now on the right wing, 10 miles from the nearest help, to make the crossing at Peachtree Creek.

Among the qualities that made Thomas an exceptional commander was his sense of anticipation—a studied readiness that prepared his army for any eventuality. With his usual thoroughness, Thomas placed cannon on a hill guarding the left flank of the Union forces that crossed the stream. At 3 p.m. on July 20, Hood attacked *en echelon* from right to left, throwing 30,000 Confederates against Thomas' 20,000. With Thomas at the front positioning troops and directing battery fire, three major attacks were thrown back in two hours. At nightfall, Hood broke off the assault. Confederate losses were heavy—nearly 5,000 by some accounts—compared with Thomas' 1,700.

After one more heavy attack against the Federals—this time aimed at McPherson's Army of the Tennessee, resulting in the Battle of the Atlanta—Hood withdrew into the elaborate inner defenses that encased the city. Sherman placed the town under siege for a month before launching the turning movement that proved to be decisive. As Sherman pushed his army to the right towards Jonesborough, Hood moved in parallel to the now extended lines, building fortifications as he went. Finally, on September 1, Thomas shattered Hood's defenses in a devastating attack that utterly defeated the Confederate forces positioned along the front. Atlanta surrendered the following day.

"Atlanta is ours and fairly won," Sherman signaled Washington. The victory might well have saved Lincoln's re-election.

During the campaign, Thomas commanded three-fifths of the Union army, won the opening and closing battles, bore the brunt of the almost daily clashes, saved the army at Kennesaw Mountain, and crushed Hood's surprise attack at Peachtree Creek.

After Atlanta, Sherman rested his forces for a time and then set out on a somewhat cursory pursuit of Hood. He soon grew weary of the chase and of attempting to prevent Hood's raids on tracks, trestles, and supply depots. Sherman's restlessness set the stage for one of the most unusual events of the war: "the March to the Sea."

Marching to the sea was not an original idea. Others, Thomas among them, had suggested doing so using a strong contingent of cavalry. It was generally agreed that the opposition would not be heavy: between Atlanta and the coast few organized Confederate forces were available to respond. Nonetheless, Sherman chose to slice through the Lower South with a huge army. An advocate of "total war," Sherman believed that the Confederacy had to be defeated psychologically as well as on the battlefield—hence the need to "make Georgia howl." While not opposed to the concept of a March to the Sea, Thomas did not view it as an opportunity for mass destruction. Throughout the war he went to considerable lengths to minimize damage to civilian property, and insisted on reparations being made when it occurred. To Thomas, a March to the Sea offered a chance to further split the Confederacy without the need to commit sizable forces.

Despite arguments to the contrary, Sherman stripped the best troops from the three armies that had forged the Atlanta campaign. Among the pieces that he took with him were Thomas' 14th Corps, perhaps the Union's best body of troops; the best cavalry mounts; almost all the heavy ordnance; and Thomas' Pioneer brigade—the envy of the Federal army. After burning Atlanta, Sherman left with 62,000 veteran troops on November 15, cutting a little opposed 60-mile path of destruction through Georgia.

Left behind was an entire Confederate army, now reinforced by Forrest's cavalry. Sherman apparently initially believed that Hood would follow his move to the sea. Hood had other ideas. He began to move west, where if he could defeat scattered forces in Tennessee and take Nashville, he could then move north, threaten or take Cincinnati, and open up numerous other possibilities. At the minimum, he could extend the war. At the extreme, he could change its direction.

The coming weeks presented a unique spectacle in warfare: two large, unfettered opposing armies moving away from one another, each seeking to wreak havoc on their adversary's countryside. Like Sherman, Hood at the start of his campaign anticipated little organized opposition.

It would be left to George Thomas to provide it.

Thomas, stripped of men and material by Sherman, was left with two corps; 5,000 cavalrymen without mounts; minimal artillery, some of it damaged; and a shortage of wagons. He immediately set out collecting forces, drawing in, among others, two divisions from Missouri. While other Federal units were in the immense area assigned to Thomas, many were needed to guard roads, communication centers, and supply depots at places like Murfreesboro, Decatur, and Chattanooga.

By mid-November, Hood's objective was clear. Nashville was the great strategic prize. Loss of the city, a center of river, rail, and telegraph communications traffic, would devastate the North and excite the hopes of the South. Hood moved into Tennessee in considerable force, nearly 40,000 veteran infantry and 5,000 cavalry.

While other Union forces were flowing to Nashville, Thomas patched together units from available resources: soldiers returning from leave, raw recruits, convalescents, and railroad guards. He took 5,000 men from quartermaster duty and put them in trenches. Along two lines of entrenchments that wrapped the city, he added earthworks and fortified strongpoints. In the interim, though, Thomas lost several thousand veterans whose enlistments expired or who were on furlough to vote.

As Hood's route became clear, Thomas bought time by ordering delaying actions aimed at slowing the Confederates' advance. General John A. Schofield with two corps at Pulaski hindered Hood momentarily before barely escaping entrapment there on November 25. Four days later at Spring Hill the Confederates mismanaged an excellent opportunity to cut off Schofield's entire force.

After Schofield's units almost literally sneaked past him at Spring Hill, Hood began an immediate, all-out pursuit. Thomas, having learned that additional forces from Missouri would not reach him until days later, asked Schofield to fight a delaying action at Franklin, Tennessee.

Schofield's units reached the town on November 30 and began hurriedly building a line of earthworks and entrenchments. Hood's advance units were close behind. By afternoon, Hood himself was on the scene and he chose to attack immediately, seeking to storm the Union positions before they were solidified. It was an impetuous, ill-advised attack made with only two-thirds of his army. The assault cost Hood heavily—some 6,300 out of 23,000 infantry engaged. Schofield withdrew that night to Nashville where his units joined other forces being assembled by Thomas. Despite his losses at Franklin, Hood pushed forward, arriving before Nashville on December 2.

Thus set the stage for one of history's most perfectly fought battles.

Before it happened though, the next two weeks witnessed another of the war's most implausible episodes. Grant, who himself had been mostly stationary before Petersburg for several months, began insisting that Thomas launch an immediate attack. The crescendo mounted daily with Grant threatening to remove Thomas from command and eventually boarding a train to Nashville to effect the relief.

Thomas, having been stripped of men and materiel by Sherman, held firm in the face of mounting pressure, using the time to assemble and train his largely recruit army. Methodically, he built a new cavalry corps: horses, including carriage horses and some found in a traveling circus, were requisitioned throughout Tennessee and Kentucky. Realistic exercises involving infantry, cavalry, and artillery acting in concert—what today would be called combined arms training—were conducted often and on a large scale. In a few short weeks, Thomas created an army.

When Schofield's divisions came in from Franklin, and with two divisions commanded by General A.J. Smith freshly arrived from Missouri, Thomas was ready. He had to wait two more days, however, while a fierce ice storm abated.

In the meantime, Hood had also been preparing his army for battle. Running east to west for five miles, his main trench line was embellished with breastworks along the front and redoubts covering the flanks. Long stretches of a stone wall shielded rifle pits in the center. Thomas would face this formidable defense line with an army composed half or more of soldiers who had never seen battle.

In the afternoon of December 14, Thomas met with his commanders to review once again his plan of attack. Innovative as always, Thomas envisioned an enormous wheeling maneuver that would strike into and around Hood's left flank. After first making a strong demonstration with his own left to hold Hood in place, Thomas' right wing, his main strength, would swing forward, rotating like a door hinge anchored to the left side of his line.

At Nashville, Thomas' attack would make history in another way as well. Thomas aligned eight African-American regiments to cover and extend his line to the left. Black units had fought in other engagements during the war, but Thomas was the only Union general who not only used them but assigned them a prominent role in a full army's battle.

Dawn of December 15 found the prospective battlefield blanketed by fog. Thomas used the cover to move his troops to within a third of a mile of the Confederate lines. At about 8 a.m. the fog lifted and Thomas' left wing smashed into fortifications on the Confederates' right. Hood, anticipating the move as foreshadowing a major attack in that sector, held his forces in place.

Soon after, Thomas sent combined infantry and cavalry attacks against the Confederate left. Two Confederate batteries were captured and their guns turned to support the Union advance. As the fight progressed, Thomas dispatched Schofield's corps, which had begun the day in the interior right of the Union line, around two other corps and repositioned it farthest on the right. The unexpected move caused Hood to stretch and thin his own lines. Despite Hood's attempted countermoves, Confederate strongpoints began to fall one after another. At mid-day, with Union forces near a key position on the Hillsboro Pike, Thomas sent cavalry units on a strike still farther to the right that threatened to enfold the Confederate line. At the other end of the line, steady pressure was applied, dissuading Hood from shifting significant forces to other places in peril along the front.

In the early afternoon, Thomas unleashed the most unusual cavalry movement of the war. Under the command of James H. Wilson, Thomas sent 12,000 Union cavalry on a right hand sweep around the Confederate left. Armed with seven-shot Spencer carbines and taught to ride to the fight, dismount, fire, and advance again, this force was the lineal descendent of the rapid strike concept first envisioned by Thomas and Rosecrans two years before.

Wilson's cavalry cut through the Confederates, overrunning redoubts and capturing artillery as dismounted infantry, then taking to their saddles to race forward and strike again. By nightfall on the wintery day, they had advanced eight miles. Their giant right hook around the Confederates placed them almost facing the lines they had departed from that morning.

Darkness found the Union forces everywhere ascendant. All along the line Hood had been forced back. In the center and on the right, his forces were battered and reeling. On the left, the Confederate flank had been swept from the field. Hood now retreated south, seeking to reform his defenses along a stretch of elevated ground known as Harpeth Hills. So overpowering had Thomas' right hand thrust been that his line now almost formed an "L" shape with the original start line. The entire left wing of Hood's army had been shoved back, collapsing into the center. The Confederates worked through the night, building a new line that bent back to protect the shattered left wing and constructing earthworks at key points on high ground.

Their efforts would be to no avail.

On the morning of the 16th, Thomas renewed his attack. On the Confederate right flank, Union forces surged forward against Hood's lines. The "black brigades" (officially the U.S. Colored Troops) attacked three times, the last assault finally breaking through under heavy fire.

While Union forces pressed forward all along the line, Thomas' main attack struck the Confederate left at an oblique angle. With his strength heavily stacked on the right side of his line, Thomas again sent Wilson's cavalry on a major sweep around Hood's fortifications.

By about three o'clock in the afternoon or shortly thereafter, Wilson's dismounted force had gained significant ground, raising havoc behind the rebel lines. Thomas chose that time to deliver the death blow to Hood's army. Thomas sent the full strength of his powerful right wing, including Schofield's entire corps, straight into the Confederate left flank. Brigade followed brigade in waves as the Union forces swept forward while in the rear Wilson's cavalry engulfed a mile and a half of the Confederate line.

On the left, the entire Confederate line gave way. On the right, Union troops moved forward, overrunning strongpoints, pushing Confederates off the high ground and forcing the shattered remnants into a wild retreat. Enveloped at both ends of his line, Hood's army came apart, racing from the catastrophe that had befallen them—one of the few times during the war that a Confederate army broke and fled from a battlefield.

Hood's army was effectively annihilated. Thomas, though, was not yet done—he dispatched cavalry that chased the scattered parts of Hood's army for 12 days and dozens of miles, ending its usefulness as a fighting force.

After the battle, when the African-American brigades marched past him on the road, Thomas moved his horse to the side, faced them, and removed his hat. He remained there until all of them had passed. It was a gesture they never forgot.

At Nashville Thomas utterly destroyed an entire Confederate army at the cost of about 3,000 men, only a small portion of whom were killed. Hood lost double that in casualties plus several thousand captured—so many were taken prisoner that housing had to be found for them in Nashville—and much of his artillery along with tons of supplies.

Nashville was the most decisive tactical victory gained by either side in a major engagement during the war. On December 24, although Grant demurred, Lincoln promoted Thomas to major general in the regular army.

After Nashville, Thomas and Wilson assembled an enormous force of cavalry and equipped much of it with Spencer repeating rifles. At Grant's order, one division of 5,000 was sent to General Edward Canby for operations against Mobile. Thomas received approval for Wilson to go after Tuscaloosa, Selma, and other remaining southern arsenals and manufacturing centers. On March 27, General George Stoneman with 10,000 cavalrymen crossed the Blue Ridge Mountains to divert Confederate forces from Sherman's move into North Carolina. Meanwhile, Wilson launched a spectacular campaign. After taking Tuscaloosa, he defeated Nathan Bedford Forrest and captured Selma on April 2 before moving on to Montgomery and finally to Macon, Georgia, taking those cities on the 12th and 21st of April, respectively.

While Lee was surrendering at Appomattox on April 9, Confederate President Jefferson Davis was attempting to escape, traveling south with a small entourage. A month later, on May 10, James Wilson, Thomas' cavalry commander, guided the dragnet of converging forces that led to

Davis' capture near lrwinsville, Georgia. Soon after, on May 26, the last Confederate army in the field, commanded by General Kirby Smith, surrendered at Galveston, Texas.

Thomas' wartime service left lasting legacies. Unlike Lee, his fellow Virginian and close personal friend, Thomas' commitment to the Union never wavered. At the outset of the conflict Thomas turned down an offer to become chief of ordnance for Virginia's embryonic army. Nonetheless, especially early in the war, Thomas' prospects for more rapid promotion may have been thwarted by officials wary of his Virginia background.

Thomas' decision to stay with the Union was of considerable consequence. Had the South possessed two generals of the quality of Lee—and Thomas was clearly of that caliber—any eventual Union victory would have been made impressively more difficult. Alternately, Lee versus Thomas—as would have been the case had Secretary of War Stanton's opinion prevailed and Thomas rather than Grant had been appointed as General-in-Chief of the Union armies—would have been a contest for the ages.

His contemporaries most often compared Thomas with George Washington. Indeed, there was somewhat of a physical resemblance: Thomas was an imposing, solid six-footer whose command 'presence' was often remarked upon. There were apparent similarities of character and conduct as well. Thomas' integrity was beyond reproach. He was a man of enormous inner strength whose calmness under fire was legendary. He exuded a sureness, a steadiness, that inspired confidence. Modest to a fault and quiet by nature, Thomas led by example. 'Old Tom' as his soldiers called him, was venerated by the men of the Army of the Cumberland. His soldiers seemed to understand that they were exceptionally well organized, trained, equipped and prepared—and that their lives would never be foolishly placed at risk. Thomas was known for his solicitous care and concern for his soldiers, frequently moving with his staff to the side of the road to yield the route to his passing troops.

Thomas was among the first of the 'modern' generals. Many of his innovations foreshadowed organizations, techniques, and equipment still present in today's army. Among many others those include: introducing the concept of remote fire control using his model signal corps; pioneering the use of combined forces and training exercises; developing portable bridges; implementing a telegraph service that facilitated command and control of dispersed forces; creating the forerunner of the modem command center; devising a movable railway base and repair facility; installing the war's most capable and best equipped hospital service, which included using railway cars as mobile field hospitals; providing a USO-like service of books and materials for his soldiers; and establishing an efficient mess service employing full-time cooks.

Grant's historic criticism, often repeated, was that Thomas was "slow." The term was true if it implied thoughtful, deliberate, meticulous, and methodical—for surely Thomas was all those things. He was the only general on either side who thought a battle all the way through, including planning for the pursuit after the opponent had been defeated. Certainly none of the Confederate generals who opposed Thomas ever described him as being slow.

Indeed, the "slow" appellation may have come from two sources neither of which had to do with speed on a battlefield or readiness to confront an enemy. As a cavalry instructor at West Point, Thomas frequently used the term 'slow trot' to conserve the usefulness of the academy's worn and aging training mounts. Others have said he used it to steady his cadets as they prepared for a practice charge. Whatever the reason, so often did he employ the phrase that his students came to use it as his nickname: "Slow Trot."

The second source was a back injury Thomas suffered in a fall just prior to the start of the war. After that, he moved more deliberately as he adjusted to the spinal discomfort. Neither the nickname nor his physical condition had any relationship to the speed with which he moved his army, but nonetheless some detractors seemed to extend the inference in that direction.

The sources of Grant's well-recognized coolness toward Thomas are uncertain. Thomas' previous service record surpassed Grant's and Thomas held superior rank. Some have speculated that Grant's embarrassment after Shiloh—when Halleck removed him from direct command and assigned four of his divisions to Thomas—may have contributed to Grant's ill-feelings. Grant was not a forgetting man.

During and after the war, comparisons of the two men were sometimes made in newspaper accounts and in the oral and written reminiscences of senior officers on both sides. Thomas almost always fared well, particularly when attention was drawn to casualty figures. While destroying an entire Confederate army at Nashville, Thomas' losses (3,000) were less than half those (7,000) lost by Grant in 30 minutes of horror at Cold Harbor.

Thomas was the only general who utterly destroyed a Confederate army in the field. That he also saved a Union army (at Chickamauga) simply adds to his luster.

Still, on the Union side it is the names of Grant and Sherman, particularly, that remain most prominently with us in the present day. Thomas did not live long after the war ended. Grant and Sherman wrote memoirs of their service. Thomas, even had he lived, had no intention of doing so. The accomplishments of Grant and Sherman are beyond question, but it is charitable to note that their memoirs are in places self-serving. Others have been less charitable labeling them 'self-lauding fiction' and, in the case of Grant's commentary, as exhibiting a 'charming indifference to fact.'

Nonetheless, with Thomas silent, and Grant and Sherman in positions of prominence with writings in circulation, their versions of history became fixed in popular perception. As the *Official Records of the War of the Rebellion* were released during the years 1880–1890, historians began noting discrepancies in their accounts. The war had been over for a long time, however, and was receding from the public eye.

In recent years, new generations of historians have delved more thoroughly into the records and at long last Thomas' name has begun to shine through.

"Time and history will do me justice," George Thomas said.

The time has long since come. Perhaps history will now catch up.

Before and After

George Thomas was born on July 31, 1816, in Southampton County, Virginia. The family farm employed 12 to 15 slaves working fields of corn, cotton, and tobacco. As a boy, Thomas had a unique relationship with the family's servants. Growing up, the Negro youths were his inseparable companions; he smuggled food and sugar treats to them and, much against the wishes of his parents, by some accounts taught them the lessons he learned each day at school. When he was older, he returned from travels with clothes, shoes, and gifts. It is interesting to speculate whether Thomas' background influenced his decision to use black regiments as an integral part of the battle at Nashville.

Thomas was 15 years old when, on August 22, 1831, he helped save his family during Nate Turner's slave revolt. Chased by Turner's men, Thomas drove a carriage carrying his family and then, about to be caught, guided them on foot through swamps and woods to the safety of a nearby town. Indicative perhaps of their relationship with the family, none of the Thomas slaves joined the revolt. In later life Thomas commented that the lesson he took from the revolt was that the desire for human freedom could not be suppressed. He regarded the institution of slavery as "intolerable."

After working for two years in a law office, Thomas received an appointment to West Point, entering the academy on June 1, 1836. His roommate was William Tecumseh Sherman. Four years later he graduated 12th in a class of 42.

Thomas' first active duty assignment was a brief stint training troops in New York. After only a few weeks he was sent to Florida where a sizable part of the small U.S. Army was engaged in a war with the Seminoles.

Everything about the meager outpost at Fort Lauderdale was atrocious: food, living facilities, and camp conditions in general. His skills were immediately apparent and because of his broad competence he was assigned multiple extra duties: commissary, quartermaster, ordnance officer, and adjutant, among others. The troops especially appreciated his successful efforts to improve the cuisine.

After a year spent sorting out supply problems and improving conditions at the camp, he accompanied one of the war's more successful expeditions. Venturing deep into the Everglades, 60 troops, with Thomas second in command, inflicted a considerable number of casualties, took prisoners, and destroyed caches of weapons, supplies, and canoes. Near the end of his tour, Colonel William J. Worth recommended his promotion to first lieutenant.

On July 1, 1842, Thomas reported for duty at Fort Moultrie, on Sullivan's Island in the harbor of Charleston, South Carolina. His assignment there was notable for his close acquaintance with then-lieutenant Braxton Bragg, who two decades later would be his opponent in some of the momentous battles of the Civil War. In December 1843 Thomas was sent briefly to Fort McHenry, near Baltimore, Maryland, for a short stint with a light artillery company. In the spring of 1844 he returned to Fort Moultrie where, with the exception of recruiting duty in New York, he remained until the outbreak of war with Mexico.

In the summer of 1845, with war on the horizon, Thomas' artillery company was dispatched to the Texas front. After landing at Corpus Christi the unit moved south to join other forces being assembled under the command of General Zachary Taylor. The conflict began in earnest in the spring of the following year when Fort Brown, a barricaded camp across the Rio Grande from Matamoros, was cut off while Taylor, with the bulk of the army, was away securing his line of supply.

Taylor's move to relieve the Fort Brown garrison precipitated the first major battles of the war at Palo Alto (May 8) and Resaca de la Palma (May 9). Both battles, American victories, were aided significantly by effective artillery support. At Resaca de la Palma, as at Fort Brown, Thomas led his gun crew with particular distinction.

With war officially declared on May 13, Taylor began his move into northern Mexico. In August, Thomas and most of his artillery battery joined Taylor at Camargo as the general prepared his army for the march on Monterrey. They arrived in front of the city on September 19, and Taylor ordered an all-out attack for the next morning. Thomas and his battery were for a time pinned in a narrow alley in the midst of a firefight. Eventually ordered to move, Thomas reloaded his weapons and slowly extracted his unit under heavy fire. The remainder of the battle was characterized by house-to-house fighting, with Thomas repeatedly putting himself and his unit in harm's way to clear barri-caded streets and rooftops.

After the battle, Taylor immediately promoted Thomas to captain for "gallant and meritorious conduct" during the fight. Late in 1846, Thomas was detailed for a time from Taylor's main army to provide artillery support for General John Quitman's move toward Tampico. Early in 1847, Thomas' unit returned to Taylor's army as it moved to reinforce the American garrison at Saltillo.

Learning that Mexican General Antonio Lopez de Santa Anna was approaching with 20,000 men, Taylor, with an army of 4,757 men and 16 guns, took up a defensive position at Buena Vista. The terrain fea-tured a high, relatively level plateau cut by ravines. Gorges on both sides ran back into the mountains. On the right, where Thomas commanded a field gun on the forward section of the American line, gullies frac-tured the landscape and hindered the massed attacks that followed the next day.

After some skirmishing, Santa Anna's assault began in the early hours of February 23. On the left the American position was turned by a mas-sive Mexican attack and the entire line was forced back. For much of the day, Thomas' artillery position became the center of the furious action. Thomas and his gun crew remained under fire for ten consecutive hours. Firing volley after volley of round and hollow shot, Thomas' men beat back repeated attacks that came upon them from forces arrayed in an enormous half circle across the American front. At times with-out infantry support, Thomas' position was nearly overrun as Mexican attacks reached within yards of his weapons before volleys of canister drove them back. Taylor's small army held on to win the desperate battle. Thomas was brevetted again, this time to major, on February 23.

Thomas remained in Mexico until August 1848. One of the first American units to move into Mexico, his company was now among the last to leave. After temporary commissary depot duties in Texas and a follow-on leave, he was posted to Fort Adams, Rhode Island, as a company commander in the 3rd Artillery.

Thomas was at Fort Adams only a short time before being dispatched to Florida where in September 1849, fighting had again flared up with the Seminoles. Thomas spent a year as a trouble-shooter, traveling from post to post around the peninsula resolving supply problems.

Three short months, January to March 1851, followed at Fort Independence in Boston Harbor before Thomas left to take a prestigious appointment at the U.S. Military Academy. He arrived at West Point in April and assumed duties as an instructor of cavalry and artillery tactics. Over the next three years, he significantly upgraded the equipment and curricula in both departments. By all accounts, he excelled in the instructor role, and Thomas' students included many who would hold senior positions in the Union and Confederate armies. After Robert E. Lee came to the academy as superintendent in 1852, Thomas and Lee became close colleagues and later continued their friendship when both were assigned to a cavalry unit in the West.

Thomas' West Point assignment ended in May 1854. Fort Yuma, a desolate post on the Arizona border near the convergence of the Gila and Colorado Rivers, followed. As post commander, Thomas led patrols, explored, gathered plants and mineral specimens, some of which he sent to the Smithsonian Institution, and learned the local Indian language. The rescue of a small Mormon child who had been kidnapped by Apaches highlighted his military activities. July 1855 brought a promotion to major and a new assignment. Thomas was posted to the 2nd Cavalry, one of the army's most elite units. A newly formed regiment, the 2nd was supplied by Secretary of War Jefferson Davis with distinctive uniforms and the army's best officers, mounts, men, and equipment. Sixteen of the 2nd Cavalry's officers would become generals during the Civil War.

A month after Thomas joined the unit at Jefferson Barracks in St. Louis, the regiment was sent to Texas and subsequently dispersed across Indian country in dozens of small outposts. For a time during the early months of 1856 court-martial boards and recruiting duties separated Thomas from his unit. Finally, on May 1, he rejoined it at Fort Mason, about 100 miles northwest of San Antonio. Over the next several months he periodically traveled with Robert E. Lee, also assigned to a Texas post, when both were assigned as members of court-martial boards. Thomas' time in Texas was generally filled with routine duties, though was also notable for extended reconnaissance scouts, the longest of which, 53 days, was dispatched against the Kiowas and Comanches.

Although he was involved in two Seminole Wars, the War with Mexico, and was consistently in the midst of some of the bloodiest actions of the Civil War, the only wound Thomas ever received in combat came from his time in Texas. On April 25, 1860, in a skirmish with a small band of Comanches an arrow glanced off his chin and lodged in his chest. Typical of Thomas, he pulled out the arrow and continued the fight.

In November 1860, Thomas left Texas on leave to rejoin his family. On his way home, a fall from a train platform caused the back injury that would plague him for the remainder of his life. Skeptical for a time that he would be able to return to active service, Thomas momentarily explored prospects for military-related employment, such as Commandant of Cadets at Virginia Military Institute, that would not require service in the field. None was forthcoming. In March 1861, shortly before the state seceded from the Union, the governor of Virginia offered him the position of chief of ordnance. Thomas declined.

Meanwhile, when Texas left the Union, the 2nd Cavalry was shipped back north. On April 13, at New York City Harbor, Thomas met the transport vessels carrying members of his regiment. From there, the unit moved to Carlisle Barracks to re-equip and train Thomas' wartime service had begun. In a quiet fashion, as was his manner, Thomas' postwar service, though tragically short, was in many ways as exemplary as his battlefield laurels.

Viewing firsthand the devastation of the populace of North Georgia and Alabama, he volunteered to serve as military governor to restore civil order and oversee elections. When soon afterward a formal system of military governments was established, Thomas' area of responsibility consisted of Kentucky, Tennessee, Mississippi, Alabama, and Georgia— more states than were assigned to any other Union general.

The initial stage of Reconstruction was particularly difficult. Clashes between repatriated Confederate soldiers and citizens who had remained loyal to the Union were frequent at first, as were hostilities between local citizens and black soldiers serving in the occupation army. Early on, Thomas warned Congress about the growing danger of the Ku Klux Klan. More violence occurred when portions of the Southern public disagreed with efforts to ratify the Fourteenth Amendment to the Constitution (guaranteeing citizenship regardless of race or previous condition of servitude). With meticulous attention to legalities, Thomas settled blacks on estates abandoned by former slave holders and provided them with equipment necessary for them to begin working the land. He was one of the few in government or the military who captured Lincoln's vision and took practical steps to transform it into reality.

Other facets of Thomas' life were equally commendable. He turned down admirers' proffered gifts of a house, silver plate, and other amenities. When supporters raised money intended for him, he insisted instead that it be given to widows and war orphans. In a reprise of his wartime decisions to refuse higher office when he believed the offer was questionably motivated, he turned aside President Andrew Johnson's attempt to appoint him General-in-Chief of the Army. Thomas believed the move, which would have installed him in the position as Grant's replacement, was a political ploy intended to sidetrack Grant's presidential ambitions. Thomas was determined to keep himself and the office he held out of politics—as was evidenced in 1867 when he refused efforts to draft him as a presidential candidate.

In 1869, Thomas took command of the Military District of the Pacific, headquartered in San Francisco. Though his health was suspect, he took on the duties with his usual thoroughness and dedication, traveling several thousand miles to visit posts in five states and territories scattered from Nevada to Washington. In the early afternoon hours of March 28, 1870, Thomas collapsed in his office in San Francisco, the victim of an apparent massive stroke.

As Thomas' remains were transported across the country, mourning crowds waited at every stop to mark his passing. His body lay in state at Troy, New York, on April 7. The visitation was attended by President Grant, cabinet members, several governors, Congressional representatives, and among other generals, Sherman, Meade, Rosecrans, and Hooker. The following day George H. Thomas was interred in his wife's family plot in Troy.

Bruce Catton said: "What a general could do, Thomas did; no more dependable soldier for a moment of crisis existed on the North American continent, or ever did exist."

DAVID PORTER

Porter helped wrest control of the great river systems in the western theater and, working with Grant and Sherman, contributed measurably to the Union victory at Vicksburg. Later, he led the naval component of the amphibious assault on Fort Fisher, "the Gibraltar of the Confederacy," closing the South's last remaining port at Wilmington, North Carolina.

The Civil War is rightfully recalled mainly for massive encounters waged across the American landscape from the Atlantic Coast to the Mississippi River and beyond. It was primarily a war of ground combat fought by infantry, artillery, and cavalry deployed in numbers unprecedented in the nation's earlier wars. Most of the war's 625,000 military deaths can be traced to those branches of the combat arms of the Union and Confederate armies. Almost all of the war's famous names are those of generals on both sides. To the extent that Civil War naval officers are remembered, it is David G. Farragut's name that is most prominently recalled—most often because of his association with a single event and a remarkable phrase: the fabled "Damn the torpedoes, full speed ahead!" command during the chaos of the attack on Mobile Bay.

The role of the U.S. Navy is too often lost amidst descriptions of titanic collisions of blue and gray armies. However, while lesser known, the navy's contributions played an important part in the North's ultimate victory. The navy's increasingly effective blockade of Southern ports along 3,500 miles of coastline on the Atlantic seaboard and Gulf of Mexico strangled the Confederacy, shutting down commerce and gradually closing off the flow of war-sustaining materials.

In the interior, the navy's control of America's great river systems fragmented the Confederate states and enabled the Union to employ freer movement of men and supplies across theaters of war notable for their vast distances. In the West, particularly, the navy directly supported the combat operations of the Federal army.

At the time the U.S. military establishment had nothing like a Joint Chiefs of Staff organization to plan, coordinate, and conduct combined operations of the nation's military services. In the Civil War in the West, cooperation evolved with considerable success primarily because of a partnership between two Union leaders: General Ulysses S. Grant of the U.S. Army and Admiral David Dixon Porter of the U.S. Navy.

Porter's name first surfaced, briefly, at the very outset of the war. When the Lincoln administration resolved on an attempt to hold Fort Pickens in Florida as well as Fort Sumter in South Carolina, Porter was one of a small group of strategists who developed a plan to re-provision and retain the Florida post. It is indicative of the internal chaos in the early days of the new regime as well as the general apprehensions of the time that Secretary of the Navy Gideon Welles, who was concurrently planning the Fort Sumter relief mission, was not advised of the efforts of Porter's group.

The key component of the Fort Pickens plan involved the use of the steam frigate U.S.S. *Powhatan*, commanded by Porter, to carry supplies and reinforcements to the fort. The attempt was successful, and Fort Pickens remained in Union hands throughout the conflict. However, given the navy's paucity of ships at the start of the war, the absence of the *Powhatan's* firepower may have precluded Union forces from making a more forceful effort to defend Fort Sumter.

In late 1861 Porter, now a commander, was in the Western Theater where with only scattered interruptions he would spend most of the war. Porter served initially under the command of David Farragut, first organizing and then commanding a flotilla of mortar boats that Farragut allowed to operate with considerable autonomy. In the closing months of the year, Porter assisted with plans and preparations to begin the campaign to pry open the Mississippi River.

New Orleans was the necessary first step. A busy port city situated several miles inland from the Gulf of Mexico, the city received goods coming down the river and commerce to and from Europe and other world markets. It was a major prize. Farragut's squadron would have to fight past two forts containing heavy guns before reaching the city's immediate defenses.

Porter hammered the forts, Jackson and St. Philip, for five days with his mortars. When the forts continued to hold out, the decision was made to run the main ships past them during the night of April 24, 1862.

Farragut successfully crashed his squadron through a barricade of logs and sunken vessels while Porter stayed in the area as a distraction and continued to shell both fortifications. Safely above the forts, Farragut sailed ahead to New Orleans. On April 29, after destroying several Confederate gunboats, he demanded and received the city's surrender.

Meanwhile, Porter's flotilla kept bombarding the lower fortifications. After the garrison at Fort Jackson mutinied, both forts surrendered to him on April 27. New Orleans to the mouth of the delta was now in Federal hands.

The next move was north up the river in an attempt to control the entire length of the Mississippi. Farragut first took his ships to Vicksburg where, with covering fire from Porter's high-arcing mortars against the city's defenses on the bluff, he passed through and linked up with Union vessels coming down the river from the north. It quickly became obvious, however, that the city could not be taken without the army's involvement. The attempt was called off and Porter, soon to be followed by Farragut, was sent east to assist General George B. McClellan's army in what came to be known as the Peninsula Campaign.

While Porter was involved with McClellan's ill-fated expedition, the U.S. Navy was being reorganized. New ranks, commands, and operational units were put in place as the navy grew and its role continued to evolve. Although relatively junior, the effect of the changes was to make Porter an instant admiral. On October 1, 1862, he was appointed commander of the newly reconstituted and retitled Mississippi River Squadron. Two weeks later, in Cairo, Illinois, he arrived to assume those duties.

The timing was propitious, as the army was turning again to prospects for opening the Mississippi. Porter was a strong enthusiast and soon developed personal and professional friendships with the two soldiers most responsible for making it happen: Ulysses S. Grant and William T. Sherman.

Vicksburg was the key that locked the Mississippi for the Confederacy. Farragut's earlier expedition as well as a failed overland attempt by Grant made it clear that a successful assault would benefit from the combined efforts of both the army and the navy: the navy to blockade the river and bombard the city, the army to invest and capture it.

As Grant was settling in to the task, Porter was detached to a side event. On January 10–11, 1863, Porter supported General John A. McClernand's capture of Fort Hindman at Arkansas Post, Arkansas. Although successful, the assault had little relationship to the Vicksburg campaign and minimal effect on its outcome. Through February and early March, Porter made runs past Vickburg's guns to disrupt Confederate river traffic below the city.

The Vicksburg campaign that followed illustrated Grant's tenacity, as several unsuccessful attempts preceded the city's fall. Beginning in February, Grant explored various routes that might take his forces close to the city. On February 4, Grant's chief engineer blew up a levee upstream that separated the Mississippi from access to the Yazoo River. The Yazoo Pass, as it was called, seemed to hold promise. If it could be successfully negotiated, the Yazoo would flow his attackers to points just north of the city.

Porter assigned Lieutenant Commander Watson Smith, with a small flotilla of 'tinclad' gun boats and two ironclads, to accompany a contingent of soldiers in an attempt to force open the prospective passage. Smith was not an aggressive commander. Several miles downstream, ships in the slow moving convoy were damaged by fire from Fort Pemberton, a Confederate fortification near Greenwood, Mississippi. After a series of tries, the effort was aborted in early April.

Meanwhile, Porter also examined possibilities for an alternative water route. On March 14, he began an attempt to push through overgrown bayous believed to be linked in a manner that would carry him close to Vicksburg. From the Yazoo River, Porter entered a narrow waterway known as Steele's Bayou with five ironclads, four mortar boats, and four tugs.

Progress, though difficult, was initially made before natural obstacles as well as Confederate barricades and sniper fire slowed and then stopped the movement of Porter's vessels. Ten days later, with additional Confederate troops on the way and the flotilla in danger of being trapped, the attempt was abandoned. At Porter's request, Sherman sent troops to cover the withdrawal of his ships.

The move that eventually brought success came when Grant shifted his army south of Vicksburg, a process that began on March 31 by marching the bulk of his forces down the *west* side of the Mississippi from Milliken's Bend to Hard Times in the area of Grand Gulf, about 40 miles below the city.

Vicksburg sits high on a bluff on the east bank, so the army would have to move back across the river to get at the city from the landward side. Porter assigned more than half of his squadron to escort a group of transport ships past the Vicksburg batteries down the river to reach the Federal forces. In a heavy, running firefight the fleet fought its way past Vicksburg's guns on the night of April 16. On April 22, a second run past the batteries was made, giving Grant sufficient transports to move his army across the river.

Grant's first attempt was at Grand Gulf on April 29. Porter's sizable flotilla, including two ironclads, four tinclads, three monitor scows, and Porter's flagship shielded 10 troop-carrying transports. Two Confederate fortifications sat nearly astride the prospective landing zone. Fort Wade sat close to the water while Fort Cobun, a more formidable obstacle, was situated higher above the river with heavy guns enclosed along a cliff face. Altogether, the Confederates had about 4,000 men well positioned behind barricades and in rifle pits. Porter split his force to simultaneously attack both fortifications. The extended barrage succeeded in reducing Fort Wade but despite considerable damage Fort Cobun held out. Porter was wounded, not seriously, by a shell fragment as he shifted vessels and redirected fire against Fort Cobun. Shells from the fort struck several vessels and damaged two during the fight.

In the early afternoon Grant broke off the encounter, realizing that sending troops on unarmed transports against Cobun's remaining heavy weapons and intact rifle pits held little promise for success. He elected instead to move 10 miles farther downstream to Bruinsburg. There, unopposed on the following day, Porter's ships, with gunboats covering transports and hay and coal barges, began ferrying Grant's army to the Vicksburg side of the river.

On May 8, as Grant's army pressed north along the east bank of the Mississippi, Porter took possession of Grand Gulf and the remnants of Fort Wade and Fort Cobun after the Confederates blew up munitions supplies and abandoned both fortifications.

One of Porter's commendable qualities was that, although under no organizational obligation to do so, he worked to understand Grant's maneuvers and their timing. Anticipating the army's movements, Porter went to considerable lengths to act in concert and lend support. In mid-May, recognizing that Grant was now moving full-out toward Vicksburg and would need food, materiel, and ammunition for the inevitable combat there, Porter established an enormous supply depot at a plantation along the Yazoo River. When Grant arrived at Vicksburg on May 18, his army was indeed in desperate need of replenishment having exhausted its supplies during a long, difficult march interspersed with major battles along the way. Grant was elated to find an enormous supply depot already in existence and available for his immediate use.

With his army fed and re-equipped, Grant made plans to attack. Porter was asked, and readily agreed, to assist by bombarding the city with his six large mortars and shelling the town's forts and batteries with his iron-clads. While Porter's ships hammered the city from the river on the west, Grant pressed his assault, investing Vicksburg with heavy, repeated attacks from the east. Days of bloody combat followed as Union forces struggled against the formidable redoubts that guarded the city. Grant tightened the ring but could not break through the defensive wall, eventually settling on a siege operation.

On June 7, in a desperate attempt to lift the siege, Confederate forces launched an attack on Milliken's Bend, a key position on the river about 15 miles northwest of Vicksburg. Union forces were first pushed back and in danger of being overrun when the giant ironclad *Choctaw*, sent by Porter, arrived on the scene. The gunboat's 100-pounder Parrot gun and large Dahlgren cannon raked the rebel attackers, breaking up the assault at great cost. The Confederates first halted their attack, then fell back, and finally withdrew completely when the eight-inch-gun *Lexington*, another vessel dispatched by Porter, also joined the fight. When Vicksburg eventually surrendered on July 4, 1863, Grant was effusive in his praise of Porter and the navy.

Although Porter and Grant believed that Mobile, Alabama, was their rightful next move, in the spring of 1864 Porter and his vessels were diverted to participate in the Red River Expedition. Led by General Nathaniel P. Banks, the campaign's major goals were to seize Shreveport, Louisiana and occupy east Texas. Banks was no Grant, and the relationship between the army and navy was often strained. Despite misgivings by many of the participants and Banks' ineptitude, some initial progress was made. Obstacles were cleared from the river and Fort DeRussy, near Marksville, Louisiana, was taken on March 14. Five days later Alexandria was captured by Union forces. On April 8, however, Banks lost a battle at Mansfield and retreated. The next day he was able to hold off the pursuing Confederates at Pleasant Hill, but then he retreated again. His withdrawal separated his force from Porter's ships moving up the river.

Banks then gave up the campaign, leaving Porter, frequently under Confederate fire, to extract his flotilla. As Porter worked to save his command, the water level in the river became precipitously low, threatening to strand the entire fleet behind Rebel lines in Red River mud. Porter had his men hastily construct a dam and flume that brought the water level high enough for his vessels to clear the shallow passage. Eventually, with help from some of Banks' soldiers nearby, Porter and his sailors succeeded in saving nearly all of his ships.

In the East, by late summer 1864 the navy's blockade had succeeded in shutting down every Confederate port on the Atlantic except Wilmington, North Carolina. Through Wilmington, blockade runners still moved commerce and war materials desperately needed by the Confederacy. The Union was determined to close it off.

Guarding the port at Wilmington was Fort Fisher, a powerful fortification situated on an inlet along the Cape Fear River. Called the "Gibraltar of the South" the fort was a massive structure protected by minefields and artillery batteries. Obvious from the outset was that a combined army-navy operation would be required to capture it.

Porter, now commander of the North Atlantic Blockading Squadron, was Secretary of the Navy Gideon Welles' hand-picked choice to lead the navy's part of the campaign. The army's initial commander was less fortuitous, as General Benjamin Butler, a political appointee with a checkered military reputation, opted to personally lead the land contingent that was drawn from his Army of the James. Butler proposed exploding a ship loaded with gunpowder near the fort, believing the concussion would flatten the structure and ease the task of his soldiers. Eager to avoid a siege or a frontal attack, Porter acquiesced.

In the early hours of Christmas Eve 1864, the aged steamship U.S.S. *Louisiana* was blown up close to the fort. The massive explosion went as planned but the fort remained standing. Butler had moved some of his force ashore, but when the explosion did not have the effect he intended, he withdrew his troops without forcing an attack.

Porter, an energetic, aggressive commander, was appalled by the feeble effort. He appealed directly to his old colleague Grant, now General-in-Chief of the Union army, asking that Butler be removed. Grant, equally incensed at Butler's incompetence, agreed. General Alfred H. Terry was appointed to command the army forces in a renewed assault that would involve about 8,000 to 9,000 men. Fort Fisher would be the largest combined operation of the war, and the 60 ships involved would be the largest fleet of warships assembled during the conflict.

Under the joint command of Porter and Terry the attack began on January 13, 1865, when Porter's ships shelled the fort for three days. In the meantime Terry, with covering fire from Porter's batteries, put troops ashore in a series of unopposed landings. On January 15, with supporting fire from Porter's ships, and after bitter close-in fighting, Union troops and marines captured the fort. Covered by Porter's flotilla, Federal forces then moved up the river toward Wilmington. On February 22, Confederate authorities abandoned the city. The loss of Wilmington, essentially the South's only remaining source of outside supply, was a devastating blow to the Confederacy.

Several innovations employed by Porter at Fort Fisher would become permanent features of the navy's amphibious landing doctrine. Each ship was assigned designated targets; counter-battery fire was emphasized; and shelling continued after the troops ashore began their attack, at which time aiming points were shifted to targets in front of the advancing units.

Porter's service during the Civil War closed with a notable episode. At Richmond on April 4, 1865, it was Rear Admiral Porter, three of his officers and 10 sailors who escorted Abraham Lincoln on his tour of the White House of the Confederacy, which was left intact when Jefferson Davis abandoned the city only two days before.

Before and After

David Porter led an eventful life even before his exceptional service in the Civil War. The son of a naval officer and the grandson of a Revolutionary War ship captain, Porter was immersed in ships and sailing from an early age.

In 1824, Porter's father resigned his commission to accept an offer from Mexico to become commander of that fledgling nation's navy. He took his son with him, and at age 12 David Dixon Porter was made a midshipman in the Mexican navy. Over the next four years Porter served on various vessels, at times participating in raids on Spanish ships sailing off the coast of Cuba.

In 1828, Porter was posted to the Mexican ship *Guerrero*, under the command of a cousin, when the ship was engaged by a much larger Spanish vessel. In the fight that followed Porter was slightly wounded. His cousin the ship captain was killed and the *Guerrero's* surviving crew members were taken prisoner. Held initially in Havana, Porter was eventually exchanged and afterward returned to the United States.

In 1829, just shy of his 16th birthday, Porter received an appointment to Annapolis. From the Academy, Porter first served on the U.S.S. *United States* before being posted to duty with the Coast Survey and subsequently to the Navy Hydrographic Office.

Early in 1846, likely because of his fluency in Spanish and his familiarity with the Caribbean, Porter was asked by Secretary of State James Buchanan to undertake an informal mission on behalf of the government. Porter's task was to assess the viability of the newly independent nation of Santo Domingo (now the Dominican Republic) and to examine an anchorage site for prospective use by the U.S. Navy. After undergoing considerable hardships, and having also mapped Santo Domingo's coastline, Porter returned in June with the information requested by the State Department.

That same month, the United States declared war on Mexico. Porter was on the gunboat *Spitfire* at Veracruz as Winfield Scott's army began the invasion that would eventually capture Mexico City and end the war. Porter was somewhat familiar with the defenses around Veracruz from his youthful experience in the Mexican navy. Porter assisted in the assault by leading a small group that sounded out a channel for later use by several ships that pounded Mexican fortifications from locations inside the harbor.

In June 1847, still on the *Spitfire*, Porter accompanied the navy's expedition against the town of Tabasco. When the landing was opposed, Porter led about 70 sailors who successfully assaulted and captured a fort that had barred entry to the city. His initiative at Tabasco led to his appointment as captain of the *Spitfire*; it was his first command.

Seeing prospects for advancement stagnate as the navy's role in the war wound down, Porter took an extended leave of absence in 1847. Over the decade that followed, he commanded a series of civilian vessels, taking ships on lengthy voyages that added to his experience and enhanced his reputation. He skippered the steamer *Panama* around the Straits of Magellan into the Pacific, made frequent voyages from New York City to Havana on the mail steamer *Georgia*, and captained the Australian Steamship Company's ship *Golden Age* between Melbourne and Sydney.

Health crises in his family eventually brought Porter back to the United States. In 1857, after 10 years away, he returned to active duty. His experiences prompted the navy to place him as captain of the U.S.S. *Supply* and assign him a most unusual mission: to transport camels to the United States. Secretary of War Jefferson Davis promoted the project, believing the animals might serve well as cavalry mounts in the American Southwest. Under Porter's command, *Supply* made two successful trips before the experiment was abandoned. He was considering an offer from a civilian company when the Civil War began, drawing his immediate involvement in the successful venture to save Fort Pickens.

At the close of the war in 1865, Navy Secretary Gideon Welles appointed Porter Superintendent of the Naval Academy, a post he held for four years. Porter was an energetic superintendent, extensively revising the school's curriculum to reflect the navy's recent wartime experience and the realities of navy life. Porter installed an honor system, revised and enforced standards of discipline, and promoted a program of organized sports.

When his wartime colleague Ulysses S. Grant was elected president, Porter was appointed Advisor to the Secretary of the Navy. In 1870, under a new system of ranks, Porter followed David Farragut as the navy's second full admiral. For the remainder of his life, Porter organized and served on several boards related to programs such as service reform, inspections, and ship repair. During his later extended semi-retirement, he wrote works of military history and fiction. Porter died on February 13, 1891, and is buried at Arlington National Cemetery.

PATRICK CLEBURNE (C.S.A.)

In addition to his exceptional leadership of Confederate forces in the west—Robert E. Lee called him "a meteor shining from a clouded sky"—Cleburne is best remembered for his electrifying proposal to free the South's slaves and grant them full citizenship.

During the course of the Civil War the military leadership of the Confederate States remained remarkably stable. Through four years of combat, the South's generals were sometimes shuffled from job to job, but the names remained essentially the same. Because the core group stayed mostly intact and because also—especially at the beginning of the war—as a group they were often more successful than their Union counterparts, the names of almost all of the Confederacy's ranking officers persist in the nation's collective memory.

To a surprising degree that recollection applies regardless of relative accomplishments or considerations of character. Whether touched with greatness like Lee or Jackson or of doubtful competence like Hood or Bragg, their names as well as those of many others whose quality ranged between the extremes—Longstreet, Stuart, Beauregard, Hill, Forrest, Early, Ewell, Johnston, and more—remain with us, instantly recognizable even to those with only casual interest in the war.

Those considerations make it more difficult to identify and assign 'unsung' labels to the Confederacy's military leaders, especially those who served at the highest levels. There are others, though, whose credentials warrant fuller consideration. One, in particular, was so skilled that American history is ill-served by his relative lack of recognition.

Because Patrick Cleburne fought mainly in the West, a theater less in the headlines and often more submerged in histories, and served under some of the South's least capable field commanders, while being denied promotion to corps command, he is more obscure than many of his contemporaries. His accomplishments, however, as well as his personal conduct and character, rank him among the best of the Confederacy's commanders.

There is much in Patrick Cleburne's brief but eventful life that is inspiring—not only to the people of the South and to the men he so ably led, but indeed to all Americans. Cleburne emigrated from Ireland at age 21. By 22 he was a popular, well respected pillar of the Helena, Arkansas community, and soon after a businessman and partner in a successful law firm.

When the war began, Cleburne volunteered as a private. He was quickly elected captain and then colonel. He was a brigadier general within 13 months and a major general nine months later. Cleburne led forces in many of the major battles in the West including Shiloh, Stones

River, Chickamauga, Missionary Ridge and throughout the campaign for Atlanta. His units frequently clashed with those of Sherman and other notable Union commanders, most often with considerable success.

Known for his intensive and exceptional training of troops and for what would now be called the "professional education" of his officers and NCOs, by war's end some authorities believed Cleburne's units were the most capable fighting force on either side. So respected was their reputation that when the Confederate government prescribed a standard battle flag, Cleburne's unit was allowed to retain its own distinct banner. Called the "Stonewall of the West," Cleburne, like Jackson, was renowned for his effective use of terrain, anticipation of enemy movements, and consistent success where other commanders failed.

Cleburne had served in the British army (as a corporal in the 41st Regiment of Foot) before coming to the United States in 1849. That experience complemented his obvious leadership talents and propelled his advancement from private soldier to major general within two years. By the time of Shiloh, his first major action, he was a brigadier general leading a brigade in the corps of General William J. Hardee.

On the morning of April 6, 1862, in the confused early stages of the battle of Shiloh, Cleburne, on the left of Hardee's corps, advanced his brigade into a maelstrom of fire while moving through woods, swampy ground, and overlapping Union positions. As the struggle surged back and forth Cleburne was for a time without artillery support as Federal gunners swept the Confederate artillery from the field. The battle raged throughout the day as both sides attacked, retreated, reorganized and attacked again. Out of 425 officers and men in one of Cleburne's regiments, the 6th Mississippi, 300 were killed or wounded. Later that day, Cleburne led the battered remnants of three regiments in an advance that carried half a mile. Low on ammunition, Cleburne replenished supplies and moved forward again before being halted by Union reinforcements and fire from Federal gunboats on the river. When the shooting died down, Cleburne attacked again, stopping as darkness approached on orders from General Beauregard (who had replaced General Albert Sidney Johnston, killed earlier in the day).

The morning of April 7 brought attacks by Union troops, now rein-forced by the arrival of an army led by Don Carlos Buell. With only a fraction of his original brigade remaining, Cleburne moved forward, advancing about a mile before halting in the face of overwhelming numbers. Still, outnumbered and outflanked on both sides, Cleburne, after protesting the futility of the order, was directed to continue his attack. Cleburne moved forward until artillery from both flanks swept his line of advance. Confederate batteries were again withdrawn from the field, and despite the lack of artillery support Cleburne's forces charged, moving forward under horrific fire. Thrown back by superior numbers and firepower, Cleburne rallied his men and led another charge that threw back a Union advance. Out of ammunition again, Cleburne halted with the remnants of his now dispersed command. One regiment, the 15th Alabama, had only 58 men remaining.

As evening fell, Cleburne assembled scattered units to help shield the Confederate army's withdrawal as Beauregard pulled his forces away from the field. Cleburne was one of the last to leave, destroying captured supplies and assisting with casualties. Cleburne's brigade, engaged without relief in heavy fighting throughout the battle, lost 188 killed, 700 wounded, and 65 missing—the heaviest casualties in the Confederate army.

Shiloh was the first major battle for most units and commanders in both armies. In its aftermath, Cleburne was one of the most highly lauded officers—cited repeatedly for his valor and achievements on the battlefield.

It was a portent of things to come.

Four months later at Richmond, Kentucky, Cleburne, now serving under the command of General Kirby Smith, organized and directed an overwhelming attack but was wounded prior to its conclusion. Cleburne's planning and leadership on the field were credited for the substantial victory. Soon after, the Confederate Congress voted him thanks for "gallant and meritorious service."

In October, recovered from the wound to his mouth and cheek sustained at Richmond, Cleburne and his unit were returned to Hardee's corps in time for the battle at Perryville, Kentucky. At Perryville, Cleburne was leading a charge when his horse was shot from under him. Scrambling up, disregarding a wound to his leg, Cleburne rallied his brigade in an assault that for a time collapsed the Union line facing him.

Despite inflicting heavy casualties on the Federal army led by Don Carlos Buell, Confederate commander Braxton Bragg decided to withdraw south into Tennessee. Cleburne was among several generals who thought Bragg had squandered opportunities and was remiss in not attempting an invasion of Ohio.

Bragg, though retreating, had captured large quantities of Union weapons, ammunition, wagons, horses, mules, and assorted materiel, all of which would be invaluable to the supply-starved rebel armies, if they could be moved to areas safely under Confederate control. So long and ponderous was the resulting train—hundreds of wagons—that transporting the treasure trove of captured goods became a major factor in the campaign. The slow-moving train was persistently harassed by Federal cavalry and threatened by approaching Union infantry.

The crisis finally came at Big Hill, Kentucky. There, a difficult feature of the terrain brought the enormous wagon train to a virtual standstill. Kirby Smith, Bragg's on-scene commander, abandoned hope of saving any part of it and gave orders for its destruction. Cleburne learned of the order and requested permission to try to save the train. Given authority to do so, he collected officers and soldiers in the area, organized work details, and carried—often literally—weapons and supplies over the mountain barrier. Cleburne directed the prodigious attempt while at the same time shielding the effort from Union attack. He saved the entire train.

Cleburne was promoted to major general in December 1862 and given command of a division, which he soon took into action at Murfreesboro, Tennessee. At Murfreesboro Bragg planned to attack the right flank of the Federal army, now commanded by William S. Rosecrans. After driving it back, Bragg intended to strike with his own right wing and pin the Union force against Stones River, foreclosing Rosecrans' avenue of retreat.

Making a night crossing of the river, Cleburne's division moved into position on the Confederate left on December 30, 1862. At dawn on New Year's Eve, Cleburne's attack struck the Federal right, pushing it back in bitter fighting that lasted throughout the day. Although again without artillery support for an extended period, by mid-afternoon Cleburne had forced the Union lines in front of him to retreat three miles. With the battle at a tipping point, the Federals were heavily reinforced with men and artillery. Newly arriving units flanked Cleburne's division on the right and Union artillery operating at close range poured concentrated fire into the advancing Confederates. Cleburne withdrew his exhausted troops, reforming them in a stand of timber about a quarter of a mile to the rear where he received orders to hold the ground and prepare for later action. During the bitter fight on the first day at Murfreesboro, Cleburne's command lost more than a third of its officers and men: 2,081 killed, wounded, and missing out of the 6,045 that crossed the river the night before.

On January 2, 1863, Cleburne led a probing attack that confirmed the continued presence of Union troops in considerable strength. That same day Bragg launched an attack with his right wing. The initial surge brought apparent success, but Rosecrans countered by placing nearly 60 artillery pieces on the other side of the river in position to enfilade the attack. Firing continuously, the massed artillery swept the Confederate lines, stopping the advance with heavy losses. Bragg again decided to retreat from the field. Cleburne was ordered to move his forces back near the river, not far from their original start point.

Later, safely ensconced in middle Tennessee, Bragg, having become aware of widespread dissatisfaction within his command, polled his generals regarding their confidence in his leadership. Cleburne, along with a majority of others, including corps commanders Hardee and Breckinridge, responded that Bragg no longer possessed the confidence of his army. Nonetheless, following an investigation by General Joseph Johnston ordered by Confederate President Jefferson Davis, Bragg was retained in command.

After the Battle of Murfreesboro (aka Stones River), there followed a six-month lull in the fighting as neither Braag nor Rosecrans took their armies into battle. Cleburne used the time to intensively drill, train, and instruct his troops. Marksmanship was stressed throughout his division and Cleburne organized an elite unit of sharpshooters.

When the armies again took the field in the summer of 1863, Rosecrans, by a series of near-bloodless moves, maneuvered Bragg out of middle Tennessee. Within a few weeks, the only section of the state remaining under Bragg's and the Confederacy's control was an area around Chattanooga. In September Bragg responded to Rosecrans' attempt to pin the Confederate forces inside Chattanooga by evacuating the city and shifting his army to Lafayette, Georgia, a bit more than 20 miles away. The effect of the move was to present the Confederacy with one of its last great opportunities in the West.

As Rosecrans pursued, he chose to come after Bragg with his army divided into three columns. Widely separated, the main elements of each wing of the Federal army were too far apart to be mutually supporting. The opportunity was there—but remained untaken—for Bragg to attack and destroy the Union columns one by one. Instead, time was allowed for Rosecrans to reunite his army and take position a modest-sized creek named Chickamauga. Bragg began moving his army across the creek during the night of September 18. One of the bloodiest and bitterest battles of the war began early the next morning.

Cleburne's division, initially on the left of the Confederate line, was first called on in mid-afternoon when corps commander Leonidas Polk ordered the unit to a new position several miles to the right. After fording the creek to get to the field, Cleburne's force formed up 250–300 yards behind a Confederate battle line already heavily engaged and falling back. At dusk, Cleburne was ordered to attack. Confronted by Federal works Cleburne's men surged across the embattled, body-strewn ground. The struggle continued into the darkness as each side hammered at the other from close range, shooting at each other's muzzle flashes. When the firing finally died down, Cleburne had advanced the Confederate line about a mile and a half. Cleburne adjusted his alignment during the night and prepared for battle the following day.

At mid-morning on September 20, Cleburne was ordered to attack in the face of concentrated artillery fire that raked the Confederate line from fortified positions to his right and right center. The devastating fire directly upon exposed units stopped the advance 100 to 200 yards in front of the Union positions. Within minutes, 500 men in one of Cleburne's brigades had been killed or wounded.

Unwilling to sacrifice further, Cleburne momentarily pulled back, reorganized his units, and formed a defensive line. In mid-afternoon his division was again ordered forward. Cleburne's advance was concurrent with a movement elsewhere on the field by Bragg's entire left wing. Led by Longstreet, the Confederates exploited a gap in the Union lines and broke through the Federal defenses. Soon after, orders came for the right wing to advance. Cleburne's artillery silenced the Union batteries that had thrown back his earlier assault. Racing forward, one of his brigades overran three Federal defensive lines and put the defenders to flight.

Now, with much of the Union army fleeing back to Chattanooga in full retreat, Bragg chose not to pursue. While the gallant stand by a portion of the Federal army led by George H. Thomas, the "Rock of Chickamauga," held the Confederates at bay, the remainder of Rosecrans' army escaped. Despite pleas by Bragg's subordinate commanders to aggressively chase down the routed Federals, Bragg halted the attack.

In the post-mortem to the South's pyrrhic victory at Chickamauga, the Army of Tennessee's generals petitioned Jefferson Davis once again for Bragg's removal. Davis met with Bragg and his assembled senior officers on October 10. A record of the meeting was not kept, but it is believed that the generals, Cleburne among them, expressed a lack of confidence in his leadership and unanimously recommended his removal. Still, Davis retained Bragg in command, allowing him one more opportunity to redeem himself and his reputation.

Chickamauga reversed the pre-battle situation: now it was Rosecrans' army in danger of being trapped inside Chattanooga. After Rosecrans retreated into the city, Bragg occupied high ground to the south and east—Lookout Mountain and Missionary Ridge—and attempted to starve Rosecrans' army into submission. He was unsuccessful. Throughout several weeks of attempted siege, Rosecrans continued to receive reinforcements, food, and materiel.

With the battlefield initiative ebbing away, in early November Bragg made a questionable decision to divide his forces, sending Longstreet to attack Knoxville and, soon after, Cleburne to reinforce the effort. Cleburne's troops were on the move when they were hurriedly recalled by Bragg to oppose heavy Union attacks at several points around Chattanooga. The morning of November 25 found Cleburne defending a key railroad bridge over Chickamauga Creek and holding the Confederates' extreme right on Missionary Ridge.

As fate would have it, the Union's main attack came straight at the Confederate right flank. William Tecumseh Sherman struck at Cleburne's four brigades with elements of six divisions in an attempt to turn the Confederate flank and fold up the entire front of the Confederate army.

Throughout a blood-soaked day at least three heavy attacks drove against Cleburne's forces, sometimes carrying to within a few feet of his lines and artillery. The last attack, sustained for more than an hour and a half, reached a horrific crescendo as Sherman pushed fresh units into the fight.

Throughout the day Cleburne launched brief counterstrikes to spoil Union attacks, often personally leading sorties into the thick of the fighting. At the end of the day Cleburne's forces, although under attack by fresh units and badly outnumbered, held their ground. In the face of enormous pressure, the Federal attempt to turn the flank was defeated.

Cleburne's heroics and those of his men would be for naught, however. While he and his men were waging a successful fight on the right, in the center Bragg's line had given way. Union forces under Hooker and Thomas broke through and put much of the Confederate army into a panicked retreat. Cleburne's brigades, having fought all day, were now tasked with covering Bragg's withdrawal across the Chickamauga.

Through the remainder of the afternoon and night, Cleburne shielded the rebel retreat from the immediate area of the battlefield, not pulling his last unit from Missionary Ridge until about 9 p.m. Several hours later he was given an even more daunting task: to position his force in Ringgold Gap, a narrow defile cut between surrounding hills, and hold it at all costs while the rest of the Army of Tennessee—troops, artillery, and wagon trains—passed through.

The gap, just east of the hamlet of Ringgold, bisected a north-south bluff called Taylor's Ridge. No more than a football field wide at any point in its half-mile length, the gap sheltered a creek, railroad track, and the all-important road.

Hurrying to the scene, Cleburne had less than an hour to familiarize himself with the terrain and position his 4,000 men in an attempt to hold back the oncoming weight of the Union army. Beginning in early morning, the initial Federal attack by Joseph Hooker's corps was launched at the gap. It was soon followed by an attempt to turn the Confederate's right flank, followed by yet another assault farther still to the right. All were broken up by artillery, counterattacks, and Cleburne's astute use of meager resources. Later in the morning, fresh Union troops tried again on the right and then on the left, only to be thrown back by Cleburne's artillery.

At midday, Cleburne received word that Bragg's army had safely made its escape. Early in the afternoon he pulled his division from the gap and rejoined the main force. His successful rear-guard action was achieved with minimal loss: 20 killed and 200 wounded or missing, after nearly six hours of combat against a numerically superior force.

The Confederate retreat eastward after the debacle at Chattanooga brought an end to the campaigning during the winter season. Cleburne used the nearly six months before fighting resumed to train and drill his division. He conducted daily instruction for his senior commanders, lessons that were disseminated through the ranks by subordinate officers. Marksmanship training was stressed as always. Cleburne waged mock battles to train new recruits and keep his veterans sharp, while devoting considerable time to keeping his division intact. Enlistments were expiring. The previous year had been a bitter one for the Confederate States of America: losses at Gettysburg, Vicksburg, and Chattanooga combined with increasing hardships at home. In Confederate military units, increasing numbers were beginning to vote with their feet—separating from, or deserting, the army. Cleburne talked with soldiers whose terms of enlistments were expiring. Few left him. It is likely that his division retained the highest percentage of soldiers in the Confederate army.

In May 1864, Sherman began his campaign against Atlanta. By this time Joseph E. Johnston had taken command of the army, Braxton Bragg having been reassigned as Jefferson Davis' chief of staff. Outnumbered at times by almost 2-to-1, Johnston sought to parry Sherman's attempts to use his numerical advantage to outflank the Confederates. A series of sweeping movements followed as Sherman attempted repeatedly to turn the Confederate left flank. Johnston defended skillfully, withdrawing slowly while keeping between Sherman and Atlanta.

Cleburne's division fought several times, at Dug Gap on May 9, at Resaca on May 14, and in a major encounter at Pickett's Mill on May 27. There, Sherman tried and failed to shatter Cleburne's force with a direct attack. In a fight that began in late afternoon and lasted well into the night, the Union advance was thrown back with large numbers of casualties and prisoners taken.

In June, Johnston drew his army back to the general area of Kennesaw Mountain. Cleburne's unit was posted south of the massif, part of the force holding the Confederate left. For one of the few times in the campaign, Sherman abandoned his flanking attempts, choosing instead to hammer straight at the entrenched Confederates. A brief engagement on June 24 was a precursor to a full-scale assault on June 27. After an extended artillery barrage, Sherman advanced in lines as many as seven deep. Driven back with enormous losses, Sherman repeated the attempt with the same results. The losses at Kennesaw Mountain induced Sherman to resume his flanking tactics, and in mid-July he finally succeeded in crossing the Chattahoochee River near Atlanta.

During the two and a half months of the campaign, Johnston had managed to retain Atlanta and hold Sherman's numerically superior force to an average advance of about a mile and a quarter a day. However, President Jefferson Davis became dissatisfied with Johnston's tactics and on July 17 removed him from command. Johnston's replacement, John Bell Hood, was a more aggressive commander but, as events would show, a less competent one.

Hood immediately took the offensive, seeking to attack George Thomas' Army of the Cumberland while it was crossing Peach Tree Creek. The assault was delayed for several hours, however, giving time for the Federals to entrench, and when the Confederates charged Union artillery was in place to hammer them from across the creek. While Thomas held his ground, James B. McPherson's Army of the Tennessee was meanwhile threatening an advance on Atlanta from the east.

The subsequent Battle of Atlanta further enhanced Cleburne's reputation and that of his division. In bitter fighting on July 21, he successfully defended Leggett's Hill against McPherson's men. That night Hood sent Cleburne and the rest of Hardee's corps on a circuitous march to be in position to slam into McPherson's left flank and rear. The next day, Cleburne's division was in the thick of the attack, the largest battle of the campaign, returning with prisoners, guns, and captured colors. Although a number of Federal units were overrun and others driven— and McPherson himself was killed—the Union army managed to rally, and then counterattack, and a complete Confederate victory once again proved elusive. The struggle for the city, which had by now taken on the character of a partial siege, raged through the rest of July and August, with Cleburne's division frequently used as firefighters, shifting from one hot spot to another.

At the end of August, Cleburne assumed temporary command of his corps, one of two engaged as Hood attempted to expel Federal troops from Jonesborough, a key railroad junction south of the city. Cleburne's attack succeeded in pushing back the Union lines and captured several cannon. However, the advance by his neighboring corps commanded by Stephen D. Lee was heavily repulsed. The loss at Jonesborough on August 31 cut Hood's supply line. On September 1, he abandoned Atlanta and moved south to reconstitute his army, rejoining Cleburne's force and other Confederate units near Lovejoy, Georgia.

After briefly attempting to chase down Hood, Sherman remained for a time in Atlanta, having helped solidify Lincoln's re-election with his victory there. After an entire summer of maneuvers and clashes, Sherman rested his troops and prepared for his next campaign.

Sherman's next move was one of the most unusual of any war past or present. In mid-November, Sherman with massive numbers and little opposition, cut loose from his base and marched almost unchecked southeast across Georgia, arriving at Savannah on the Atlantic coast on December 21. Hood chose not to follow, instead moving his army west, where at the outset little visible opposition stood between him and a potential drive to the Ohio River. Sherman's departure left somewhat isolated, smaller, and hastily assembled forces to oppose Hood, who was now reinforced by cavalry led by Nathan Bedford Forrest.

It fell upon Union General George H. Thomas to assemble a hastily extemporized army to confront Hood. Seeking to buy time, Thomas sent John Schofield to track Hood's movements and, where possible, to delay his advance. At the end of November an apparent opportunity presented itself for Hood to trap Schofield's force. At Spring Hill, Tennessee, however, a series of events mismanaged by Hood and his staff allowed Schofield to slip away to safety.

As was typical of John Bell Hood after his numerous setbacks, he lashed out at his staff and subordinate commanders, blaming them for debacles often of his own making. It was apparently Cleburne's intention to confront Hood when the movements of the armies and a break in the fighting presented an occasion to do so.

That opportunity never came.

Hood followed as the Federals withdrew north, on the afternoon of November 30 coming up with Schofield's force positioned behind prepared fortifications at Franklin, Tennessee. Against the unanimous advice of his assembled commanders, Hood chose to launch a frontal attack across two miles of open ground. At Gettysburg, the assault that has come to be known as Pickett's Charge covered about a mile and at one point the undulating terrain provided brief shelter. At Franklin, the distance was twice as far and the level ground provided little respite from the fire.

Cleburne's division was posted just to the right of center in the attacking line, along the right edge of a road that split the expanse of open ground. His unit was one of the first to make contact, driving back Union troops positioned in front of the main line of defense. Cleburne continued to press the attack, eventually reaching the main line where fighting became hand to hand.

Around Cleburne's troops the Confederate assault began to collapse, bled away by distance, intense fire, and mounting casualties. The corps to the right of Cleburne was driven back, enabling Union defenders to place Cleburne's division under a devastating crossfire. After two horses were shot from under him, he continued to press forward on foot, waving his cap and rallying his men to advance. Minutes later, lost somewhere in the smoke and fire, Cleburne was killed.

Seldom has a battle been more costly or needless. Of the 23,000 or so engaged in the fight, Hood lost more than 6,000 soldiers killed, wounded, or captured. Cleburne was one of six Confederate generals killed in action.

The men of Cleburne's division recovered his body the following day.

After the battle Schofield, having succeeded in delaying Hood, withdrew further to Nashville where his forces were merged with Thomas' army. In a battle fought on December 15 and 16, Thomas enveloped both Confederate flanks and in the most tactically decisive victory of the war effectively destroyed Hood's army.

While Cleburne's combat record is among the most sterling in either army, his name is most often attached to a proposal with monumental non-military implications.

On January 2, 1864, Cleburne recommended that in return for full emancipation of all loyal slaves, the South enlist blacks in the Confederate army.

Drained by three years of combat, and lacking manpower and resources comparable to the North's, Cleburne foresaw the inevitable decline and defeat of the Confederacy unless extraordinary measures were taken. Cleburne was not a slave owner nor an advocate of slavery as an institution. In addition to his belief in states' rights, he had apparently sided with the South mainly because of his affection for the people of Arkansas who had befriended him as a young immigrant and enabled him to prosper in their midst. Now, with the South's prospects waning, he proposed enlisting blacks in the Confederate army. It was a stroke, Cleburne believed, that would not only help redress the South's manpower disadvantage, but at the same time defuse the arguments of Northern abolitionists. Perhaps, he thought, it might even remove the reluctance of foreign powers to support the Confederate states.

Cleburne read his proposal to a meeting of the assembled generals and regimental commanders of the Army of Tennessee. Some agreed; others, adamantly, did not. His recommendation was not forwarded, the stated rationale being that it was a political, not a military treatise. However, an opponent at the meeting sent a copy to President Jefferson Davis. Davis ordered that it be suppressed, and all known copies were destroyed. While Cleburne's proposal was known and discussed among senior ranks at the time, it was not until more than 30 years after the war that a copy was found and published.

Cleburne believed that given the choice between securing independence or preserving the institution of slavery, the South would choose independence. At the time, slave holders and other power brokers in the Confederacy did not agree—or at least did not frame the discussion in those terms. When eventually they did concur—on March 13, 1865, the Confederate Congress passed legislation authorizing enlistment of slaves in the army—it was far too late. The following month Lee surrendered at Appomattox.

There is a sentiment among some scholars that Cleburne's radical proposal was the cause of his not being promoted to lieutenant general.

In the months that followed the January meeting, two of three openings were filled by officers junior to Cleburne and one was left vacant.

That Cleburne made his recommendation with little regard for its potential effect on his prospects for advancement did not surprise his contemporaries. Almost universally he was regarded as an officer of the highest character and ethical standards.

Throughout the conflict, stories abounded of Cleburne's exceptional sense of honor. In Kentucky early in the war, when Cleburne learned that some of his soldiers had stolen property from civilians, he made restitution out of his own pocket. Later, one of his solders took a hat and blanket from a Union officer prisoner. Cleburne gave his own hat and a set of blankets to the captive officer. At Kennesaw Mountain, Cleburne readily acquiesced to a truce initiated by one of his officers that allowed Union troops to remove their wounded colleagues from a battlefield about to be ravaged by flames from a fast moving fire—and then further contributed Southern troops to help in the effort. When Union General McPherson was killed along Cleburne's front during the Battle of Atlanta, under a flag of truce Cleburne sent McPherson's gold watch back to the Union lines for later return to his family.

There was considerable nobility in Patrick Cleburne's short life— and much in his accomplishments and conduct that linger across the generations to instruct and inspire North and South alike. 'A meteor shining from a clouded sky,' was Robert E. Lee's epitaph for Patrick Cleburne. But, it was a junior officer who may have said it best of all: Cleburne was 'The perfect type of a perfect soldier.'

Before and After

Patrick Cleburne was born in County Cork, Ireland on May 17, 1828. Orphaned by age 15, he was unsuccessful in his attempt to study medicine at Dublin's Trinity College. Two weeks before his 18th birthday he enlisted in the British army, serving in Her Majesty's 41st Regiment of Foot. On July 1, 1849, a few months short of three years of service, he was promoted to corporal. In November of that year he purchased his discharge from the army, and a month later he sailed for the United States. After landing in New Orleans, Cleburne went first to Cincinnati, Ohio, staying only four months while he worked in a drug store. By April 1850 he was in Helena, Arkansas, which became his permanent home from the time of his arrival at age 22 until his death at age 36.

At Helena, Cleburne worked first in a drug store. Later he acquired his citizenship, studied law, and became a partner in a respected law firm. His famous proposal to emancipate the South's slaves unfolds in large measure like a well-reasoned legal argument.

The battle at Franklin, Tennessee that cost Cleburne his life began at about 4 p.m. when the Confederate units began their move forward across two miles of open ground. Cleburne was killed an hour or two into a fight in which shooting persisted until well after 9 o'clock at night.

After Cleburne's troops recovered his body the following day, he was interred not far from the battlefield at a site on whose beauty he had remarked only a short time before. In 1869, his remains were moved to Helena, Arkansas, and reburied in his adopted home city.

Deeper in the Shadows...

EMORY UPTON

During the course of the war, Upton held senior positions in each branch of the army—infantry, artillery, and cavalry. His innovative infantry tactics were widely adopted throughout the army.

Union general Emery Upton was the only officer on either side in the Civil War who successfully held senior command positions in all three combat branches of the U.S. Army: infantry, artillery, and cavalry. Commissioned as a second lieutenant on May 6, 1861, by the end of the war he was a brevet major general. He was 25 years old.

Upton graduated from West Point with a commission in the artillery, and eleven weeks into his military career he saw his first action at Bull Run. Wounded twice in the fighting around Blackburn's Ford, he refused to leave the field. Upton commanded an artillery battery through the Peninsula Campaign and the Seven Days Battles. By the fall of 1862, he was in command of an artillery battery at Antietam.

Late that year, his reputation established, Upton was promoted to command of an infantry regiment, the 121st New York, and advanced to the brevet rank of colonel. In December he led his regiment at Fredericksburg. By the following July he was a brigade commander—the 2nd Brigade, 1st Division of the VI Corps—at Gettysburg. After moving his unit 35 miles in a night march to position it on the battlefield, his brigade was held mostly in reserve during the battle. In November 1863, the excellent performance of his unit at Rappahannock Station earned Upton further favorable attention.

In 1864, with Grant now General-in-Chief, the Union army began to exert continuous pressure on Confederate forces. Upton led his brigade through the horrific fighting in the Wilderness as Grant moved against Lee in the Overland Campaign, from May 4 to June 12.

While Upton's service throughout the war was consistently of the highest caliber, he is mainly remembered for his actions on one bloody day at Spotsylvania Court House. On May 10, 1864, Upton employed a new tactic for attacking heavily defended positions. Instead of assaulting Confederate breastworks in the 'Mule Shoe' salient with the standard extended battle line moving slowly and firing as it advanced, Upton devised something radically different: he massed his assault force in a tighter cluster, aimed at a small, clearly defined position in the enemy line, and then rushed it at full speed without pausing to fire. Upton's innovation exceeded beyond expectations: his 12-regiment force overwhelmed the Confederate defenders and achieved a considerable breakthrough.

Unfortunately, as was often the case on both sides during the war, the successful attack was not supported. Lacking help from nearby Union forces and faced with increasing numbers of Confederate reinforcements rushed to the scene, Upton, wounded in the fight, withdrew his units from the field.

Two days later he was promoted to brigadier general. On that same day, May 12, General Winfield Scott Hancock used Upton's tactics in a corps-strong attack against the Mule Shoe, capturing almost an entire division and nearly cutting the Confederate army in half. Subsequent fighting raged for nearly 20 continuous hours as Lee counterattacked to plug the gap.

Upton's wounds kept him briefly out of action, but he returned to his command when Grant began the siege of Petersburg. In June the VI Corps, Upton's parent unit, was pulled away to help turn back Confederate General Jubal Early's move toward Washington, D.C. The corps remained detached from Grant, fighting Early's army in the Shenandoah Valley and reducing it as a source of sustenance to the South's armies.

On September 19, 1864, at the Third Battle of Winchester, Upton took command of the 1st Division when its commander was killed early in the fight. As combat continued, Upton was severely wounded but refused to leave the field, choosing instead to lead the division from a stretcher for the remainder of the battle. Soon after, Upton was brevetted to major general. His promotion came three years and four months after his graduation from West Point.

After convalescing, Upton returned to the war, this time assigned to a cavalry unit. For the remainder of the conflict Upton led the 4th Division of James H. Wilson's cavalry corps.

He took command at an eventful time. As the war was drawing to a close, Wilson led an enormous raid against Selma, Alabama, one of the South's few remaining munitions-producing and manufacturing centers. Wilson's Raid, as it came to be called, involved the largest cavalry force (13,000 men) assembled during the war.

Beginning on March 22, 1865, Wilson pushed his corps south in three division-sized columns against a Confederate force under the overall command of Nathan Bedford Forrest. At Selma, an additional 5,000 Confederates—mainly hastily armed civilians—manning breastworks and gun batteries, confronted the Union advance.

After breaking through Forrest's mounted units, Wilson reached Selma on April 1. He moved the following day, assaulting the city in a three-pronged attack. From his position on the Union left, Upton led his division through gaps in the Confederate lines during a fight that lasted through the day. When it was over, the Federals had achieved a considerable triumph. Union cavalry took 2,700 prisoners while capturing 102 cannon along with an immense quantity of military supplies.

Wilson's Corps, with Upton's 4th Division often at the point, followed the victory at Selma by sweeping almost at will for five weeks through central Georgia, capturing cities, taking prisoners, seizing artillery pieces, and destroying locomotives, factories, arms, munitions, and other sustenance intended for Confederate forces.

Upton had fought in the first large encounter of the war at Bull Run. Now it was his fate to participate in one of the last large engagements as well. On April 16, 1865, a week after Lee surrendered at Appomattox, Upton's division made a rare night attack on Confederate fortifications and depots near Columbus, Georgia. Fighting in and around the city, Upton's men took 1,500 prisoners, captured large quantities of military supplies, and burned a Confederate naval vessel.

The 25-year-old general was held in such high regard that in May he was assigned to arrest Alexander Stephens, the vice president of the Confederacy. Soon after, for a time, Jefferson Davis was placed under his overall custody.

Within the U.S. Army Upton is remembered as much for his seminal writings after the war as he is for his notable service during it. Based on his study of the Franco-Prussian War and his observations of military organizations around the world, Upton wrote *The Armies of Europe and Asia*, a treatise that advocated professional military education, officer fitness reports, and promotion by examination for American Army officers. For the army as an institution, Upton suggested a general staff system.

Upton's magnum opus, *The Military Policy of the United States*, incomplete at the time of his death in 1881, was published posthumously in 1904. *Military Policy* reiterated many of the same proposals outlined in his earlier work as well as advocating a strong standing army to be augmented by conscription during major conflicts and compulsory age-related retirements for officers.

Many later reforms of the nation's armed forces can be traced to Upton's proposals.

Sixteen years after the war ended, Upton's final assignment was as commander of the 4th U.S. Artillery. At the Presidio of San Francisco, in intense, near-continuous pain from headaches likely caused by a brain tumor, Upton took his own life. He is buried at Auburn, New York.

A SPECIAL CASE:
BENJAMIN F. ISHERWOOD

The U.S. Navy's greatest engineer. Navy vessels with steam-propelled engines designed by Isherwood gained control of America's river systems and sealed off a coastline extending 3,500 miles along the Atlantic Seaboard and the Gulf of Mexico.

Rear Admiral Benjamin F. Isherwood never commanded a ship, sank an enemy vessel, or fired a weapon in anger during the Civil War. Few leaders, though, played as consequential a role in the navy's ultimate success.

Soon after the Civil War began, Isherwood was named engineer-in-chief. It was a post he would hold through the entire war. So valued was Isherwood's service and so vital were his contributions that an entire organization, the Bureau of Steam Engineering, was established to more fully exploit his talents and leadership.

Before the war Isherwood had been a prodigious writer of technical and scientific treatises related to steam engineering, steam propulsion, and his own experiments with thermodynamics. Assigned for a time to the Washington Navy Yard where he helped design ships and conduct experiments with steam propulsion, Isherwood combined theoretical concepts with practical experience as an engineering officer on several warships. In the decade before the war his extensive studies on the comparative efficiency and performance of various engine types made him uniquely qualified for his wartime position.

As the war progressed, shutting down Confederate access to commercial goods and military supplies became a primary focus of the U.S. Navy. Blockading the South evolved into an enormous undertaking. A coastline 3,500 miles long had to be sealed off and entry denied to ports scattered along the Atlantic Seaboard and Gulf of Mexico. Eventually, as ports, inlets, and channel islands were quarantined, the South's economy was progressively strangled.

Isherwood's contributions were the stuff of legend. He designed ships and steam engines capable of chasing down Confederate blockade runners and patrolling vast expanses of ocean. The Union began the war with less than 30 steam-powered vessels. When the conflict ended, the number exceeded 600 steam vessels of all types: fast, powerful ocean-deployed ships designed to close off Southern ports as well as shallow draft boats that ultimately gave the Union control of the South's rivers. Isherwood's contributions shaped the capabilities of the United States Navy. At the end of the war, not a single port on the Atlantic or the Gulf of Mexico remained open to Confederate commerce or blockade runners.

Lauded by some as perhaps the navy's greatest engineer, Isherwood died in 1915 in New York City at age 92.

A SPECIAL CASE:
MONTGOMERY C. MEIGS

At the outset of the Civil War, the U.S. Army numbered 16,367 officers and men. Two million would serve during the course of the conflict. As Quartermaster General, Meigs transformed them into the world's best equipped army. His astute use of the North's extensive railway system funneled supplies to Federal armies on the move across America's vast landscape.

Identifying a quartermaster as one of the nation's unsung military leaders may be without precedent; however, Montgomery C. Meigs, Quartermaster General of the Union army, warrants the exception. Officials in the Lincoln Administration and his military colleagues regarded Meigs' achievements as vital to the triumph of the Union cause. One member of Lincoln's cabinet, Secretary of State William Seward, believed the war might have been lost without Meigs' services.

General Meigs' career followed an unusual pattern. When the conflict began in 1861, he was serving as a military engineer in Washington, D.C. On May 14, he was appointed colonel in the infantry, but the very next day he was promoted to brigadier general and named Quartermaster General of the Army, a position he held throughout the war.

Meigs and the army began with almost nothing. On January 1, 1861, only weeks away from the first shots being fired, the U.S. Army was essentially a small constabulary force numbering 16,367 officers and men—and many of those would leave when the Southern states began seceding from the Union.

When Lee surrendered four years later, the Federal government had more than a million men under arms (more than two million served during the course of the war), all of whom were equipped with weapons, uniforms, blankets, canteens, tents, shelter halves, and all the other paraphernalia associated with a modem industrial-age army. The cavalry received horses, saddles, blankets, horseshoes, nails—a seemingly endless list. Under Meigs' oversight, the thousands of items were requisitioned, paid for, transported, allocated and forwarded to depots and front line units. Except for ordnance, through the months of conflict Meigs was responsible for supplying almost every item required to sustain the Union army's massive war effort. In the four years of war, the Union army was arguably transformed into the best equipped and provisioned fighting force in military history.

Making that happen was Montgomery Meigs' great contribution to the Union's victory.

From the outset, the North had an advantage in manufacturing capacity; however, translating that latent capability into tangible military strength was another matter entirely. Meigs' abilities were quickly recognized and were so well regarded that he was retained in the quartermaster position for the duration rather than being assigned as commander of a combat unit. As an organizer and administrator, he was known for his forcefulness and efficiency. As a public servant he was renowned for his personal integrity. As Quartermaster General, Meigs likely disbursed more money—billions of dollars in today's currency—than any other official in the nation's history up to that point. Contemporary sources indicate that it was properly spent and exhaustively accounted for. On occasions when suppliers provided sub-standard goods—instances were perhaps inevitable given the number of military procurements and the speed with which they were ordered and produced—contracts were terminated or quickly adjusted.

Many of his department's innovations remain with us to this day. Under Meigs' oversight, standard sizes for uniforms were introduced, as were shoes specifically designed to fit both left and right feet. Likewise, Meigs was ahead of his time in appreciating and exploiting the tie between campaign planning and logistics. His abilities became evident early in the conflict when his stellar planning and preparations enabled General George B. McClellan to move 100,000 men with associated supplies and ammunition by boat during the Peninsula Campaign. As the war progressed, Meigs was often immersed in preparations for forthcoming operations, spending considerable time at Grant's headquarters directly handling the Army of the Potomac's major supply depots. Under his stewardship the supply and replenishment cycle was transformed: the process of requisitioning and disbursing equipment and transporting troops and war materiel grew consistently faster as the war progressed.

Meigs made exceptional use of the Union's railway system. When the war began, the Lincoln administration quickly put the North's railroads under government control. That gave Meigs and Union commanders priority to move troops and supplies over more than 22,000 miles of track. The South, reluctant to impinge on the prerogatives of the states, and further hampered by rail gauges that varied in size across the Confederacy, never enacted a similar measure.

As the war progressed, Meigs' exhaustive preparations were increasingly complemented by an astute sense of timing and an ability to anticipate the warfighters' needs. At Savannah in January 1865, he met Sherman—who had cut loose from his supplies and lived off the land during his fabled 'March to the Sea'—and personally supervised the resupply and refitting of his army. Two months later he did it again as Sherman moved out of Georgia into the Carolinas.

Meigs never led troops in combat. At the very outset of the war, he was one of a small group, along with Navy Captain David Porter, who planned and executed the provisioning of Fort Pickens, Florida. In July 1864, when Confederate General Jubal Early made a strong thrust toward Washington, D.C., Meigs served as commander of a division of hastily assembled War Department employees to help defend the city. Early's threat, however, was pushed away before he penetrated the city's defenses. Clearly, however, the North's regard for Meigs' achievements more than compensated for his absence of frontline experience when he was named to the honor guard at Abraham Lincoln's funeral.

Beyond his quartermaster duties, Meigs left notable legacies in other areas as well, although they, too, are not well remembered. As an engineer before the war, Meigs supervised the construction of both wings and the dome of the U.S. Capitol. During the war, it was his recommendation, intended at the time at least in part as a riposte to Robert E. Lee, which led to the grounds around the Custis-Lee mansion being transformed into Arlington National Cemetery.

Meigs died in 1892, and is buried at Arlington.

A SPECIAL CASE:
JOSHUA LAWRENCE CHAMBERLAIN

At Little Round Top on the second day at Gettysburg, Chamberlain's leadership may have saved the battle, and perhaps the war, for the Union. During the course of 20 major battles, he was wounded six times and was the recipient of the Medal of Honor. At Appomattox, Grant chose him to preside over the formal surrender of the Army of Northern Virginia.

Thanks to Michael Shaara's Pulitzer Prize-winning book *The Killer Angels* and the movie *Gettysburg*, Joshua Lawrence Chamberlain is perhaps more familiar to the American public than many of the other leaders chronicled in this book.

Chamberlain's life defied conventional norms. A professor at Bowdoin College, he spoke 10 languages and taught every course in the school's curriculum except mathematics. During the war he fought in 20 battles, had six horses shot from under him, was wounded six times, and was brevetted to major general. Cited four times for bravery, he received a Medal of Honor for his actions at Gettysburg.

From the totality of Chamberlain's remarkable wartime service, two events warrant special recognition and a place in the collective memory of all Americans. The first occurred on July 2, 1863, at Gettysburg. Amidst the horror of one of the bloodiest days in American history, Chamberlain saved the battle, and with it quite possibly the war.

On the second day of the battle Chamberlain, commanding the 20th Maine, was assigned to hold the extreme left of the Union line. His was the last regiment on the flank at Little Round Top, the southern-most point in the "fishhook" that, beginning at Culp's Hill in the north and traversing along Cemetery Ridge to Little Round Top, formed the Union's defense.

Through some of the most severe fighting of the war, Chamberlain's regiment held against repeated Confederate attacks that came in waves throughout the day. At times, Chamberlain's line was bent almost back on itself as the rebels repeatedly threatened to batter past his position. Had they done so, the left flank of the Union defense would have been smashed, exposing the entire Federal line. Confederate control of Little Round Top would have enabled the rebels to roll up the Union front, destroying Meade's army or forcing it into surrender or retreat. Late in the day, with half of his men killed or wounded and the remainder nearly out of ammunition, Chamberlain met the final Confederate attack with a tactic that made him famous, and perhaps saved the Union army.

By this time in the battle, Chamberlain's line was formed into an "L" configuration to prevent rebel attackers from flanking the position on the west side. With the Confederates again moving up the hill in large numbers, Chamberlain ordered his troops—many of them completely out of ammunition or down to their last few bullets—to fix bayonets. As the Confederates drew near, he had his soldiers on the extreme left, beginning with those farthest out on the base of the "L", swing outward in a wheeling motion. When their movement brought them even with the rest of the line, which acted like a hinge on a swinging door, the entire regiment charged. The rebels, exhausted, now themselves flanked by a regiment coming down at them from higher ground, broke and ran. The 20th Maine's bayonet charge swept the Confederates from the hill.

When the fighting resumed the next day, Lee chose to try the center of the Union line with the assault known as "Pickett's Charge." When that attempt failed, Lee withdrew.

Thus ended Lee's cosmic throw of the dice—an attempt to end the war with a decisive victory on Northern soil. In the greatest battle ever fought on the North American continent, the Union army survived the storm. At Appomattox two years later, with growing strength in men and materiel and at long last led by effective commanders, Lincoln's soldiers finally prevailed.

The second event that limns Chamberlain's legacy occurred at Appomattox after the bloodshed had ended. In recognition of his extraordinary service, Chamberlain was chosen to preside over the ceremony formalizing the surrender of the Army of Northern Virginia.

In the early morning hours of April 12, 1865, with Union troops lining each side of the road, the remnants of Lee's proud army marched toward Appomattox Court House to surrender arms, colors, and battle flags. Led on horseback by the great cavalier of the Southern cause, General John B. Gordon, the Confederate ranks, sad and despairing, trooped up a slight hill and then followed the small lane onto the level ground near the court house.

What happened next became a sublime moment in American history. Although aspects of the story have at times been told or interpreted differently, the versions offered by both Chamberlain and Gordon are generally consistent in their major details.

As Gordon at the head of the column drew even with him, Chamberlain called the Union troops to attention and ordered them to "Carry Arms"—a move in which troops in formation snap their rifles against their right shoulders and hold them vertically as a form of salute.

Surprised and deeply touched, Gordon responded with the classic salute of the cavalry leader, wheeling his horse and dropping the tip of his sword to his stirrup. Gordon then ordered the Southern column to 'Carry Arms', dipping the Confederate colors as they passed between the lines of Union troops.

Thus, the final scene at Appomattox was one of reconciliation. For a country torn apart by four years of carnage that took the life of one out of every 33 Americans, Chamberlain's gesture began the process of healing the nation.

A FAMILIAR NAME IN A LESSER KNOWN ROLE:
WINFIELD SCOTT

Scott's "Anaconda Plan" to choke off access to Southern seaports and split the Confederacy by gaining control of the Mississippi River became an essential element of the Union's war-winning strategy.

When the Civil War began, Winfield Scott had been a general in the Army of the United States for 47 years, and General-in-Chief for 20. Brevetted to brigadier general in 1814, Scott played important roles in three of the nation's first four major conflicts.

At the time of Fort Sumter, Scott was 75 and in poor health. Obese and infirm, he could no longer mount a horse. It was apparent that he could not take operational command in the field. In November, Lincoln named George B. McClellan to replace him. The consequences remain uncertain. McClellan proved to be an adept trainer and organizer of armies but a most timid and unsteady commander in the field.

Scott was one of the few officials, military or civilian, who understood from the outset that the war would be long and difficult and would require an unprecedented allocation of the nation's resources. During the six and a half months of the conflict in which he held significant official responsibilities, Scott devised a strategic plan for the conduct of the war that proved prescient. Dubbed the "Anaconda Plan" by the press, Scott's proposal was in essence an encirclement strategy that called for a blockade of Southern ports and control of the Mississippi River. The blockade would choke the Confederacy; control of the Mississippi would cut it in half.

Scott was hoping to avoid major bloodshed and some thought his plan would take too long, but as the war lengthened it became an essential element of Union strategy. Grant's victory at Vicksburg in July 1863 put the Mississippi firmly under Union control. When the conflict ended nearly two years later, every port in the Confederacy had been captured and the South's coastlines on the Atlantic and Gulf of Mexico were sealed by Union warships.

Justifiably recalled as the genius of the war with Mexico, Scott also deserves to be remembered for devising a national strategy in the Civil War that was well conceived and executed.

Scott lived until 1866, long enough to see the Union's triumph. He is buried at West Point.

CHAPTER 7
THE INDIAN WARS OF THE WEST

RANALD MACKENZIE

Cited by U.S. Grant as "the most promising young officer" in the Union Army at the close of the Civil War, Mackenzie became the army's primary "firefighter" during the Indian Wars of the West. Sent to trouble spots across the Southwest, Great Plains, and Rocky Mountains, he was never defeated. In a decade and a half of warfare, he lost fewer men than did Custer in one horrific hour of combat.

The Indian wars of the American West were fought across an immense landscape remarkable for its varied geography and climate and for the cultures of the Native peoples who inhabited it. The wars were also waged by a surprisingly small military force. During the 25-year period following the Civil War, the U.S. Army seldom numbered more than 15,000 officers and men. Those few soldiers manned the nation's 150 forts, posts, camps, arsenals, and armories; guarded 6,000 miles of frontier and coastline; escorted wagon trains, stage coaches, and survey parties; shielded the construction of railroads, trails, and bridges; protected settlers and settlements; scouted; and, when called upon, fought Indians.

By one count, they were called upon 1,067 times during the course of 13 major campaigns. Their losses are believed to have numbered 923 killed and 1,061 wounded. Casualties among civilian scouts and contractors added another 577 to the total. Army records estimate that more than 5,500 Indians were killed or wounded during these encounters.

While identical sets of circumstances seldom existed, several frequently recurring conditions served as triggers for many of the wars. These factors varied in intensity from region to region and conflict to conflict. Foremost among them were the westward migration of the nation's growing population—a journey that took thousands of immigrants across Native regions; the discovery of gold or silver on historically Native or treaty land; and the rapid destruction of the continent's great bison herds.

The government's attempts to address the "Indian problem" by relocating the tribes or moving them to reservations were often resisted by the free-roaming and fiercely independent tribal groups. The Natives who signed treaties and moved to agencies sometimes faced an additional irritant: government functionaries did not always supply the annuities promised in treaty provisions.

Indeed, treaty violations (sometimes in response to incidents perpetrated by the other party) were not unknown on either side. Native actions most often took the form of thefts of livestock and killing raids on homesteads, settlements, outposts, and immigrant travelers.

The conflicts on the Great Plains and in the West and Southwest would present the U.S. Army with a different form of warfare than its officers and men had experienced during the Civil War—and they would confront a difficult foe. Inherent in the culture of many of the Native tribes was perpetual warfare with rival groups. Nomadic, tenacious, aggressive, their warriors formed "the best light cavalry in the world."

Ranald Mackenzie was one of the first of the U.S. Army's senior field commanders to wage war against the Indians with consistent success. Having taught himself to "think like an Indian," he turned many of the Native tribes' warfighting methods against them and was undefeated in encounters that spanned much of the American West. Despite darker sides to Mackenzie's service, there can be no questioning his accomplishments, his brilliance as a commander, or his personal bravery. On battlefields throughout Texas, the central Plains, and the Southwest, Mackenzie was often the government's "firefighter," given the most difficult tasks in the most dire circumstances. During the course of his career fighting Indians across a substantial part of the continent, he lost fewer men than did Custer in one horrific afternoon of combat.

Still, there were aspects to his service that make his career more difficult than most to place in balance. At times his discipline was so harsh that he was known to his soldiers as the "Perpetual Punisher"; he took his forces on extra-legal, cross-border excursions; and he was sometimes criticized for his treatment of the Native tribes that he was sent to subdue. His legacy is further blurred by the mental instability that afflicted him in later years and forced his retirement from the army.

Judgments, though, about Mackenzie the officer and his legacy are less than clear-cut. While chafing at times under his harsh discipline and high standards, Mackenzie's soldiers respected his courage and appreciated his ability to keep them alive. Throughout his career, his losses in combat were remarkably light. Recent scholarship has affirmed that Mackenzie's cross-border excursions had the tacit (or more) approval of President Ulysses S. Grant and General Philip H. Sheridan, Mackenzie's superior in the chain of command. Eventually, Mackenzie negotiated "hot pursuit" protocols with Mexican authorities. Finally, there is the interesting footnote that Mackenzie, the harsh, implacable warrior on the battlefield, regarded his successful efforts to prevent war with the Ute tribe as his proudest achievement. Thus, the ambiguities remain.

Mackenzie's career is perhaps best recalled for his leadership on battlefields and in campaigns against opponents adept in guerrilla warfare. There he was without peer.

Mackenzie's service following the Civil War was almost entirely in the West. From 1867 to 1875, first as commander of the 41st Infantry, a Buffalo Soldier regiment, and later as commander of the 4th U.S. Cavalry, Mackenzie was posted at various times at Fort Brown, Fort Clark, Fort McKavett, Fort Concho and Fort Richardson in Texas, and at Fort Sill in Indian Territory (present-day Oklahoma). In October 1871 Mackenzie was wounded for a seventh time during a skirmish with Comanches at Blanco Canyon. His service during this period was highlighted by triumphs at the Battle of the North Fork of the Red River (1872) and at the Battle of Palo Duro Canyon (1874).

Two aspects of the Battle of the North Fork brought Mackenzie notoriety as an Indian fighter. The first was that the campaign and its climactic struggle were waged in the *Llano Estacado*, the "Staked Plains" of West Texas, an immense region of rugged, inhospitable terrain that had long been the nearly impenetrable stronghold of the warring bands. The second was that it was likely during this expedition that Mackenzie developed a strategy for defeating the Plains Indians.

Striking out of the *Llano Estacado*, for years the Comanches had raided ranches, stolen cattle, and indulged in illicit *Comanchero* trade. From the time of the U.S. Army's arrival in the region, the Staked Plains had been a forbidden zone—a sanctuary from which Comanches operated with near-impunity from refuges in hidden canyons, seemingly swallowed up in the vast, flat emptiness. On July 21, 1872, Mackenzie with 284 officers and men of the 4th Cavalry and 24th Infantry, plus Indian scouts, began a reconnaissance that stretched all the way west to Fort Sumner, New Mexico, then north, and finally back east to the Texas Panhandle. After resupplying and resting his command, on September 21 Mackenzie moved north toward the headwaters of the Red River, along the way leaving a supply cache and a security detail near present-day Clarendon, Texas.

On September 29, leading a force of seven officers, 215 enlisted men, and nine scouts, Mackenzie came upon a substantial Indian village located near present-day Lefors, Texas. The 262 lodges, probably housing well over a thousand Indians, were situated on the North Fork of the Red River about seven miles from the mouth of McClellan Creek. After first resting his men and horses, Mackenzie formed his troopers into columns of four and prepared for a charge.

Mackenzie's attack took the village completely by surprise. One company made straight for the Indians' horses, stampeding or capturing the herd. Meanwhile, Mackenzie's remaining columns tore through the village before fanning out in pursuit of the masses of Indians that were put to flight. Except for a group of 80 or so warriors who were killed or scattered after a brisk fight near a creek bank, major resistance was quickly overcome. It is likely that the most intense combat lasted for no more than half an hour. Lodges, stores of meat, robes, clothing, camp supplies, and utensils were burned. Hundreds of horses and mules were captured, although some were recovered by Comanche raids on Mackenzie's camp the following night.

Mackenzie's after action report cited 23 Comanches confirmed killed, although other bodies may have been hidden to prevent desecration by Mackenzie's Indian scouts. Some estimates place the Comanche dead at 50 or more. The 130 Comanches taken prisoner were later exchanged for the band's promise to go back to the Indian agency and to return white captives held by the tribe. Mackenzie's losses were two troopers killed and two seriously wounded. (Some sources say three killed and three wounded.)

The victory at the North Fork was of special significance. For the first time, the army had struck at the heart of the Comanche fortress, and Mackenzie had mastered terrain that the Indians had considered inviolable. The *Llano Estacado* was no longer a sanctuary. Capturing the horse herd took away the Indians' mobility and with it their capability to hunt and conduct raids. With their horses gone, and their supplies and their village destroyed, the Indians could not survive except on the reservations. It was a lesson that Mackenzie and other commanders would apply often in the future.

The battle of the North Fork was a precursor to the forthcoming Red River War, and to the way that conflict would be fought by the army. Conditions in the region had steadily worsened following the 1867 Medicine Lodge Treaty that established two reservations in Indian Territory. Some Comanche, Kiowa, Southern Cheyenne, and Arapaho bands moved to the reservations. Other sub-tribes, though, refused to sign and remained hostile. Indian raids from inside and outside the reservations followed. For the reservation Indians, strife was sometimes a response to the tardiness in receipt—or pure absence—of the food and provisions promised by the government.

For both treaty and non-treaty Indians, war was a reaction to encroaching white settlement and to the hundreds of commercial buffalo hunters who swarmed through the area, ignoring treaty provisions. Between 1874 and 1878, hunters all but exterminated the great southern herd of American bison. As conditions deteriorated, large numbers of Indians from several tribes resolved to make a final attempt to drive the intruders from the Plains. Conversely, for the army the year 1874 brought a concerted attempt to pacify the Texas frontier.

An attack in late June by several hundred Indians on a buffalo hunter encampment at Adobe Walls provided the catalyst for government action against the southern Plains tribes. Eventually, five columns of troops moving from different points of the compass converged on the Texas Panhandle and tributaries of the Red River. Mackenzie's column, sweeping north from Fort Concho (near San Angelo), was part of a plan aimed at maintaining a continuous offensive, pressuring the Indians from all directions until they were forced into submission.

The army on this occasion was well-provisioned for an extended campaign. The army's unremitting pursuit and the tightening ring thrown across the panhandle made it a scene of frequent clashes. More than 20 battles were fought before the Red River War officially ended in June 1875. The decisive one came at Palo Duro Canyon, and the U.S. forces that fought and won the battle were led by Ranald Mackenzie.

In late September, Mackenzie moved north toward the canyon with his column, comprised mainly of the 4th U.S. Cavalry accompanied by infantry and associated scouts. Long regarded as a safe haven by Native tribes, Mackenzie believed, correctly, that large number of Indians would be assembled there. After first defeating Comanches in a small encounter in Tula Canyon on September 26, Mackenzie continued his pursuit and two days later reached the rim of Palo Duro Canyon. There, he found bands of Kiowas, Comanches, and Southern Cheyennes spread over as many as five villages scattered along the canyon floor.

At the point at which Mackenzie's troopers reached it, the canyon was about a half mile wide with towering 500-foot walls that in places were almost vertical. Straddled by the Indian camps, a small stream trickled along the canyon floor.

Mackenzie's attack at sunrise on September 28 was aimed at taking the sleeping villages unaware. The attempt at surprise met with only partial success, however, when the soldiers' presence was detected by an Indian chief or, in another version, a sentry. Although immediately killed or put to flight, the warrior got off a warning shot that alerted the first village. Sweeping over the rim, some of Mackenzie's troops followed a path of sorts leading down to the canyon floor. Others simply charged down the wall of the canyon before racing through and destroying the village.

The shock and chaos of the assault on the first cluster of Comanche lodges spread panic through the other villages. Lodges were abandoned and flight began almost immediately as large numbers attempted to escape Mackenzie's trap and reach the open plains. Few succeeded. Resistance was scattered and ineffectual and by nightfall Mackenzie's soldiers had taken the five villages and destroyed their contents. Perhaps as many as 2,000 Indian ponies were captured. More than 1,400 were eventually shot to prevent them from falling again into Indian hands. The devastation was total. In addition to horses and camp paraphernalia, the Indians' entire winter food supply was destroyed.

The casualties at Palo Duro canyon were remarkably light as Mackenzie lost only one soldier. Overwhelmed almost immediately, only three Indians were killed. Still, the defeat was total. The loss at Palo Duro Canyon along with unrelenting military pressure from several directions decided the campaign. Dismounted and hungry, pursued incessantly, within a month large numbers of Indian bands began returning to their reservations. When Quannah Parker's band surrendered the following summer, the Red River War was officially over.

Mackenzie returned to Fort Sill in Indian Territory after the clash at Palo Duro Canyon. Ironically, many of the Indians from the Palo Duro encampments were initially interred there. Frustrated with the reservation system and the deplorable conditions he found, Mackenzie ordered his soldiers to build houses for the Indians and, despite objections from the Indian Bureau, issued rations from military stores to the internees.

While at Fort Sill, Mackenzie suffered a near-fatal accident, striking his head after a fall from a wagon. He remained in a near-coma for two or three days. The severity of the accident has led many to conjecture that the fall contributed to the mental problems that afflicted him a few years later.

In 1873, in the interregnum between the battles at the North Fork and Palo Duro Canyon, Mackenzie was posted to Fort Clark, near Brackettville, with orders to stop the theft of livestock from Texas ranches by Indians raiding across the border from Mexico. On May 18, in an extralegal excursion (several sources make it fairly certain that raids of these kinds received at least tacit approval from higher authorities), Mackenzie struck across the border into Coahuila, Mexico. Finding the raiders' village near Remolino, he burned it and returned with 40 captives. The presence of the hostages combined with Mackenzie's aggressive border patrolling put an end to the raids.

Following Custer's defeat at the Little Big Horn in June 1876, Mackenzie was sent north to Camp Robinson in the northwest panhandle of Nebraska. (Camp Robinson would be officially designed a fort in January 1878.) The Great Sioux War was raging and although Wesley Merritt's victory at Warbonnet Creek in July had stopped the flow of Indians leaving reservations to join the warring bands, conditions remained unsettled. Hundreds of hostiles led by Crazy Horse, Sitting Bull, Dull Knife, and other war chiefs posed continuing threats.

After a failed attempt the previous year, in 1876 government commissioners met with representatives for a second time to negotiate a treaty that would relinquish Sioux claims to the Black Hills. In late September, after several days of confusion and disputes, commissioners secured sufficient signatures from the reluctant and sometimes bewildered chiefs to claim dubious title to the Black Hills region.

The negotiation process was hostile from the start; after one particularly angry session an embittered Sioux chief walked out, taking his followers with him. More importantly, after the treaty was signed two influential Indian leaders, Red Cloud and Red Leaf, infuriated by the results, took their followers away from the Red Cloud Agency. Thirty miles from the post, along Chadron Creek, they established new camps and demanded that government rations be delivered to them at those locations rather than at the agency.

General George Crook, department commander, arrived at Camp Robinson in mid-October. Perhaps fearing the precedent and a breakdown in the government's reservation system if the situation was left unaddressed, Crook concluded that the Indians must return to the agency, even if force was required to make them do so. Concerned also that the bands might break away to join the still-hostile groups farther north, Crook determined on immediate action.

On October 22, Mackenzie led a sizable force on a fast-moving night march that took them to the Chadron Creek area. There, close against the hostile camps, eight companies from the 4th and 5th U.S. Cavalry accompanied by 40 Pawnee Scouts waited for daybreak. At sunrise, in a daring and well-conceived strike, the scouts captured the Indians' pony herds while four companies of cavalry surrounded each camp.

Both villages surrendered immediately. The firearms of 150 warriors were confiscated along with more than 700 horses. The Indians were taken back to the agency the same day, with women and children and the aged and infirm permitted to ride. Warriors, marvelous horsemen who practically lived on horseback, were required to walk the entire 30 miles.

As best as can be determined, not a shot was fired; but, for the Indians the defeat was crushing, as total surely as if bodies had been left strewn on the battlefield.

The effects were felt almost immediately.

Red Cloud from that point resumed his role as an advocate for cooperation, and the door was slammed on the possibility that the bands might unite with Crazy Horse or other groups still at war.

A month after his successful raid on the camps along Chadron Creek, Mackenzie moved from Camp Robinson against a large group of hostiles believed to be congregating near present-day Kaycee, Wyoming. Led by Dull Knife and Little Wolf, the band of Northern Cheyenne was thought to number about 400 warriors. With a force of 1,000 consisting of elements of four cavalry regiments accompanied by Indian scouts, Mackenzie tracked west into Wyoming Territory. In late November, Pawnee scouts found the Cheyenne along a fork of the Powder River in the southern Big Horn Mountains.

Located in a gorge bounded by towering walls and bisected by a swift, ice-choked river, the Cheyenne set their camp in a relatively open area where the canyon widened out. The site was difficult to approach, as the main canyon was further cut by several smaller lateral chasms, each with fast-moving streams that fed the larger river. The Cheyenne considered the place impregnable.

Mackenzie attacked the encampment of 173 lodges at dawn on November 25. Numbering 1,300 inhabitants, the village was home to almost the entire Northern Cheyenne tribe. In bitterly cold weather the initial assault drove some of the warriors, many of whom were ill-clad, into the frozen countryside. Mackenzie's troopers captured the camp's pony herd early in the battle. Soon after, Company A of the 4th Cavalry was sent to prevent the Indians' desperate, nearly successful, attempt to retrieve it. The Northern Cheyenne resisted fiercely and at one point trapped the company in a steep ravine, firing down at it from both sides.

As the fighting intensified, Mackenzie sent one, then two companies into the fray. The relief force charged on foot and the fighting became hand to hand as the struggle continued to escalate. For a time the battle hung in the balance as the entire cavalry force was committed to the struggle in the ravine and to other fights around the campsite. Eventually, with the assistance of several of his Indian scouts who provided heavy covering fire from nearby high ground, Mackenzie's 5th Cavalry troopers rescued their embattled comrades, killing about 20 Cheyenne as they cleared the ravine.

Meanwhile, a cavalry company raced through the encampment, eventually taking two hillocks that commanded the immediate battle area. After a difficult struggle Mackenzie's men secured the village, although they were harassed for a time by Cheyenne warriors who fired from nearby rocks and high ground before retreating from the area.

The battle, which became known as the Dull Knife Fight, was prolonged and bitter. Mackenzie lost six killed and 26 wounded. Losses among the Northern Cheyenne were put at 26 killed with an additional unspecified number wounded. Mackenzie's troopers burned all the lodges and their contents and took with them 600–700 captured horses. The Dull Knife Fight essentially ended major Cheyenne participation in the Great Sioux War, leaving only Crazy Horse's band of Lakota Sioux as the major hostile band continuing to resist the government.

In 1877, Indians resumed cross-border raids from Mexico into south Texas, and in March 1878 Mackenzie was sent to Fort Clark to deal with the incursions. As before, he instituted a system of active, far-ranging patrols and in June led an expedition into Mexico. His foray, aimed at causing the Mexican government to take action against the Indians, had the desired effect. By late fall of that year the raids had ceased.

In October, again functioning as the army's trouble-shooter, Mackenzie was sent with six companies of cavalry to the Los Pinos Agency in Colorado. Utes at the agency were refusing to follow the provisions of a recent treaty that required the tribe to move to Utah. Mackenzie averted the threatened uprising by advising the chiefs that the only alternative was war. Two days later, the tribe began its move. Mackenzie regarded the peaceful solution to the Ute controversy, where one wrong move would have led to war, as one of the great achievements of his life.

The final stages of Mackenzie's career as an Indian fighter continued to be crowned with success. In the fall of 1881 he moved with his cavalry to Arizona to command field operations aimed at subduing warring Apaches. In September of that year fighting had again erupted when Apaches killed U.S. cavalrymen at a bloody fight at Cibecue Creek. On September 25, Mackenzie arrived at Fort Apache, having moved his battalion nearly 1,000 miles, mostly by train, from Gunnison, Colorado. Overcoming a convoluted organizational structure, Mackenzie positioned troops at key locations, worked effectively with Mexican authorities, and using techniques perfected earlier, rather quickly quelled the modest uprising. In October, after conducting a short but effective campaign, he was reassigned to command the District of New Mexico.

Once again tasked with pacifying Apaches who were launching cross-border raids, as well as putting down a threatened uprising by restless Navajos, within a year the army was firmly in control.

Before and After

Ranald Mackenzie was born July 27, 1840 in New York City. After attending Williams College for a time, he received an appointment to West Point where he graduated at the top of his class in 1862. Mackenzie's extraordinary talent as a combat leader came as a surprise to many who had known him before he entered the military. Shy and reserved, with delicate features, as a youth Mackenzie was afflicted with a speech impediment (a slight lisp) and had a rather high, shrill voice that never completely changed. Although he grew tall and rugged in appearance, issues with his speech and voice persisted and he never became comfortable speaking in public. Friends from his youth described him as quiet and modest and remembered his smile and earnest gray eyes.

West Point and, perhaps especially, his Civil War experience seem to have changed him. In later years his military colleagues would characterize him using phrases such as "alone and aloof," and "cold and efficient." By temperament he became high-strung—nervous, impatient, and irritable.

Referred to by Ulysses S. Grant as "the most promising young officer" in the Union army, Mackenzie was brevetted repeatedly for his leadership and bravery. Within two years he had fought in eight major engagements including Bull Run, Antietam, and Gettysburg. Later, he led cavalry forces in the Shenandoah Valley Campaign, at the Battle of Five Forks, and in the war's concluding encounters near Appomattox. With Lee's surrender, Mackenzie took custody of captured Confederate property. When the war ended he was a brevet major general at the age of 24.

From his earliest days in the military, Mackenzie gained a reputation for his meticulous approach to duty and for his willingness to assume responsibility and take the initiative, with or without orders. The men who served under Mackenzie often disliked him, sometimes intensely, for his harsh discipline. Almost all, however, recognized his exceptional abilities as a trainer and leader and greatly respected his bravery under fire. In balance, many of his soldiers may have seen the latter qualities as more compelling—when Mackenzie served as commander of the 41st Infantry, the regiment had the lowest desertion rate in the army.

In the words of his major biographer, "They never loved him, none of his soldiers ever would, but they would follow him anywhere."

Mackenzie's long service as a field commander in the Indian wars ended in 1883. By then a brigadier general in the regular army, he was reassigned from New Mexico to duty as commander of the Department of Texas. Within weeks his mental state rapidly deteriorated, however, perhaps as a consequence of the head injury suffered from the fall at Fort Sill. His behavior increasingly erratic, he was retired from the army and placed for a time in an asylum.

Mackenzie's death on January 19, 1889 left to history's judgment a military career that was an intriguing blend of harshness and brilliance. Mackenzie's aggressive disposition to wage total war was abetted by his unquestioned personal courage. Counterbalancing his willingness to stretch legalities and invite criticism for his tactics was a record of sustained success on the battlefield. If the surest measure of a combat commander is how he is judged by his opponents, then surely Mackenzie was paid the highest of compliments. Dull Knife, the famed Northern Cheyenne chief who during the course of a long and eventful life faced many of the army's foremost leaders, said to Mackenzie, "You were the one I was afraid of."

Mackenzie is buried at West Point.

EUGENE A. CARR

*Counting the Civil War and his service on the frontier, Carr participated in more than
40 major battles. Culminating with a major victory at Summit Springs, Colorado, his leadership
of the Republican River Expedition cleared a vital region and paved the way for settlement.*

Few officers in American military history have led forces in harm's way on so many occasions and for such an extended period of time as Eugene Asa Carr. His career included an impressive record as a combat leader during the Civil War as well as on the Great Plains and in the Southwest. Most notably, he led the campaign that cleared the Cheyenne from their fortress-like area along the Republican River in Nebraska and Kansas, and defeated Tall Bull's Dog Soldiers in a classic encounter at Summit Springs, Colorado. Altogether, he participated in 40 major battles.

Arcing north and south out of Kansas across most of southern Nebraska, the strategic value of the Republican River Valley was obvious long before a series of military campaigns brought notoriety to the region. From time immemorial, the Indians had used the valley as fortress, shelter, and hunting ground. It was a citadel: the Gibraltar of the Plains Indians.

The military importance of the area increased with each passing year as the frontier moved westward. Beginning in the 1850s, U.S. forces in considerable strength scouted the region in isolated forays that inevitably provoked clashes as the military units moved through the valley. After the Civil War separate patrols escalated into a series of campaigns. Conducted each year, the expeditions were part of a larger whole, linked together by the military's overall strategic objective of subduing the tribes in the valley or driving them from it.

The first expedition, in 1867, led by George Armstrong Custer with six companies of the 7th Cavalry, was inconclusive, notable mainly for, in Custer's words, "a particularly sharp conflict" against several hundred Sioux at the forks of the Republican near present-day Benkelman, Nebraska. The following year's expedition, led by Carr, while not yet decisive, would prove to be more significant.

Despite attempts by a Congressional committee to reach agreement with the warring tribes, in 1868 large bands of Indians resumed hostilities along and below the Republican River. To oppose them, Carr, a major in the Regular Army at the time, took the field with a contingent of the 5th U.S. Cavalry.

Carr was soldierly in appearance with a piercing gaze and full beard turned from black to gray in his later years. Less than average in height, his erect carriage made him appear taller. Carr was a soldier-scholar, widely read and intellectually curious, and fearless on the battlefield. Unlike his contemporary, Ranald Mackenzie, Carr was also known for his kind and considerate treatment of his officers and men. During a cholera outbreak at Fort Riley, he had personally ministered to several of his stricken soldiers. He was a less than docile subordinate, however, and was a frequent thorn in the side of those above him in the chain of command.

In early October, Carr, posted in Washington, D.C., received orders to join the 5th U.S. Cavalry, "the Dandy Fifth," on the Kansas plains. On October 18, 1868, with an escort of 100 troopers, he was hurrying to locate and join his command, already in the field, when his force was attacked by a large Sioux and Cheyenne war party near Beaver Creek, Kansas. Carr formed his supply wagons in an oval, placed his horses and mules inside, and for the next eight hours fought off repeated attacks by the 700 or more warriors who rode in constricting circles around his makeshift stockade. After a struggle through the heat of the day, the Indians withdrew in the face of increasing losses. Three of Carr's troopers were wounded.

Carr caught up with his command, seven companies and a contingent of scouts, on October 22 at Buffalo Tank, a railroad stop on the Kansas Pacific Railroad. Carr immediately set the force in motion towards Nebraska and the Republican River Valley. On October 27, not far from the Solomon River in northern Kansas, the cavalry's advance guard ran into a substantial force of Sioux and Cheyenne. The initial skirmish grew quickly into a full-fledged battle as 500 Indians joined the fray and Carr poured his entire command into the fight. A large, confused running melee then resulted that continued for about six miles. At nightfall the Indians broke off the action after losing about 30 warriors killed and wounded.

Unlike many battles on the Plains, which were intense spasm exchanges that were seldom of long duration, the first day's encounter was only the beginning of a prolonged period of violent, near-continuous action. For the next four days a furious running battle raged, tracing a long northward crescent across the Republican into Nebraska, west through the valley and then back again south to Beaver Creek.

The Sioux and Cheyenne losses were thought to be significant, and when the cavalry prepared to resume the attack at dawn on October 31, the Indians had vanished. Carr's efforts scattered the bands, pushing many of them south, driving them against Sheridan's forces waiting in Indian Territory.

From the government's perspective, the 1868 expedition had been more successful than the campaign of the previous year. Still, while the Indians had suffered substantial losses and had been temporarily dispersed, the danger along the Republican River valley had not been removed. Indeed, as events would show, the threat would soon reappear larger and more ominous than before.

In 1869, a short distance south of present-day Orleans, Nebraska, the Sioux massacred a party of United States surveyors near where Sappa Creek flows into the Republican River. Every member of the survey party was killed.

In the spring, Cheyenne Dog Soldiers, the tribe's elite warrior society, led by Chief Tall Bull and accompanied by large Sioux war parties, moved aggressively into the Republican Valley. Beginning on May 21, 1869, they launched a campaign of terror that cut a swath of destruction from the Saline River in Kansas to the Big Sandy in Nebraska. Moving swiftly, the Indians struck hunting parties, burned homesteads, derailed and nearly wiped out the crew of a Kansas Pacific train, and killed 13 persons in raids up and down the river. On May 30, war parties destroyed a Kansas settlement, killing an additional 13 settlers and kidnapping two women. David Butler, governor of the two-year-old state of Nebraska, wrote to General C.C. Auger, commanding officer of the Military District of the Platte, imploring the army to provide immediate assistance.

General Auger replied the following day, assuring Governor Butler that help would be quickly forthcoming from Fort McPherson, near present-day North Platte, Nebraska. Eight days later, Auger made good his promise. On the 9th of June, a force under Carr's command left the post, moving first south and east along the Platte, then south to Medicine Creek, and then toward the lush valley of the Republican River. Their trek took them across rolling plains that rise gradually in elevation until they reach the foothills of the Rocky Mountains. Unknown to them at the time, underneath the coarse, unplowed prairie grass lay some of the most fertile soil on the continent. They skirted slow-moving, muddy streams that ran full in the spring but were now shallower in the summer, their channels often cut by sandbars overgrown with scrub willows.

Here and there, they crossed buffalo trails that ran north and south—deep, dusty paths formed by great beasts moving on their journeys over the millennia: north in the spring to reach the summer grass, then south again in the fall. Along these trails were buffalo "wallows"—depressions worn by bison as they rolled about in the soil. Some of the older, more permanent wallows, their bottoms packed hard by use over the years, held water run-offs from the surrounding prairie.

Carr's troopers reached the Republican on June 13 and camped at a point about four miles below the junction of the river and the mouth of Beaver Creek. These steps were the first in a series of moves that eventually formed an enormous horseshoe-shaped track that ranged over parts of Kansas, Nebraska, and Colorado. The campaign became known as the Republican River Expedition.

The frontier army was small, impoverished, and desperately under-manned at the time—the demobilization following the Civil War had been massive in scope and size—and throughout the five-week campaign Carr sent repeated requests for additional weapons, ambulances, and assorted provisions. Still, in the context of the times it was a sizable force that Carr took with him from Fort McPherson: eight companies of the 5th Cavalry (although none of the companies was at more than half its authorized strength), two companies of Pawnee Scouts, 54 overloaded wagons pulled by mule teams, and a complement of teamsters, wagon masters, and herders.

Midway through the expedition—an indication of how thinly stretched the army was at the time—one veteran cavalry company was withdrawn from Carr's force and sent for duty along the Little Blue River. That unit was replaced by a third company of Pawnee Scouts. Initially, Carr had misgivings about the quality and competence of the Pawnee contingent. As the campaign progressed, the caliber of the Pawnees' service became more evident and Carr's concerns were considerably reduced. In later campaigns he would explicitly request their presence.

Carr was well-chosen to lead the expedition. The most famous per-sonage on the campaign, however, was William F. Cody, Chief of Scouts of the 5th Cavalry. Carr and "Buffalo Bill" had previously served together, and Carr, impressed with Cody's "skill, fighting, and marksmanship," requested that Cody lead the cavalry's contingent of scouts.

Carr, Cody, and the "Dandy Fifth" were unquestionably moving in harm's way. The Republican River Valley had long been a refuge for the Plains Indians. It sheltered them from blizzards in winter and provided food, water, and lodging grounds in the summer. Now, in the spring of 1869, it was their last stronghold in the central Plains. They would not relinquish it easily.

Carr's force moved across terrain that was alternately rugged and sandy and, at the time, not well charted. The harsh landscape and the absence of roads and trails made it difficult for the wagons to keep up with the main body of troops. Breakdowns were frequent and the mules often played out from dragging wagons through the sand. To maintain the momentum of the pursuit, on two occasions Carr left a cavalry company and the wagon train behind with orders to catch up later.

The journey to the south provided evidence of Cheyenne presence in the area. On the morning of June 12 a cavalry patrol was scouting along Deer Creek when it ran into a hunting party of about 20 Indians who fled before an attack could be organized. The trail was soon lost as the Cheyenne dispersed and little of consequence resulted from the campaign's first, fleeting contact.

For two days after entering the valley, Carr moved mostly west, crossing over Deer Creek before stopping early on the 15th to rest his troops at a campsite along the banks of Prairie Dog Creek. The troops bivouacked along the stream, with the Pawnee Scouts camped about a half mile from the cavalry. The wagon train was positioned between the two camps. Apparently hidden in the tall grass throughout the day, Indians attacked the wagon train area in late afternoon as Carr's men settled down for supper. In the shooting and melee of the first few minutes, a teamster was wounded and Carr's troopers struggled to respond. The sudden attack was aimed at driving off the mule herd and thus immobilizing the wagon train carrying Carr's supplies.

Quick reaction by the Pawnee Scouts foiled the plan. Before the cavalry could react, the Pawnees raced to their ponies and went after the attackers. Along with Bill Cody—who had left his horse saddled—and the scouts' commander, Major Frank North, the Pawnees engaged the Cheyenne in a running battle that extended over several miles as the raiders raced away to the south. Cody and the Pawnees were joined by several companies of cavalry before darkness fell and the chase was broken off. The Pawnees killed two of the marauders before night obscured the trail.

At three the next morning, the main force turned south toward Kansas, tracking Indian "sign" to the north fork of the Solomon River. After 25 miles, they lost the trail as the Indians scattered and blurred their path. Three days later, after scouring the area, Carr turned back north, crossing again into Nebraska and returning to the Republican River with the intention of scouting along it and clearing it to the extent that his manpower and supplies allowed.

For the next several days, Carr's troops moved in a series of long marches, 25 to 30 miles a day, tracking generally west along the river. Patrols were dispatched daily, scouting ahead and to the north and south of the main body. At the end of the month, Carr brought his force to a pre-arranged rendezvous at a place called "Thickwood" in southwestern Nebraska. There, he was re-provisioned by a wagon train sent from Fort McPherson. Carr sent his sick and injured back to the fort with the return train and rested his men in the timbered area for most of two days.

On July 2, the troops resumed the march, moving westward toward the Colorado border. The following day a large, promising trail was discovered. Signs indicated that the tracks might have been made by the Dog Soldiers who had raided the settlements. Although the party was obviously large, the Cheyenne again did a masterful job of disguising their path: scattering, driving livestock over the trail and traveling on hard ground before reassembling at night.

Nonetheless, Carr's men were narrowing the gap. Carr again stripped a group free of the main body and wagon train, sending three companies of cavalry and one company of Pawnee Scouts with three days of packs in pursuit of the Cheyenne. On July 4 the detached force came across a 12-person war party carrying a wounded brave on a litter. The Pawnee Scouts ran the Cheyennes down, scalped three of them and captured eight horses, two with army brands.

Although skeptical of catching up with the main body of Cheyenne, who probably would have been warned by the surviving members of the Deer Creek hunting party, Carr put his entire force on the march. After backtracking momentarily to find a better route for his wagons, Carr then led his main body west through the difficult, sandy, inhospitable terrain of what is now eastern Colorado—a high, barren plain that further west rises gradually into the foothills of the Rocky Mountains.

Clashes were soon forthcoming. On the 8th, four men were detailed from the column to retrieve a horse that had strayed. Several miles from the main body, they were jumped by eight Indians. The small detail sought refuge in a rock outcropping and killed the horse they had only recently recovered, using the carcass for shelter. The Cheyenne eventually left the sharp fight after two warriors were wounded.

Late that night, Carr's main camp again came under attack. In an unusual night foray, a group of Indians—by most accounts five to seven, by one version as many as 30—rode from east to west sweeping through the entire camp. Hollering and shooting as they raced among the tents and wagons, they attempted to stampede the horses and cause casualties in the resulting confusion. The attack was over as quickly as it began as the raiders disappeared into the night.

Other than one Pawnee Scout wounded by "friendly fire" from a cavalryman, the attack did little material damage. The brazenness of the raid, however, signaled that Cheyenne were nearby in substantial numbers.

Determined to maintain the pursuit, Carr moved at dawn the next day. Turning north, he began a series of forced marches through the desolate country of northeastern Colorado that each day brought him closer to Tall Bull's Dog Soldiers. Signs of recently abandoned campsites were discovered. The prints of a white woman's shoe were found, reaffirming the possibility that Carr was on the track of the Dog Soldiers who had raided, killed, and kidnapped in Kansas and Nebraska. Carr's fast-moving soldiers continued their relentless pursuit, often covering distances in a single day—as many as 65 miles on one occasion—that the Indians traveled in two or three.

On July 10, troopers found a camp that the Indians had apparently abandoned earlier the same day and a heel mark left by a white woman's shoe. Carr halted at the encampment and readied his command for action.

Meanwhile, in recent days Tall Bull had first taken his band east toward Nebraska and the South Platte. Finding the Platte and other streams running too full for safe crossing, and worried that the route would take him in the direction of known military presence, he changed course. Lulled possibly by Carr's momentary backtracking in the past week into thinking that at least some of the force was being withdrawn, Tall Bull went into camp at White Butte Creek near Summit Springs, Colorado.

Carr was now 20 miles away.

Carr's provisions were running low and his men were tired. More critically, the cavalry's horses were by now ill-fed and exhausted. Carr formed his command, sorted it by the physical condition of troopers and their animals, and chose to take to battle with him "those whose horses were fit for service." There were not nearly as many as he would have liked: only 244 out of 400 men from his seven cavalry companies, and only 50 of 150 warriors in the three companies of Pawnee Scouts would accompany him when the force left at dawn on the 11th.

By evening, they were victorious.

At Summit Springs, Carr and his men surprised, out-fought, and over-whelmed their Indian adversaries. Guided by Bill Cody to the Cheyenne camp in a small valley about 14 miles southwest of Sterling, Colorado, Carr's outnumbered force of less than 300 cavalry and Pawnee Scouts slammed into Tall Bull's 500 Dog Soldiers from three sides, thoroughly routing them. The fight was brief and violent. Tall Bull and 51 other Cheyennes were killed. The remainder fled or were taken prisoner. Carr's after action report listd 274 horses, 144 mules, 9,300 pounds of dried meat, 84 complete lodges, 56 rifles, 22 revolvers, 40 bows and arrows, 50 pounds of gunpowder, 20 boxes of percussion caps, 17 sabers, 9 lances, and 20 tomahawks captured in the attack.

Troopers also freed Maria Weichell, one of the women captured in Kansas. She was found wounded but alive near Tall Bull's lodge where, by some testimony, the chief had shot her during the attack. According to some participants, a second woman prisoner, Susanna Alderdice, was tomahawked by one of Tall Bull's wives and died soon after the battle. Carr's cavalrymen sustained only one casualty, a minor wound inflicted by an arrow.

Initiated by a classic cavalry charge, the battle was one of the few in the history of the frontier where reality would match the scenes depicted in western fiction.

For years a bastion of the Plains Indians, the Republican River Valley was finally cleared for settlement. Carr's expedition broke the strength of the Cheyenne Dog Soldiers and eliminated the last Indian stronghold on the central Plains.

Before and After

Carr was born in Erie County, New York, on March 20, 1830. At age 16 he entered West Point, graduating 19th of 44 in the class of 1850. Nicknamed the "Black-bearded Cossack" for his most prominent physical feature, after graduation Carr was posted to duties on the frontier. He was one of the few commanders whose extensive career as an Indian fighter included service in the West prior to the start of the Civil War. Carr served in Kansas, Nebraska, and Texas, seeing his initial action as early as 1854 against Apaches near the Sierra Diablo Mountains. On October 10th of that year, Carr, part of a 40-man cavalry company tracking a band of 300 or so Lipan Apaches that had stolen cattle from nearby ranches, was severely wounded. Typically, he stayed on the field leading his men. Soon after, he was on the Great Plains participating in Harney's Sioux Expedition in 1855 and shepherding Fort Riley, Kansas, through a cholera outbreak later that year. In 1856–1857, Carr helped maintain order on the Kansas border and led a company in the so-called Mormon War. In 1858, he accompanied Colonel Edwin V. Sumner on the army's first major reconnaissance of the Republican River Valley, an area whose name would later be inextricably linked to his own. At the outbreak of the Civil War he was in a command position at Fort Washita in Indian Territory.

Carr's Civil War service began early in the conflict and covered the duration of the war in the western theater. He saw action at Wilson's Creek, Pea Ridge, Port Gibson, Champion's Hill, Vicksburg, Camden, Little Rock, Fort Blakely, and was part of the final drive towards Mobile. His actions at Pea Ridge, where he was wounded several times while leading a division in the fierce fighting around Elkhorn Tavern, were eventually recognized by award of the Medal of Honor. Carr held a series of major command assignments throughout the war. He was commander of the cavalry division in VII Corps, commander of the District of Little Rock, and finally commander of the 3rd Division of the XVI Corps during the campaign against Mobile near the end of the conflict. By war's end, he was brevetted to general.

For two years following the war, Carr was posted to Reconstruction duty in Arkansas and North Carolina. In 1868, he was again sent west to the frontier. There, along the Republican River, he would lead the two expeditions that would forever tie his name to the military history of the central Plains.

In December 1868, between Republican River expeditions, Carr led a difficult reconnaissance from Fort Lyon, Colorado, to the Canadian River. Plagued throughout by severe weather, the campaign was notable mainly for having had for a time both "Buffalo Bill" Cody and "Wild Bill" Hickok assigned as scouts.

Carr was never very far from the action. Typical was an episode in south central Nebraska early in 1869. Spring of that year found the 5th Cavalry transferring from Fort Lyon, Colorado, to Fort McPherson, Nebraska, to take part in the Republican River Expedition. On May 14, soon after the unit had crossed into Nebraska, scouts came across an Indian trail of considerable size near Medicine Creek. Still some distance south of the fort, Carr, then serving as the operational commander of the "Dandy Fifth," sent his pack train on to Fort McPherson and detailed seven companies of cavalry to follow the trail.

Led by "Buffalo Bill" Cody, the troopers pursued the difficult trail for two days, tracking the Indians several miles in an easterly direction. While the rest of the command watered its horses at a ford along Spring Creek, Carr sent a small group that included Cody on an advance scout to check on five Indians who had been seen in the far distance. A short time later, Carr, anticipating trouble, sent a full cavalry company under the command of an experienced Civil War veteran, Lieutenant John Breckenridge Babcock, to support the reconnaissance. Carr's instincts proved correct.

Two miles from Spring Creek, as Babcock's troopers made contact with the scout party, both groups were ambushed and surrounded by an estimated 200 Indians who poured into the cavalrymen from hiding places in nearby gullies and ravines. Carr's arrival with the rest of the regiment ended a desperate struggle notable for "Buffalo Bill" being wounded in action and a Medal of Honor later being awarded to Lieutenant Babcock for his leadership in responding to the attack.

By 1870, Carr was commander of Fort McPherson on the Nebraska frontier. In 1876, he was with Colonel Wesley Merritt and the 5th Cavalry at Warbonnet Creek, where he led the last great charge of the U.S. Cavalry, helping Merritt turn back the hundreds of Cheyennes attempting to join Crazy Horse and other "hostiles" on the warpath further north. Carr accompanied the "Dandy Fifth" through the Sioux Campaign and led it at the Battle of Slim Buttes. He was in charge of the small garrison at Fort McPherson throughout the Cheyenne Outbreak from Indian Territory during the fall and winter of 1878. In 1879, he was named commander of the 6th Cavalry at Fort Lowell, Arizona. He served there for five years until being posted to Fort Wingate, New Mexico, in 1884.

Carr's service in the Southwest included the Victorio Campaign and, most notably, the battles of Cibecue (alternately, Cibicu) Creek and Fort Apache.

In late August 1881, Carr led a force comprised of five officers and 79 enlisted cavalrymen on a mission to apprehend a powerful Apache medicine man suspected of planning an uprising. Nock-ay-det-klinne (or, variously, Nook-ay-det-klinne, or Nochaydelklinne), mentor to Cochise and Geronimo, was a White Mountain Apache whose village was near Cibecue Creek in the interior of the Fort Apache Indian Reservation in eastern Arizona.

Carr left Fort Apache on August 29, taking soldiers drawn from two troops of the 6th Cavalry and Company D, 12th Infantry. He was also accompanied by Indian scouts, at least some of whose loyalty was suspect: 12 of the 23 were Cibecue Apaches, known followers of Nock-ay-det-klinne.

Tracking through rugged country cut by sharp canyons, Carr made 29 miles the first day. It was later conjectured that an ambush had been avoided by an inadvertent choice of trails made at the last minute during the march.

The following day, Carr took his men across Cibecue Creek where it flowed only a short distance from the Apache village which sat on a long, narrow bluff about 20 feet above the creek bottom. Following a narrow path, Carr's men reached the village about three o'clock in the afternoon.

After a parley, Nock-ay-det-klinne agreed to accompany Carr back to the fort. As the column moved along the trail away from the village, it became stretched out and broken as the medicine man, under guard by a sergeant and eight troopers near the rear of the file, found reasons to delay his departure. When the full procession was eventually in motion, the entourage was periodically joined or shadowed by increasing numbers of armed Apaches.

As the front of the file moved toward Carr's planned campsite about two miles south of the village, a sharp bend in the trail momentarily blocked it from sight by the remainder of the column. It was apparently at this time that fighting erupted, with the Apaches initially focusing their attack on the rear of the column where Nock-ay-det-klinne rode with the contingent of nine soldiers. The Apache scouts mutinied, either instigating the assault or immediately joining in it. While much of the full encounter was fought at some distance with long range rifles, the initial clash involving the scouts—riding nearby or intermingled with the cavalrymen—was a violent, close-in encounter.

Despite the initial surprise, Carr rallied his troops, and although some historians have criticized his handling of the episode, brought the separated parts of the column together and succeeded in driving off the attackers. Seven soldiers were killed at the scene and another later died of his wounds. Two more were wounded but safely evacuated. Eighteen Apaches, including Nock-ay-det-klinne, were killed.

Carr, concerned about the threat to Fort Apache, only lightly held by 60 soldiers, and wary of a potential ambush on the way back to the fort if he lingered at the scene of the fight, decided on a surprise night march to separate himself from the attackers, whose strength he estimated at 60 during the initial attack, later joined by 200 or more during the course of the battle. After burying the dead, Carr fed his troops, rearranged his packs and supplies—42 horses and seven mules had been lost during the fight—and destroyed the provisions that could not be carried by his remaining pack train. At 11 p.m., he began his move back to the fort, reaching it without incident in the afternoon of the following day.

Carr's premonition about a threat to the fort proved correct. Two days later the Apaches attacked in considerable force, making several assaults mostly at long range. The raiders were eventually driven off by heavy counter-fire after a struggle that lasted through the day and into the early evening. Three soldiers were wounded. Apache losses were unknown.

Cibecue Creek and Fort Apache would be the last of Carr's 40 major encounters. He retired from the military as a brigadier general in 1893.

Carr died in Washington, D.C. on December 2, 1910, and is buried at West Point.

WESLEY MERRITT

At Warbonnet Creek, Nebraska, the first battle after the Little Bighorn, Merritt shut off the flow of reinforcements to hostile bands operating in the north. After Warbonnet Creek, the Indians never again prevailed in a major engagement.

On July 17, 1876—three weeks after the Little Bighorn—a slender, soft-spoken cavalry officer defeated hundreds of Sioux and Northern Cheyenne attempting to join Crazy Horse, Sitting Bull, and other noted war chiefs. His triumph at the little known and vastly unappreciated battle at Warbonnet Creek, Nebraska, shut off the flow of Indians to the battlefields further north. Wesley Merritt's victory was the beginning of the end for the Plains Indians, as after Warbonnet Creek, they never again prevailed on a major battlefield. By the following summer, the war on the Plains was over.

Waged near a small stream in extreme northwestern Nebraska, the Battle of Warbonnet Creek came after a series of calamitous defeats inflicted on U.S. military forces sent to quell the massive uprising that had exploded across the plains. Culminating with the catastrophe at the Little Bighorn, Indians repeatedly battered army units led by some of the nation's most famous commanders.

Fighting had begun late in the preceding year when, outraged by the intrusions of gold seekers and settlers into the Black Hills, hundreds of Sioux and Cheyenne left their reservations. Conditions continued to deteriorate after government-sponsored talks at the Red Cloud Agency aimed at buying the Black Hills failed. Emboldened by victories won during the spring and early summer, they refused orders to return.

In early 1876, seeking to strike while the hostiles were in stationary camps and their pony herds weakened by winter weather, General George Crook sent a column under the direct command of Colonel Joseph J. Reynolds north from Fort Fetterman, Wyoming Territory, to attack hostile Sioux known to be wintering in the southeast corner of Montana. On March 17, Reynolds was defeated in a disastrously mishandled battle along the Powder River.

After re-provisioning, Crook put forces in motion as part of a grand strategy intended to crush the major Indian threat once and for all. As conceived by Lieutenant General Philip H. Sheridan, Commander of the District of the Missouri, three columns moving from different directions would converge on the Yellowstone-Powder River area where large numbers of "non-treaty Sioux" along with other bands that had left reservations were believed to be gathering. Sheridan's plan sent Crook north from Fort Fetterman; meanwhile, Colonel John Gibbon would move east down the Yellowstone River from Montana; and Brigadier General Alfred Terry would drive west from Fort Abraham Lincoln in Dakota Territory. Caught between the converging wings, the hostiles would either be destroyed or forced back to their agencies.

Crook's force made first contact, a brief skirmish along the Tongue River on June 9. On the 17th, a much larger and more consequential engagement occurred near the headwaters of Rosebud Creek in south-eastern Montana between the Powder River and the Little Bighorn. At the Rosebud, Sioux and Cheyenne launched a day-long attack on Crook's column. While Crook still possessed the ground at the end of the day, his combat losses and expenditures of supplies and ammunition induced him to abandon his portion of the offensive. He turned his force south to Goose Creek, Wyoming, where he waited for provisions and, with more than a thousand men already under his command, asked for reinforcements. His request for additional troops would play a part in the drama that was to unfold on Warbonnet Creek the following month.

More importantly, by moving south, Crook took his army away from the vicinity of the Little Bighorn, where Custer was annihilated eight days later.

Believing that Crook was still moving towards him, General Terry sent Custer and the 7th Cavalry up Rosebud Creek to locate and pursue Indians thought to be concentrating in the valley of the Little Bighorn. Custer found a huge trail and followed it west. Unwilling to wait for Terry's and Gibbon's now-combined force to reach him, Custer came upon one of the largest encampments of hostiles ever assembled on the North American continent. In the ensuing battle, Custer and every one of the more than 200 men under his immediate command were killed.

The Little Bighorn left the nation thunderstruck. By the standards of Plains warfare, the casualties were staggering—and amid shock and anger came calls for action. More ominously, as word of Custer's defeat spread through the tribes, hundreds of warriors made preparations to leave their reservations and join the hostile bands on the warpath in the north.

Wesley Merritt's connection with the central Plains began on July 1, 1876, when he took command of the 5th Cavalry, engaged in operations in the western panhandle of Nebraska. However, even before the debacles at Rosebud Creek and the Little Bighorn, Sheridan, concerned by reports of Indians leaving the Red Cloud and Spotted Tail agencies in northwestern Nebraska, had ordered the 5th Cavalry to move to the region and cut the "feeder-trail" linking the reservations with the Powder River area where large numbers of hostiles were rapidly assembling.

Initial elements of the 5th Cavalry, sent from posts scattered across the central Plains, arrived in Wyoming in early June. Subsequently, at Fort Laramie, eight full companies came together. Soon after, the force moved out to take blocking positions along the Indian trail. In the face of rising tensions, they would remain in that location for about a month.

On July 1, as the unit maintained its vigil on the trail, Colonel Merritt took command, replacing elderly Colonel William Emory, an 1831 graduate of West Point, who retired after having for several years exercised only administrative command of the unit. Operational command in the field had been held by Lieutenant Colonel Eugene A. Carr. When Merritt assumed command, he chose to exercise operational as well as administrative control. Carr nevertheless remained with the unit and fought with it at Warbonnet Creek. During the following campaign and the Battle of Slim Buttes, Merritt commanded the expedition's combined cavalry contingent while Carr led the 5th Cavalry component.

Quiet and unpretentious, noted for his coolness under fire, Merritt was highly regarded, having been brevetted to major general for his exceptional service during the Civil War. Dark-haired, of average height and build, Merritt was clean-shaven early in his military career before allowing himself a modest mustache as he grew more senior in rank. Merritt knew the territory well, having spent several months in the area serving as Cavalry Inspector for the Military Department of the Missouri, serving under department commander Sheridan— duties that enabled him to function as Sheridan's personal investigator and troubleshooter.

At the 5th Cavalry's main camp northwest of the Red Cloud Agency in Nebraska, brief lulls were broken by intermittent skirmishes as groups of warriors pushed away from the agency. Merritt responded by moving the camp closer to the Indian trail and launching an aggressive series of scouting forays. The move to the new camp brought with it an added sign of peril: Merritt's soldiers found recently dug rifle pits and the bodies of Black Hills miners killed by the Indians.

Merritt kept his troops at the new campsite for the next several days while patrols scoured the area. Those activities ended on July 12, when Sheridan, apparently responding to Crook's continued pleas for reinforcements, ordered Merritt to return to Fort Laramie to refit and then to join Crook in northern Wyoming.

The return to Fort Laramie was well underway and the unit was going into camp after a march of 16 miles when Merritt received word from the commander of Camp Robinson that hundreds of Cheyenne were planning to leave the Red Cloud Agency and join the warring bands farther north. Merritt reacted quickly. Advising Crook and Sheridan of his decision, over the next two days he backtracked 51 miles to a point on the road between Fort Laramie and the Red Cloud Agency. There, he camped the night of July 14. Concluding that a further advance of his entire force toward the agency might provoke a fight before he was ready—and determined to verify the accuracy of the information he had received—Merritt sent a cavalry company to investigate the situation at the agency.

By midday on July 15 he had received word that 800 or more Cheyenne and Sioux led by Chief Little Wolf were planning to leave the agency that day or soon after. Merritt realized that it was crucial to shut off the flow of additional warriors to the hostiles who had already fought the cavalry to a standstill.

Within an hour of receiving the news, Merritt personally led seven companies deep into northwestern Nebraska. If he could beat the Cheyennes to the trail, he intended to meet them head on and force them back to the agency.

Time was of the essence. Even if they left on Sunday July 16, the Indians would need only a 28-mile ride to reach the junction of the trail. Merritt would have to travel three times that distance. To do it, he needed to retrace his path to the north and turn east across the Indians' most likely route. Leaving a small detachment to guard much of his wagon train, whose commander was told to follow and catch up when the cavalry halted or went into camp, by 10 o'clock that night Merritt had taken his men 35 miles. After a brief stop to rest and feed the horses, by five in the morning they were on the march again.

At midday they reached a palisaded camp along Sage Creek guarded by a company of infantry. There, they rested for an hour, ate a quick lunch, and further lightened their loads. Merritt's cavalrymen broke open ammunition boxes and stuffed their pockets and belts with cartridges.

At Sage Creek, Merritt decided to leave his heavy supply wagons and take only light company wagons with three days' rations. The infantry company was loaded into the bigger wagons and added to the contingent already assigned to guard the train. Directed to follow the cavalry, their approach toward Warbonnet Creek the next morning would influence events in the battle that followed.

That night, July 16, at 8 p.m., Merritt's cavalry reached Warbonnet Creek. They had marched 85 miles in 31 hours—and they had beaten the Indians to the vital crossing.

Bill Cody and his men, well out on the eastern flank as Merritt drove his force toward the junction, returned from a scout that night, assuring Merritt that the Indians were still positioned southeast, between Merritt's troops and the reservation. Large numbers of hostiles were moving towards them, however, and would probably reach the crossing

Warbonnet Creek (tree line) flows in a series of loops and curls around the perimeter of the battlefield. The two unusual cone-shaped hills played prominent roles in the battle.

early the next day. Indeed, Little Wolf's Cheyenne, having heard of the battle with Custer, were already on the move, hurrying to add their numbers to the hundreds already on the warpath in Wyoming and Montana. That night they were camped about seven miles southeast of Merritt's men on Warbonnet Creek.

The 5th Cavalry bivouacked in light timber on a small plateau near a line of bluffs. Shielded behind the western slope of the ridges, Merritt's encampment could not be seen by hostiles moving up the trail from the east and southeast. Only a few fires were allowed, and those were dug deep into holes so the flames could not be seen. One entire company was placed on guard duty, positioned in hollows, ravines, and scrub timber where they could see objects silhouetted against the sky.

In the pre-dawn hours, details in the landscape began to emerge as the blackness receded. To the west, the lightening sky revealed the rolling hills of the higher ground crossed by the regiment the night before. Immediately to the east, Warbonnet Creek extended across the 5th Cavalry's front in a series of loops and curls that began in the southeast and traversed north before twisting back toward the left edge of Merritt's camp. A portion of the creek to the north was rimmed by a thin, snake-like tree line as the stream bent back and twisted its way to the South Fork of the Cheyenne River. Beyond the creek was a relatively flat area that extended 300 to 400 hundred yards before meeting a series of low ridges that pointed in the direction of the creek. The ridges varied slightly in height and the space between them was flat. In some places, the field of vision from these low spots and from the smaller ridges was obscured by the slightly higher ground on either side.

Merritt's sentinels were placed on two small, sharply pointed hills that formed distinct spikes in the skyline. Unusual features in the landscape, the southernmost one was about 90 feet high and 400 yards away from the tree line and ridge that hid the 5th Cavalry. The second hill, not quite as high, was about 100 yards closer to camp.

The knolls provided unobstructed views to the southeast, the direction from which the Indians would most likely come. The trail the Indians would use passed only a short distance to the right of the southernmost knoll. There it crossed a shallow ravine. As the ravine and the

The large conical hill in the background served as Merritt's observation post. Troopers from three companies swept around its sides in the last great charge of the U.S. Cavalry. The small fenced memorial in the foreground marks the scene of the Buffalo Bill Cody-Yellow Hair fight.

trail wound their ways separately north, the ground between them rose sharply, concealing one from the other.

Merritt had been up since 3:30, joined within an hour by the entire 5th Cavalry. In the pre-dawn quiet, the troopers huddled around shielded fires boiling coffee and frying salt pork. Soon, the "Dandy Fifth" was ready to mount up: 330 enlisted men, 16 officers, a doctor, and five scouts including, and led by, "Buffalo Bill" Cody.

At about 4:15, as sentries watched from the top of the tallest hill, several Cheyenne warriors in groups of two or three appeared at the head of a ravine about two miles to the southeast.

Merritt was instantly notified and came to the knoll with three of his staff, quickly followed by two scouts and about a half dozen cavalrymen. They were soon joined by Cody, returning from an early morning scout during which he had located the Indians' main camp. The entire group had dismounted behind the hill and crawled to a vantage point at the top, peeking over at the spectacle unfolding before them. At the first sighting of Indians, Merritt ordered the 5th to saddle up and mount, the order passed quietly from trooper to trooper. Six companies then moved forward, angling south, hidden by the sheltering bluffs as they waited in line only 200 yards from the trail and the ravine crossing.

The Indians, sent by Little Wolf to scout ahead, rode slowly in the direction of the outpost on the hillock and the 5th Cavalry's encampment. Moving in a pattern momentarily inexplicable, a number of warriors suddenly darted halfway up the wall of the ravine and began looking intently to the west. The initial band moving up the draw was soon joined by others. By 5 a.m. dozens of Indians were visible, lining the hillsides a mile and a half away, all fixated by some occurrence out on the western horizon.

The explanation soon became clear. Merritt's supply train—the heavy wagons he had left at Sage Creek—were coming into view as tiny dots far out on the higher ground of the western rim. In a superb logistical feat, after tending his mules and piling infantrymen on top of his supplies, Lieutenant William P. Hall had brought his train ahead on an all-night march. From a distance, with the infantry in the wagons concealed beneath wagon tarps, the Indians likely believed it to be a civilian train bound for the Black Hills, and ripe for the picking.

Moments after daybreak, additional excitement occurred. As Merritt and the small group with him watched, several warriors broke away from the main body on a facing ridge. Charging headlong down the slope, the party raced directly towards them at full speed. Again, the observers on the hill were left with no immediate explanation. Again, when it came, the answer lay to the west. Behind them, popping up suddenly over a high point on the prairie, no more than a mile to the southwest, two couriers carrying dispatches to Merritt galloped into view, visible not only to the cavalrymen on the hillock but also to the Cheyenne who were moving swiftly to intercept them. The Indians were not seen by the couriers who, believing Merritt's camp was near, had hurried ahead of the protection of the oncoming supply train. To those on the knoll it was apparent they would meet near the junction where the trail and the ravine came together.

Some contemporary accounts credit Cody with proposing that he, along with two scouts and six troopers, cut the Indians off before they could surprise the couriers. Seeing the same opportunity, Merritt immediately ordered Lieutenant Charles King, in charge of the sentries on the hill, to signal when the time was right for Cody and his party to burst from cover and confront the fast-approaching Indians.

Staying out of sight, Cody and his men scrambled down the backside of the hill, mounted their horses and, still concealed, rode to a spot near the head of the ravine. There, they waited for the signal from King. As the Indians raced headlong down the draw, the lieutenant raised his hand, delaying until the moment was right to achieve maximum surprise. When the Cheyennes were about 90 yards away, he brought his hand down, yelling for Cody to attack. Cody's party sprang from their hiding place, tore headlong around the shoulder of the bluff and, firing as they rode, charged straight towards the onrushing warriors.

Startled, the Cheyennes momentarily halted and began answering the attack, firing volleys toward Cody and at the hillside outpost. Their leader, Yellow Hair, bent low over his pony's neck, fired a round that narrowly missed Merritt as he ran to join Lieutenant King at the top of the knoll.

Cody's charge carried his squad straight into the advancing Cheyennes. In the melee that followed—an episode still wrapped in controversy— Cody and Yellow Hair engaged one on one. Accounts vary as to the nature and duration of the individual combat that resulted in Yellow Hair's death.

The developing clash between Cody's small force and Yellow Hair's Cheyennes caused action to erupt both west and east from the scene of their encounter. Out on the prairie to the west, at the sound of the first volley and with Indians now visible to them, Lieutenant Hall broke his infantry out from under the wagon tarps and deployed them in skirmish position to protect the supply train. To the east, the mass of Indians on the ridge opposite Warbonnet Creek began a dash to the scene of the fight.

The Indians' bid to rescue their colleagues had carried them about halfway across the open ground toward the creek when Merritt ordered the 5th Cavalry to move against them. Sweeping both north and south around the tallest conical hill, three companies—B, K, and I—reached open ground, formed into line, and charged. Line abreast, guidons snapping in the breeze, in a classic cavalry charge—possibly the last in American history—the three veteran companies of about 147 troopers lit into the oncoming Indians.

Stunned by the sight of the wave of blue about to slam into them, the Cheyenne turned their ponies and took flight. Merritt's cavalry chased the Indians closely for about three miles as the Cheyenne abandoned their possessions and raced in panic to the southeast toward the reservation. Sounds of the battle from Warbonnet Creek and the chase that followed carried to Little Wolf's camp seven miles away. Realizing that their path was now blocked and the goal of joining their allies was no longer attainable, they hurriedly dismantled their village and began the trek back to the Red Cloud Agency, leaving behind several lodges and hundreds of pounds of provisions.

Correctly sensing that the fight had gone out of the Indians, Merritt directed the cavalry to follow the Cheyenne in a loose pursuit over the next 30 miles, intent mainly on keeping them on the move toward the agencies. Stringing out his forces over an extended front to prevent flanking attempts by groups of hostiles, Merritt's wide net rolled southeastward, folding the mass of Indians within it and keeping them always pointed toward the reservations. There, without further opposition, they arrived that night and the following day.

Losses on both sides were minimal. Merritt's only casualty occurred during the chase when a cavalryman's horse fell down an embankment, injuring the trooper. Several accounts cite the Indians' only loss as Yellow Hair. Others indicate that during the chase, at least six Cheyenne were killed and perhaps another five wounded. Soon after the battle, Eugene A. Carr, who led the 5th Cavalry's charge that morning and participated in the pursuit, wrote to his wife that three Indians were killed.

The next day, July 18, Merritt telegraphed the results of the battle to Sheridan in Chicago and to Sherman and the administration in Washington. The same day, the 5th began the trip back to Fort Laramie, arriving there on July 21. As was usual with Merritt, he did not tarry. The 5th took on supplies and re-shod their horses the next day. At 6 a.m. on July 23rd, they marched north to join Crook.

Merritt's conduct immediately following the battle was noteworthy. During the Indians' panic-stricken flight, it would certainly have been possible to have killed or maimed them in large numbers. Merritt chose instead to simply follow and push them back to their agencies. Given that Warbonnet Creek occurred less than a month after the Little Bighorn and the public likely would have supported a more aggressive outcome, his restraint was commendable.

Merritt was initially criticized in some quarters for not immediately responding to Crook's pleas for reinforcement. Time has muted that criticism. Crook continually appealed for additional manpower although he remained static in garrison with more than 1,000 men—already too many to chase quick moving and rapidly dissolving bands of hostiles. Merritt's victory at Warbonnet Creek prevented large numbers of Cheyenne and Sioux from combining with the hostiles that tormented Crook that summer, and provided far more effective service than joining him quickly in an already cumbersome camp.

Merritt's legacy, and that of the 5th Cavalry, was that for more than a month they blocked the vital trail used by the Indians to reach the hostiles in Wyoming and Montana. Then, when the first major war party headed northwest, the defeat that Merritt and the 5th Cavalry inflicted on them was decisive, both militarily and psychologically. After Warbonnet Creek, the Cheyenne and Sioux made no other significant attempts to leave their agencies and join their allies in combat.

The stone memorial is located on the site of the encounter between cadres led by Buffalo Bill Cody and Northern Cheyenne warrior Yellow Hair. Yellow Hair was killed during the combat.

Less than a month after achieving their greatest victory at the Little Bighorn, for the Plains Indians Warbonnet Creek was the "beginning of the beginning of the end." Never again would they come together in such large numbers or prevail in a major battle.

For the military, and the country, Warbonnet Creek played an important role in helping restore morale and confidence. Merritt and his 5th Cavalry outgeneraled, outrode, and outfought a dangerous foe. Their actions turned large numbers of hostiles around, prevented others from joining, and took all of them permanently out of the war. The masterful triumph was, in the words of one scholar, "timely, professionally executed, and desperately needed."

After the fight at Warbonnet Creek, Merritt moved north with Crook and on August 3 joined General Alfred Terry. For a time, the two columns joined and moved generally eastward with more than 4,000 men. After Terry split off, dispatching units in an attempt to prevent hostiles from reaching Canada, Crook's contingent continued a difficult trek toward the Little Missouri. Crook stripped his force of non-essentials, intending to travel fast and light. Their grueling, controversial pursuit was maintained in the face of horrific weather. In its latter stages the expedition, with Merritt leading the combined cavalry division of 10 companies of the 5th Cavalry, five companies of the 2nd Cavalry, and 10 companies of the 3rd Cavalry, was reduced to half rations supplemented by mule and horse meat from cavalry mounts played out by starvation and exhaustion.

In early September, 150 troops dispatched on a supply replenishment mission ran into a Sioux village near present-day Reva, South Dakota. The troops surrounded the village, located near a geologic feature called "Slim Buttes," and attacked at dawn on September 9, inflicting several casualties.

Indian survivors made contact with Crazy Horse who, with 600–800 warriors, moved quickly toward the destroyed village. In the meantime, Crook's full contingent, including the 5th Cavalry, along with various other cavalry, infantry, and artillery units—totaling slightly more than 1,000 combatants—arrived on scene.

During the fight at Slim Buttes, Merritt's troops pushed the Indians initially from the high ground and, ultimately, from the field. Later, he took command of the entire expedition, guiding it back to Fort Robinson, as Crook departed for other duties.

While Merritt's victory at Warbonnet Creek had shut down the flow of Indian reinforcements, the victory at Slim Buttes was the first for government forces over hostile groups who were in the field at the time of the Little Bighorn. Merritt's leadership played a vital role in each triumph. In the turbulent history of warfare on the Great Plains, both battles were significant. By the middle of the following year, Crazy Horse, leading one of the last major hostile groups, surrendered at Camp Robinson, Nebraska.

Aside from his achievements at Warbonnet Creek and Slim Buttes, Merritt's most notable service on the Plains took place three years later during the Ute War of 1879. In early October of that year, he led a relief force of 250 troopers of the 5th Cavalry on a 170-mile forced march to rescue 200 or more soldiers trapped and besieged after a six-day battle with Utes along the Milk River in northern Colorado. Merritt's march, from Fort D.A. Warren near Cheyenne, Wyoming, would in later years be studied for the speed and consummate professionalism with which it was conducted. Merritt's timely arrival on the scene prompted the surrender of the Ute chief and essentially ended the war.

Before and After

Wesley Merritt was born in New York City in 1836 and graduated from West Point in 1860, ranked 22nd of 41 in class standing. After initial postings with cavalry units in Utah, he was recalled to Washington, D.C., at the outbreak of the Civil War. He remained there until April 1863, when he was named adjutant to the commander of the Army of the Potomac Cavalry Corps. In May, he participated in Stoneman's Raid during the Battle of Chancellorsville. Soon after, Merritt was given command of the 2nd Cavalry. He led that unit at Brandy Station, the largest cavalry battle of the war, and at the Battle of Upperville. He was cited for his "gallant and meritorious service" in both battles.

In the cavalry reorganization that followed, Merritt was jumped in grade from captain to brigadier general. Collectively, Merritt, along with Elon Farnsworth (later killed at Gettysburg), and George Armstrong Custer were known to the American public as the "boy generals."

At Gettysburg, Merritt's unit guarded Union lines of communication during the opening phase of the battle and participated in an attack on the Confederate right flank on the final day of combat.

In December 1863, Merritt took command of the 1st Division of the Cavalry Corps and led it during Grant's Overland Campaign. He and his unit saw major action at the Battle of Yellow Tavern, during which Confederate cavalry leader J.E.B. Stuart was killed.

In August 1864, Merritt's division was transferred to General Philip Sheridan's newly formed Army of the Shenandoah and served there throughout the Valley Campaign. Sheridan quickly came to respect the young officer and the two of them formed a friendship that lasted throughout their lifetimes. Merritt received a brevet promotion to major general after routing Confederates at the Third Battle of Winchester on September 19, 1864.

As second in command to Sheridan during the Appomattox Campaign that closed the war, Merritt was again cited for bravery at the Battle of Five Forks. He was named as one of the commissioners to oversee the Confederate surrender at Appomattox Court House.

In mid-1865, Merritt was given command of the cavalry forces of the Military District of the Southwest, commanded by Sheridan. In July of that year he led his cavalry units on a month-long 600-mile trek from Shreveport, Louisiana, to San Antonio, Texas, where they formed part of the Union's occupation forces in the region. Merritt remained in Texas for nearly a decade, serving as commander of the newly-formed 9th Cavalry, a "Buffalo Soldier" unit charged with tracking down renegades and Indian raiders.

After duty as General Sheridan's "troubleshooter" on the plains, Merritt was assigned to the 5th Cavalry and began the service at Warbonnet Creek, Slim Buttes, and the Ute War that would bring him his greatest recognition. Merritt served on the frontier until 1882 when he was named Superintendent of West Point, a post he held until 1887. Merritt is sometimes credited with inaugurating the army's first war game maneuvers. He was an advocate for continuing professional education for the officer corps.

In April 1887, Merritt was promoted to brigadier general in the Regular Army and assigned as Commander of the Department of the Missouri. In 1889, he accompanied troops to present-day Oklahoma to help maintain order during the land rush that opened the territory to settlers.

With the outbreak of the Spanish–American War, Merritt was given command of the U.S. Army's VIII Corps. After Admiral George Dewey defeated the Spanish fleet at Manila Bay, Merritt's forces took the city in August 1898. Merritt served briefly as military governor of the Philippines and later advised the U.S. commissioners who negotiated the Treaty of Paris that ended the war.

Merritt retired from the army in 1900. Like his contemporary, Eugene A. Carr, he died in 1910 and was buried at West Point.

NELSON A. MILES

Miles' victory over Crazy Horse at Wolf Mountain, Montana, was but one of his triumphs over prominent Indian leaders on battlefields that spanned much of the western half of the present-day lower continental United States.

Few combat leaders during the nation's Indian wars fought on so many battlefields over such varied landscapes as Nelson Miles. Fewer still did so with more consistent success. On fields of strife across Texas, the central and northern Plains, Arizona, and the Pacific Northwest, Miles led U.S. Army forces to an uninterrupted string of victories.

Miles was known as a highly competent, innovative combat leader who led from the front. He was wounded four times during the Civil War while fighting in all of the Army of the Potomac's major battles except Gettysburg (when he was recovering from wounds received at Chancellorsville, where he won the Medal of Honor). Some biographers have commented that unlike many successful military commanders, Miles actually *looked* like a hero. Tall and muscular with broad shoulders, intense blue eyes and a jaunty mustache, he cut a dashing figure.

There were, however, episodes during the course of his long and remarkable service that temper his legacy. There were, for example, life-long feuds with other senior officers about who should receive credit for victories to which each of them contributed. There were later questions about credit withheld from a deserving subordinate and about the handling of a peace agreement. Later still, at Wounded Knee, there were disputed murmurs that his aggressiveness as overall director of operations may have contributed to the violent outcome.

To many, Miles seemed an abrasive personality. Although grade reductions and restorations of permanent ranks were pro forma during the army's massive drawdown after the Civil War, he was vocally indignant about his reduced rank. (Miles was promoted to colonel in the Regular Army in 1866. He had been advanced to brevet major general during the war.) By some accounts, he was unabashed in his efforts to accelerate his own advancement. Married to the niece of General William Tecumseh Sherman and the governor of Ohio, he was not above appealing directly to them as well as to President Ulysses S. Grant for assistance with his career. Vain and ambitious, he spoke openly about his aspirations for high political office. Because of his political networking, Miles was not well liked by many of his senior officer colleagues. He was, however, popular in the ranks and well-respected by his troops who recognized his obvious competence and valued his experience.

Miles' service after the Civil War was almost entirely on the nation's frontier, as he saw action on battlefields that extended from the Plains of Texas westward across the continent.

In the Red River or Buffalo War of 1874–1875, a conflict primarily aimed at forcing belligerent Kiowa, Comanche, and Cheyenne bands onto government agencies, Miles led a mixed unit of cavalry and infantry from Fort Leavenworth, Kansas, to the Texas Plains. Miles' force was one of five columns that pressured the warring bands and, aided by Ranald Mackenzie's victory against Comanches in the Battle of Palo Duro Canyon, forced their surrender.

On the northern Plains, the early months of 1876 brought a string of defeats to the U.S. Army that culminated in the disaster at the Little Bighorn. Along with other units sent from distant locations, Miles and the 5th Infantry were called from Kansas as the army attempted to regain the initiative.

Major goals of the campaign were to bolster the garrisons at each Indian agency and establish a permanent presence on the Yellowstone River. Like the Republican River in the central Plains, the Yellowstone area was of special importance to the nomadic tribes. The region's grass, water, and plentiful buffalo provided shelter and sustenance to the warring groups. Now, aroused by several victories and led by legendary war chiefs, thousands of Lakota Sioux and Northern Cheyenne warriors waited along the Yellowstone and its tributaries for the army's arrival.

Miles, with six companies of the 5th Infantry, arrived in the area in early August aboard the steamer *E.H. Durfee*. Initially given command of a 10-company wing of a large expedition under the overall command of General Alfred Terry, Miles remained with the massive force for only a short time. On August 10, Terry's column met with that of General George Crook coming up from the south. The two units moved together for a time but the 4,000-man combined force was too large for tracking, chasing, and fighting small, fast-moving bands of hostiles.

Miles was soon released to return to the Rosebud Creek area. Transported from there downriver on the steamer *Far West* he, along with Colonel Elwell S. Otis, established posts along the Tongue River where that stream emerges from the Yellowstone. The cantonments—on the north bank of the Yellowstone, at the mouth of the Powder River, and at O'Fallon's Creek (later moved to the Glendive Creek area)—covered major fords and were intended to keep hostiles from using them as escape routes. Miles also kept a company aboard the *Far West* as a floating, mobile reserve.

Miles quartered the bulk of his troops at an extensive camp on the Tongue River. From there he headed up four major expeditions against the Sioux. Aimed at ultimately driving the hostile bands back to the agencies, Miles' sorties pursued the Indians relentlessly, destroying provisions and keeping the hostiles constantly on the move.

From the Tongue River, Miles struck one of the campaign's first successful blows. When a replenishment wagon train failed to reach his encampment as expected, he put the 5th Infantry on the march. Moving down the Yellowstone, his troops found the train besieged by Sitting Bull's warriors. Miles' soldiers rescued the train and then followed Sitting Bull's band as the Indians moved north.

At Cedar Creek on October 21, Miles destroyed Sitting Bull's village in a battle conducted in textbook fashion. Miles assigned five companies as skirmishers across a broad front, skillfully deployed three others as reserves, and made exceptional use of two artillery pieces. Two additional companies shielded the artillery and guarded the supply train. The Sioux were likely surprised by the accurate, sustained firepower of well-trained infantry equipped with long-range Springfield rifles. Though heavily outnumbered, Miles' troopers pressed the attack, forcing the Sioux back. Several strong counterattacks led by Gall and other war chiefs eventually failed after heavy fighting, though before scattering, the Sioux attempted to set fire to the prairie. When that failed they fled, abandoning their camp, which Miles quickly burned.

By this time the massive coalition of Indian forces that had fought on the Little Bighorn had dispersed into smaller, but still lethal, bands. The scattering of the hostile groups changed the nature of the Great Sioux War. Campaigns were now characterized by multiple operations against separated bands moving across a landscape so immense it was called the "Big Open" by the Native tribes.

In early November, Miles returned briefly to the Tongue River to resupply before moving back north to the Missouri. To more effectively scour the countryside, he separated the 5th Infantry into three independent commands. On December 18, one of those columns—three companies commanded by Lieutenant Frank Baldwin—caught Sitting Bull's Hunkpapa Sioux on Ash Creek near the Yellowstone divide. Sitting Bull's village of about 120 lodges was destroyed as were many of the band's horses and mules. Bereft of food, shelter, and supplies, Sitting Bull's military strength was effectively negated. Not long after, wary of the army's persistent aggressiveness even in the face of horrific weather conditions, he took his followers to Canada and removed himself from the war.

It had long been Miles' contention that if Sitting Bull and Crazy Horse—the charismatic leaders of the warrior bands—were defeated, the scope of the Native uprising would be materially diminished if not ended entirely. Now, having dispatched Sitting Bull, Miles set his sights on Crazy Horse.

Late in 1876, with Crook still in the field and Ranald Mackenzie having defeated Dull Knife and the Northern Cheyenne at the Dull Knife Fight, Miles learned of Crazy Horse's presence along the Wolf Mountains. On December 29, Miles took seven companies and artillery in pursuit, moving southwest through the Tongue River Valley. His men were superbly equipped for the arctic-like conditions. Blankets had been cut up for underwear; buffalo overcoats had been issued as had overshoes, leggings, woolen face masks; and fur was provided for caps and gloves. Miles forced a relentless pace, tracking hostiles who had been pillaging near the cantonment, believing that the raiders would lead him to Crazy Horse and the main encampment of Sioux and Northern Cheyenne.

However, by contemporary accounts, Crazy Horse had apparently envisioned the raiders as a decoy party intended to lure Miles away from his post and into an ambush—a reprise of the ploy used in the Fetterman Massacre along the Bozeman Trail a decade earlier.

As events unfolded, the ambush plan went awry when, on January 7, 1877, a handful of scouts sent ahead by Miles captured a small group of Indians along the suspected route to Crazy Horse's camp. In a subsequent attempt to rescue the captives, the decoy party launched a premature attack, striking the troopers before Crazy Horse and the main body of warriors were on hand to fully spring the trap.

Although the major components on neither side had reached the scene, the preliminary battle on January 7 was hotly contested. Jumped by 40–50 warriors hidden in brush, the scouts sought refuge in a thin line of timber a few hundred yards distant, having two horses shot from under them along the way. Making barricades of fallen trees and boulders, the outnumbered scouts fought off several attempts to rush and overwhelm their position. As the shooting grew more intense, additional numbers of Indians, likely 100 or more, joined in the attack, taking up positions in surrounding rocks and on nearby hillsides.

At the sound of firing, Miles, camped a short distance away, sent an infantry company and an artillery piece to relieve the besieged scouting party. Heavy small arms fire persisted for an hour or more before shells from Miles' artillery piece induced the Indians to break off their attack and begin a slow retreat. By nightfall, the valley was quiet and the scouts and the relief force sent by Miles had returned safely to camp.

After leaving the main cantonment in late December, traveling through periodic snow flurries and temperatures that sometimes reached 30 degrees below zero, Miles had brought his 436-man force to a horseshoe bend in the Tongue River. His troops were making an early camp there when fighting began between the scouts and another decoy party.

Miles had chosen excellent defensive ground for his encampment. The horseshoe configuration of the river shielded the camp on three sides. To the southwest, a plateau topped by a small knoll—later to be known as Battle Butte—provided a mostly unobstructed view of the valley. After sending troops to assist the scouts, Miles had formed skirmish lines that wrapped the bivouac site in a protective ring. When the shooting ended at dusk, Miles—anticipating a possible assault on the camp the following day—put two full companies on guard duty along the projected line of attack.

Miles' premonition was correct: Crazy Horse did indeed attack the following day, although the assault did not come completely from the quadrant he anticipated.

Crazy Horse, unaware that the decoy party had already skirmished with elements of Miles' force, planned to follow the Tongue River to within a few miles of the army camp, where the force would split. Half of the 800 warriors, mostly Northern Cheyenne, would cross the river, use the hills to mask their approach, and move against the soldiers' encampment from the south. Crazy Horse with his 400 Lakotas would continue along the river and attack from the west.

Believing an assault would come entirely from that direction, Miles sent Company E, 5th Infantry to the high, unobstructed ground on Battle Butte. The 80-foot sheer face on the west side of the butte would channel any frontal assault to a quarter-mile wide opening between the butte and a line of bluffs north of the camp. To cover that gap, Miles placed Company K in a group of cottonwood trees along the river bank.

Apparently thinking he had achieved surprise, Crazy Horse and his Lakota warriors streamed along the northern bank of the river, making no attempt at concealment as they neared Miles' fortifications. Miles, though, had his force up at 4 a.m., and had immediately sent out scouts to scour the area, a task made more difficult by three feet of recently fallen snow.

Despite the cold and the masking snow cover, Miles' veteran contingent of scouts detected Crazy Horse's advance and raced back to warn the camp. Miles quickly rode to the Battle Butte plateau where, through field glasses, he watched Crazy Horse's large force move through the foothills west of the cantonment.

Miles later commented on an interesting aspect of the battle: many of the Indians dismounted and fought on foot, forming firing lines a few hundred yards from Company K's position in the cottonwoods.

Miles quickly positioned his units to receive the attack. Pointing with a small stick that he carried with him through the battle, he sent Company A, 5th Infantry, and some mounted infantrymen to join the company and artillerymen already stationed on Battle Butte, then shifted his two artillery pieces to the northwestern edge of the plateau. He next sent two additional companies to support Company K, now heavily dug in among the cottonwoods. On the opposite river bank, Company E, 22nd Infantry, moved to Company K's left. On the right, on the south bank near the supply wagons, Miles posted Company F, 22nd Infantry. Two companies, C and D of the 5th Infantry, were kept in reserve inside the horseshoe formed by the bend in the river.

Miles' dispositions were timely and well-conceived. At around 7 a.m., the Indians' initial assault, mounted by Lakotas and Cheyennes in large numbers led by Crazy Horse, struck Company K's entrenched positions in the trees along the river. The heavy attack was thrown back by Company K's riflemen, supported by Companies E and F on the flanks and well-placed artillery rounds from the cannon atop Battle Butte.

Driven back by intense fire, the Indians retreated into the nearby hills, regrouped, and charged again. The second of several subsequent assaults struck the far eastern extremity of Company K's position in an attempt to collapse the line and force the unit to retreat across the river. Each attempt was blown apart by heavy rifle fire and shells from Miles' artillery.

Fighting near Company K's section lasted through the early morning. Eventually, Crazy Horse shifted his attack still further east, occupying bluffs that overlooked portions of Miles' camp. Covering fire from the heights enabled groups of warriors to cross the river and move through the valley to high ground southeast of the campsite.

While the battle raged to the west, a group of 400 or more Indians, mostly Northern Cheyenne led by Medicine Bear, crossed from the north bank of the frozen river and moved toward the hills south of Battle Butte. Their approach was seen by the Company F commander atop the plateau, who shifted his line, extending it from the center of the mesa and wrapping it amid rugged outcroppings along the southwestern edge. The rocks in the sector formed a natural barricade from which Miles' riflemen met Medicine Bear's approach with volley fire aided by artillery support.

As the Indians pressed forward, Company E shifted to the southern base of the knoll to meet the attack. Medicine Bear's assault now reached a key point: if the Indians overran the defending company, Miles' troops and his artillery positions elsewhere north on the plateau would be exposed to attack with little cover. Miles was now ringed in on three sides: Medicine Bear's warriors pressed forward from the south while others under Crazy Horse held the valley to the northwest and, after crossing the river east of the camp, now controlled a line of bluffs to the southeast.

With the nearest assistance several hundred miles away, Miles boldly took the offensive. First taking on the most ominous threat, he sent Company A against the large numbers of warriors now gathered on three ridges arrayed one behind the other about a quarter of a mile from his post on Battle Butte, and pulled his two reserve companies to positions on the plateau.

Company A moved over mostly open ground to attack the ridge line 400 yards distant. Clad in heavy buffalo coats as protection against the bitter cold, the skirmish line trod across snow-covered ground, pressing their attack while taking fire from Indians shooting down from the heights.

The company's determined attack cleared the first of the three ridges, smaller by half than the two immediately in back of it. However, the company's follow-on attack on the two higher ridges eventually stalled, the victim of numbers, natural obstacles, and exhaustion. Miles saw the attack losing momentum and sent Company D, 5th Infantry to reinforce the assault.

After crossing the valley floor, Company D moved to the left of the embattled unit already fighting on the ridge and continued up the face to the second, taller hill. Meeting fierce resistance, the troops slowly inched their way up the steep, icy slope.

As D Company struggled its way up the hill, an unusual episode took place that influenced the future of the battle. In an attempt to rally the warriors fighting on the ridges, Big Crow, a prominent, much-venerated Northern Cheyenne medicine man, began to dance atop the third, highest ridge. Clad in vivid red, he believed himself immune from harm by the soldiers' rifles. For a considerable time, fully exposed to fire, Big Crow did indeed seem to be impervious to injury. Eventually, however, shells from two troopers firing from 200 yards away struck him and he fell mortally wounded in the snow. The loss of their medicine man seemed to dishearten many of the Northern Cheyenne warriors, some of whom began to drift away from the battlefield.

The fighting ebbed for only a moment, however, as Crazy Horse, who had circled around from the fighting in the northern part of the valley and crossed the river east of the soldiers' camp, led a ferocious attack that threatened to overwhelm the soldiers on the ridge. Rallying 300 or so Lakotas, he boldly struck at the two embattled companies. Moving over a terrain feature that connected the two ridges, Crazy Horse's assault carried to within 50 yards of D Company's forward line.

Again the battle hung in the balance. Although fighting continued to the north around K Company's entrenchments in the cottonwoods, and in the south where Medicine Bear's men moved against Battle Butte, Miles saw that the two companies, A and D, struggling on the ridge were in jeopardy. Indeed, his entire force would be threatened unless Crazy Horse's Lakotas could be driven from the third ridge. Miles committed his last reserve unit, Company C, to the fight.

Instead of launching C Company to directly reinforce the troops already engaged on the ridges, Miles sent it straight at the third ridge. The C Company commander took his unit to the base of the ridge and then ordered his men to charge. Although the commander's horse was shot out from under him, the company moved inexorably up the hill under heavy fire.

As Company C fought its way up the ridge, troopers found a drainage runnel that provided access to the Lakotas fighting on the connecting ground between the second and third ridges. At this point, 500 combatants were mixed in a desperate struggle that lasted through the morning. The Indians fiercely held their ground before continued pressure from the advancing troopers caused them to fall back to positions along the crest of the third ridge. There, concealed among jagged outcroppings, fallen trees, and hidden ravines, they established a formidable redoubt and held the advancing troops at bay with plunging fire from their Winchester and Sharps rifles.

The warriors' strong fortification and heavy, sustained fire was visible from Miles' command post on Battle Butte, so he ordered the position shelled by his two artillery pieces. Explosions in the rocks and timber eventually began to take a toll, causing the Indians to begin a slow retreat off the ridge and into the valley. Their withdrawal was orderly and well-conducted; the warriors periodically halted, reformed their firing lines, and continued the battle against the advancing troops.

The army pressed the pursuit for about an hour, until around noon, heavy snow began to fall. With visibility increasingly poor, his troops exhausted, ammunition low, and the Indians moving away from the battlefield, the chase was called to a halt.

As the weather rapidly deteriorated into blizzard conditions, warriors fighting Miles' troops in the north along the cottonwoods by the river and in the south close to Battle Butte also withdrew from the area, using the blinding snowfall to shield their retreat. After five intense hours of combat, the battle was over.

Despite the large numbers of combatants and the enormous expenditure of ammunition by both sides, the casualties were fairly light. One soldier was killed on the scene, another later died of wounds, and seven others were wounded. The extent of Indian losses is uncertain.

The next day Miles led a six-company reconnaissance in force through the valley along the Indians' line of retreat. Carcasses of dead horses were found as were numerous pools of blood congealed on the frozen ground. The pools marked locations where the Sioux and Cheyenne wounded had been dragged through the snow. Miles noted that the blood trails continued for five miles.

Crazy Horse's retreat took him and his followers toward the Big Horn Mountains 70 miles to the south. In the midst of a Montana winter, it was an inhospitable place with little game, marginal shelter, and implacable Crow enemies. Losses in supplies and ammunition precluded Crazy Horse and his Sioux and Cheyenne followers from resuming their attacks.

Wolf Mountain and similar clashes subsequently affirmed General Philip Sheridan's conviction—firmly shared by Nelson Miles—that the best way to defeat the wide-ranging Plains Indians was to wage war year-round, including, most particularly, campaigning through the deep winter months when the Indians were in semi-permanent camps, food was scarce, and the pony herds were weak. It had taken a considerable time, but Mackenzie, Sheridan, and Miles (those three in particular) had figured out how to fight and win on the Plains.

Later, the significance of the battle would become fully apparent: Wolf Mountain was Crazy Horse's final attempt to wage offensive warfare against the U.S. Army. Four months later, in May, he surrendered with 800 followers and 2,000 ponies at Camp Robinson, Nebraska.

By April 1877, Minneconjou Sioux Chief Lame Deer and his followers were regarded as the most threatening band of hostiles still at large. Lame Deer had sworn never to surrender.

Miles now made Lame Deer and his band his personal focus. Difficult tracking through the Tongue River Valley to Rosebud Creek and subsequently down a small tributary today called Lame Deer Creek, brought Miles and his troopers to the hostiles' village. Miles attacked the 60 lodges at dawn on May 7, killing Lame Deer and several others and destroying the Minneconjou's pony herd.

Except for the few scattered survivors of Lame Deer's camp, after Miles' victory warring bands almost entirely disappeared from the "Big Open." Through the summer and fall of 1877, Miles coordinated what in a later time would be called "search and destroy" missions, keeping independent columns on constant move through the region. On July 3, the last shots in the war were exchanged when one of Miles' detached units traded fire with a small band of Sioux.

By September, the remainder of Lame Deer's band turned themselves in at the Spotted Tail Agency in Nebraska. The army, well equipped, adequately provisioned, highly mobile, striking regardless of terrain or weather conditions, had at long last adopted a strategy that led to victory. The Native bands, weary, hungry, and suffering, were now all in Canada or on reservations.

Across the "Big Open" there remained only abandoned campsites. The Great Sioux War was over.

The end of the war brought little respite for Miles and the 5th Infantry. Violence had flared that summer in the Northwest, where portions of the Nez Perce tribe objected to General Oliver O. Howard's demand that they move to government agencies. Evading Howard's pursuit, the tribe had engaged on a legendary trek. Led by Chief Joseph and others, their journey had brought them all the way from their homeland near Wallowa Valley, Oregon, across the Idaho and Montana Territories. By the end of September, after several battles and narrow escapes, they were only 40 miles from Canada and safety.

Lagging behind in the chase, on September 12 General Howard had sent a message to Miles at Fort Keogh, Montana, asking for his assistance. Miles received Howard's note on September 17 and left the following day with a force of 520 soldiers, civilian employees, and scouts.

Moving northwest, diagonally with the Nez Perce's anticipated line of march, Miles took his mixed cavalry/infantry force on a rapid 160-mile march toward the Canadian border. On September 29 in the midst of a heavy snowstorm, scouts found the Indians' trail. The following day, north of the Bear Paw Mountains along Sand Creek, they located their encampment.

Fearing that the tribe would resume their flight, Miles moved out at 2:30 a.m. As his column approached the village he ordered an attack, sending a battalion of the 2nd Cavalry, about 160 troopers, to assault the camp. A battalion of the 7th Cavalry, with 100 troopers, was assigned to follow the 2nd Cavalry's charge and support the attack. The remainder of Miles' force, about 145 mounted infantrymen from the 5th Infantry, followed in reserve bringing with them a cannon and the pack train. First at a trot, then at a gallop, and finally in an all-out charge, the first wave of cavalry raced toward the fortified camp.

Believing they had eluded Howard and not anticipating Miles' approach, the Nez Perce were resting prior to making a final, short push into Canada. Only minutes before the attack, Nez Perce scouts detected Miles' column advancing toward the village. The Nez Perce were among the most militarily proficient of all the Native tribes; despite the brief warning time, warriors responded quickly and well. From rifle pits, rugged ground, and a ravine near the ridge traversed by the cavalry, they rose up and fired on the onrushing horsemen. Renowned throughout the region as superb marksmen, their steady fire killed and wounded several soldiers, forcing the first-arriving company to withdraw to a distance 250–300 yards away. Two other companies then struck at the front and were similarly repulsed by Nez Perce firing from behind a near-vertical embankment.

Miles then sent two dismounted companies of cavalry and his infantry units to occupy high ground and form a fighting front. By about three o'clock in the afternoon all was in place for an attack by the combined force. The attack, against well-conceived barricades manned by skilled fighters, was thrown back with heavy losses. By nightfall on September 30, Miles had lost 18 dead and 48 wounded. The Nez Perce were thought to have lost 22 warriors killed, including three of their most prominent leaders. They had also lost much of their horse herd, captured by Miles' scouts and a small unit of cavalry around the time of the initial attack.

Both sides fortified their positions during the snow and bitter cold of the night that followed. Nez Perce dug shelters for the women and children and rifle pits that covered all approaches to the camp, which measured about 250 yards along each side in a nearly square configuration. The rifle pits were manned by about 100 warriors, each armed with three or more weapons—largesse from successful encounters during their epic march.

By now, Miles had the camp surrounded. Rather than storming the village and subjecting his troops to further lethal fire from the well-positioned defenders, he shifted tactics and placed the encampment under siege. Miles' 12-pounder Napoleon cannon arrived that evening and the following morning Miles began shelling the village.

Fitful negotiations began fairly soon but agreement was not initially forthcoming. Shelling continued through October 3, but the Nez Perce were well dug in and the firing, though prolonged, did little physical damage. Psychologically, however, the pounding may have exacted a toll; apparently at about that time many of those inside the besieged camp began to despair of their circumstances.

Their prospects were further dimmed with the arrival of General Howard and an advance force in the evening of October 4. Howard, the senior officer on the field, allowed Miles to retain tactical control of the siege.

Miles agreed with Howard's suggestion that two friendly Nez Perce who accompanied his column be sent to the village to plead for an end to the fighting. On October 5 at 8 o'clock in the morning, firing ceased as the envoys made their way into the camp. This time, with the Nez Perce cold, hungry, and having lost most of their horses, Chief Joseph agreed to surrender.

Joseph's agreement covered only that portion—a substantial majority—of the Nez Perce tribesmen who were directly affiliated with him. Altogether 431 Nez Perce—79 men, 178 women, and 174 children—surrendered or were captured by Miles' troops. Another smaller group, led by White Bird, did not surrender and managed to slip through army lines and reach Canada. Miles' scouts reported that the soldiers had captured more than 1,500 horses during the course of the battle.

Miles provided food and blankets to the Nez Perce and promised Chief Joseph that the tribe would be allowed to return to reservations in their homeland. Over the forceful objections of Miles and Howard, General William T. Sherman, Commanding General of the United States Army, overruled that decision. Instead, the Nez Perce were first sent by train to Fort Leavenworth, Kansas, and later to Indian Territory (present-day Oklahoma). They were eventually allowed to return to the Pacific Northwest in 1885.

Although some sources place the figures higher, total losses from the five-day siege are thought to number 21 soldiers killed and nearly 50 wounded (three of whom would die later). Most of the casualties occurred during the cavalry charge on the first day of fighting. Nez Perce losses are not known with certainty, but probably numbered about 25 killed, with another 50 or 60 wounded.

Miles was effusive in his praise of the Nez Perce warriors, describing the fight at Bear Paw as the fiercest of any Indian battle in which he had ever been involved. His view that the Nez Perce movement was unequalled in the history of Indian warfare was shared by several others. General William T. Sherman commented that the "Nez Perce fought with almost scientific skill, using advance and rear guards, skirmish lines and field fortifications."

The war's aftermath was not without controversy. Although Colonels John Gibbon and Samuel Sturgis had also led forces pursuing the Nez Perce, Miles and Howard precipitated an argument that lasted the rest of their lives about which of them should receive credit for Chief Joseph's surrender.

Miles' Nez Perce expedition was noted for his pioneering work with heliograph communications. A decade later in the Southwest his adroit use of signal mirrors to communicate over long distances—a facility acquired from his experience against the Nez Perce—would play a role in the campaign against Geronimo's Apaches.

On April 28, 1886, Miles arrived in the Southwest to replace General George Crook as commander of U.S. forces in the region. Hostilities had resumed on May 17 of the previous year when Geronimo with about 35 warriors and 100 or so followers fled the San Carlos Reservation in Arizona. Over the next several months of fitful encounters, promises of surrender made and broken, and extended chases over rugged country along the border and into Mexico, Geronimo raided settlements, stole livestock, and killed 75 American citizens, 10 soldiers, 12 Apaches, and an unknown number of Mexicans.

Crook had relied primarily on Apache scouts in his efforts to track down Geronimo. Miles chose not to do so, or at least not to emphasize their use to the same degree. Instead, he posted infantry at key passes and water holes. As in Montana, he made effective use of heliograph equipment placed on mountain tops to communicate over the territory's vast distances. Miles formed a special unit to track Geronimo's band.

Chases, often anti-climactic, covered hundreds of miles and took Miles' special force well across the border. Much of April through August was spent in Mexican territory. After weeks of fruitless efforts, Miles' unit made contact with Geronimo and his followers, now worn down by constant pressure and movement.

In mid-July, Miles sent Lieutenant Charles Gatewood, an Apache-speaker knowledgeable of the tribe's customs, to negotiate with Geronimo. On August 24, after an arduous journey, Gatewood found the Apache chief. Despite difficult negotiations and several changes of mind, they reached agreement the following day. Geronimo formally surrendered to Miles on September 4 at a site south of Rodeo, New Mexico, near Apache, Arizona.

Geronimo's surrender brought closure to an epic period in American history. His raids were the last significant guerrilla activity in the United States. Where once thousands of Native warriors roamed and raided the Plains east to west from the Missouri River to the Pacific Coast and north to south from the Canadian to the Mexican border, Geronimo's band at the time of his surrender consisted of 16 warriors, 12 women, and six children.

Miles' actions during and after Geronimo's surrender have sometimes been called into question. By several, but not all, accounts he withheld credit from Lieutenant Gatewood for that officer's role in negotiating the surrender. When Geronimo and his followers were sent to Fort Marion, Florida, the exiled group included Apaches who had helped Miles during the conflict. Some versions of the episode have Miles proposing that action or agreeing with it, even though sending them with the hostiles was contrary to an agreement made with them earlier. Crook bitterly opposed the incarceration of the scouts, and the resulting enmity between the two men lasted until Crook's death four years later.

In 1890, Miles directed the army's overall response to the "Ghost Dance" scare then sweeping across the Plains tribes. The Ghost Dance was part of a mystical set of beliefs preached by a Paiute Shaman named Wovoka. Wovoka, also known as Jack Wilson, prophesied that the entire Indian race, living and dead, would be reunited on·a regenerated earth free from death, disease, or misery. When that cosmic event occurred, the buffalo would be restored and the white men would disappear. The dance was an important part of the prophecy; the more often it was performed, the sooner the prediction would come to pass. There were variations in the dance ritual; unique to the Sioux was the belief that Ghost Shirts would protect them from soldiers' bullets.

The Ghost Dance originated in western Nevada among the Paiute tribe, and by the spring of 1890 it had reached the Pine Ridge Reservation in South Dakota. The Ghost Dance provoked concern bordering on hysteria from settlers and Indian agents who interpreted the promised disappearance of the white man as a violent threat to their safety.

In response to appeals for protection, the government moved large numbers of additional troops into the region. On December 15, Sitting Bull, a Ghost Dance advocate, was killed during an altercation when tribal police attempted to arrest him.

Amidst confusion and rising tensions the tragedy at Wounded Knee occurred two weeks later.

Miles was not at Wounded Knee and not in direct command of forces in the field. He criticized the on-scene commander, Colonel James Forsyth, and later filed charges against him. (Secretary of War Redfield Proctor eventually dropped the charges and exonerated Forsythe.) In later years Miles' harshest critics suggested that his aggressive actions to contain the Ghost Dance scare might have panicked the Lakota Sioux and set in motion the events that culminated in bloodshed. Others find the alleged connection less than distinct. In any event, the Wounded Knee aspersions did not prevent Miles' later selection as Commanding General of the United States Army.

Wounded Knee was the last major encounter between government forces and Indians in the United States, and the Ghost Dance movement died out soon after. Its demise also closed Miles' career as an Indian fighter.

Before and After

Miles was born in 1839 on a farm near Westminster, Massachusetts. For a time in his youth, he worked as a clerk in a crockery store. Unlike the majority of his army contemporaries, Miles did not attend a military academy. Rather, on his own initiative, he secured military instruction from a former officer in the French army. His service during the Civil War was noted for its extent and for his personal heroism. With the Army of the Potomac, he fought at Fair Oaks, Antietam, Fredericksburg, Chancellorsville, the Wilderness, Spotsylvania, Petersburg, and the closing campaign at Appomattox. For a short time immediately following the war, Miles commanded the District of Fort Monroe where he supervised the incarceration of Confederate President Jefferson Davis. Miles drew criticism for having for a time placed Davis in shackles.

In 1894, after his service in the Indian Wars, Miles directed the 12,000-man force assembled by the government to put down the Pullman Strike. On October 5, 1895, he was appointed Commanding General of the U.S. Army, a post he held until his retirement as a lieutenant general in 1903. In 1898 he led the U.S. forces that captured Puerto Rico during the Spanish-American War.

Miles' brusque manner made him few friends. Already made uncomfortable, or envious, by his political connections, many of his fellow officers were openly wary. Negative views of Miles' actions and accomplishments expressed by contemporaries, though perhaps animated by their personal discomfort with him, make aspects of Miles' career difficult to assess.

The one sure measure was his consistent success on the battlefield.

Miles died in 1925 in Washington, D.C., and is buried at Arlington National Cemetery.

Deeper in the Shadows…

WILLIAM S. HARNEY

Harney led the U.S. Army's first campaign against the Plains Indians. His victory at the Battle of the Blue Water enabled travel along the Oregon Trail to proceed relatively unimpeded for nearly a decade.

Brigadier General William S. Harney led army forces on the federal government's first military campaign against the Plains Indians. On September 3, 1855, near present-day Lewellen, Nebraska, Harney's force defeated bands of Brule and Oglala Sioux led predominantly by Chief Little Thunder.

Called the Battle of the Blue Water, or sometimes referred to as the Battle of Ash Hollow because of its proximity to the famous Oregon Trail site, the expedition was mounted to avenge the so-called "Grattan Massacre" of the previous year. In 1854, Lieutenant John Grattan was sent from Fort Laramie, Wyoming, to extract restitution for a cow that had wandered away from a party of Mormon travelers and fallen into the hands of a band of Sioux led by Chief Conquering Bear. During the confused, ambiguous confrontation that followed a shot was fired and in the resulting melee Grattan and his entire party of 29 soldiers were killed.

When news of the incident spread, the public demanded retribution for Grattan as well as for other depredations—attacks on travelers, ranch burnings, and livestock thefts—that followed. In response, Secretary of War Jefferson Davis recalled General Harney, who was on leave in Paris. At Jefferson Barracks in St. Louis, Missouri, Harney assembled a force of 600 men consisting of the 2nd Dragoons, five companies of the 6th Infantry, one company of the 10th Infantry, and a battery of the 4th Artillery. When Harney crossed into present-day Nebraska, he had with him the largest force that had ever entered Indian Territory.

Eventually, along a small tributary of the North Platte River now called Blue Creek, Harney caught up with the band of Sioux led by Little Thunder that was believed to contain participants from the Grattan incident as well as perpetrators of later raids on travelers and ranches. On the morning of September 3, the Indians were clustered in two villages along the west side of Blue Water Creek. Forty-one Brule lodges were located four miles north of the North Platte River. An additional 11 Oglala lodges formed a smaller camp three miles further north.

When the troops crossed the North Platte River, the terrain they moved through was shaped by the meanderings of Blue Water Creek. At the time of the battle, the creek was "about 20 feet wide and 2 to 10 feet deep flowing over a rocky or sandy bottom." The banks were "abrupt and 3 to 4 feet high". The stream makes a series of mostly mild curves back and forth along the east and west walls of a small valley as it runs its 10 to 11-mile course to the north.

The valley itself is about a half mile wide, bounded on the east by low sand hills. On that side, toward the north end of the valley, there is a gap between the sand dunes. At that point, hills momentarily soften and the ground levels out, falling away in a gradual slope to the east. The soil in this area has a springy, marshy texture associated with it. North of this meadow-like breach the sand hills resume and continue with the stream until it ends a few miles in the distance. The hills on the east are modest in height and have the appearance of gentle, rolling mounds.

There is little that is gentle about the bluffs that form the west wall. They are steep, rugged, cut by narrow ravines, and characterized by sharp outcroppings of rocks whose twisted crags form small caves or niches between the coarse formations. Small mesas periodically appear along the west face; the tops of the bluffs are relatively flat as they continue north through the valley.

The battle that erupted that morning was one of the most savage of all encounters between the U.S. Army and the Plains tribes. By the usual standards of Plains warfare the numbers involved were huge and the casualties were high in a fight that eventually covered acres of ground

One of a series of rugged bluffs along Blue Water Creek (in trees in foreground) assaulted by Harney's infantry companies. As the battle developed, cavalry units swept over the top of the bluffs trapping the Indians between converging forces.

both at the scene of the main combat and during the pursuit that followed.

After an early, confused series of parleys between Harney and Little Thunder failed to avert hostilities, Harney attacked at sunrise. Harney pushed his infantry diagonally north and west across the valley floor against Sioux parties firing from caves, crevasses, and outcroppings on the rugged bluffs that bordered the stream on the west. Meanwhile, at Harney's direction, his cavalry, led by Philip St. George Cooke (later to become Confederate general J.E.B. Stuart's father-in-law), circled around the two villages and struck from the north and west. Cooke's charge took the cavalry over the top of the bluffs, pinning the Indians against the on-rushing infantry. As the cavalry raced south, the Indians were caught inside Harney's rapidly closing vise. In a matter of minutes, as the trap swung shut, the valley of Blue Water Creek and its adjoining western bluff became the scene of carnage.

Exposed to withering fire in the open and about to be overrun from the north and south, most of the Indians fled initially to the caves and rocky outcroppings on the heights along the west side of the valley. There they were soon assaulted by the two companies of infantry moving up the valley floor and by the three companies of Cooke's cavalry coming over the tops of the bluffs behind them. Heavy fighting quickly spread across the hillsides as the Indians fired from rock formations and niches in the jagged limestone in a desperate attempt to repel attackers now enveloping them from both front and rear.

The first phase of the battle was notable for its fury. The infantry employed recently issued long-range rifles—the U.S. Rifle-Musket Model 1855, a .58 caliber muzzle loading percussion rifle. Harney's cavalrymen were armed with the Sharps Carbine, Model 1852, a .52 caliber breech loading percussion weapon. Together, their rifles and carbines extracted a fearful toll as targets presented themselves along the hillside and in the crags, crannies, and underbrush on the faces and tops of the bluffs. It is possible that the Indians were surprised by the range of the new weapons and underestimated the extent of their lethal fire. Heavy broadsides into the caves and twisted rocks caused horrific casualties from ricochets as well as from direct fire.

Harney placed his artillery at the south end of the battle area on a small mesa at the base of the hills where the Indians had fled. That vantage point enabled the batteries to maintain a steady fire into the caves and rake the hillsides where a rain of arrows and bullets was coming from the Indian defenders.

The fight along the bluffs was short but vicious as the Indians resisted fiercely, returning the concentrated fire being poured into their lodgments up and down the bluffs. Eventually, the fire from the cavalry shooting down from the top of the hills and the increasingly heavy assault by the infantry as more and more soldiers reached the bluffs became too severe to withstand; the intensity of the attacks coming from both the front and the rear forced the Indians to abandon their positions. They fled—desperate, headlong, and mostly unorganized—away from the hillside, racing towards and then across the creek, seeking escape through the gap area between the sand hills on the east rim of the valley. Warriors with fresher ponies managed to escape, although "there was much slaughter in the pursuit, which extended from five to eight miles."

Eighty-six Indians were killed during the fight and perhaps as many as 50 more during the pursuit that followed. Harney's losses numbered four killed and four severely wounded, one of whom may have died later. Search parties found articles that established the presence of hostiles in Little Thunder's camp and confirmed their connection with the Grattan Massacre, mail train murders, and other atrocities. The scalps of two white women were discovered on the body of a slain warrior.

Harney's expedition was one of the most effective ever undertaken against the Plains tribes. The scope of his victory so shocked the Sioux nation, the largest and most belligerent of the Native bands, that its 10,000 warriors remained relatively peaceful, and travel on the overland trail was mostly unmolested for almost a decade.

Although the significance of the battle has long been apparent, confusion remains regarding several of its features. For example, the encounter is increasingly referred to as the Battle of Ash Hollow. In reality, the battle occurred about six miles northwest of the famous site, across the North Platte River in a broad valley formed by a creek referred to in the 1850s as the Blue Water.

Outcroppings and caves in the rugged bluffs provided firing positions for Oglala and Brule warriors and momentary shelter for women and children. Ricochets from small arms and cannon fire striking the limestone caused many casualties.

The popular perception of the clash has also changed over the years. The initial public reaction—widespread acclaim—was later followed by labels such as "Harney's Massacre." For a time, soldiers who fought in the battle were sometimes branded "butchers" and "squaw killers." In recent years those harsh judgments have mostly reversed. Most current assessments conclude that Harney and his troops were unjustly accused. As was often the case in Plains warfare, strangeness in dress created confusion during the chaos of the running fight. Some women and children were struck while sheltering alongside warriors firing at their attackers from caves and crevasses. Contemporary accounts indicate that Harney was prompt in detailing soldiers to recover the wounded on both sides. In the aftermath, the expedition's medical officer was officially commended for being "indefatigable in his attention to the suffering of wounded, both of our troops and the enemy."

After leaving a small force at a newly constructed sod fortification named Fort Grattan, on September 9, Harney, with the main body of his troops, left the Ash Hollow area and moved northwest toward Fort

Laramie. There, marauding Sioux had recently made off with 80 head of the fort's livestock. Other bands of Sioux, however, traveled to the fort to negotiate a peaceful settlement.

Harney met with the non-belligerents, smoked the peace pipe, and directed that the Sioux return stolen property, turn over the Indians guilty of murder, and make no more attacks on the overland trail. The chiefs present at the meeting were not able to answer on behalf of the greater Sioux nation. Determined to send a message and prosecute the guilty, Harney took 450 soldiers and 25 mountain men scouts and set out in pursuit.

The weather was already marginal—28 degrees—when Harney left Fort Laramie on September 29. Nonetheless his troopers moved quickly. The mountain men scoured enormous areas in a series of scouts, soon confirming that the Indians had dispersed into small bands. Harney sent a portion of his force back to winter at Fort Laramie, then continued with the remainder of his troops tracking east across the Dakota Badlands towards Fort Pierre. Snow fell as early as October 4, but Harney persisted, reaching the outpost on October 20. No soldiers were lost on the journey. Harney had taken astute precautions, sheltering his men in Indian animal skin lodges while on the march and paying special heed to supplies and material. Still, it was an exhausting trek that taxed soldiers, equipment, and horses. Importantly, Harney had demonstrated that military operations could be conducted on the northern Plains even under the most bitter conditions. It was a lesson that Mackenzie, Miles, Sheridan, and others would apply in full measure in the years that followed.

During Harney's stay in Fort Pierre, he visited isolated outposts in the dead of winter. At an encampment near the Niobrara River, in temperatures near zero and with three feet of snow on the ground, he arrested the post commander for insufficient care of his soldiers while having taken personal shelter in the cabin of a nearby river steamer. Harney stayed at the location for two months, building a sheltered enclosure for the soldiers.

In February 1856 he returned to Fort Pierre and arranged for a spring council with Sioux leaders. Nearly all the Sioux bands attended. This time their leaders arrived at Fort Pierre with a better understanding of Harney's temperament and intentions. They complied with Harney's demands, surrendering three warriors implicated in stagecoach attacks and returning several of the animals stolen from Fort Laramie the previous fall.

Earlier, during Harney's trek to Fort Pierre, other Sioux, Minneconjou this time, had arrived at the fort under a white flag, stating to Harney's representatives that they wanted nothing more to do with "Mad Bear" (Harney). On November 2 the group returned additional horses stolen at Fort Laramie.

Looking from the top of the bluffs across Blue Water Creek. The Indians' escape route is at the top left center of the photo.

Six days later another Sioux band arrived intending to sue for peace. Harney, who by then had arrived at the post, told the assembled Sioux leaders that he would meet with representatives from the entire Sioux nation in 100 days, asking that 10 leaders from each band meet with him in council at that time. Harney sent word to the major chiefs that he would consider their failure to attend the meeting as an indication they were still at war.

The Indians honored Harney's request, meeting with him at Fort Pierre on March 1. As was usual with Harney, he spoke in blunt terms telling the chiefs that he believed the buffalo would disappear and that eventually the Sioux would have to adapt to a different lifestyle. Harney laid out several conditions to the assembled leaders: their thefts of horses must stop; attacks on the Pawnees, their historic rivals, must end; the goods they had stolen must be returned; the warrior who had stolen the Mormon's cow (and precipitated the "Grattan Massacre") must be surrendered, and that there must be no more attacks on travelers along the overland trail.

In return, Harney promised that the government would protect them from white intrusions, resume their annuities, and return all Indian prisoners of war not involved in the stagecoach attacks. Harney selected Sioux leaders and assigned each of them 100 warriors to help carry out the terms of the agreement. As a further gesture of goodwill, Harney began using Indians as couriers to deliver military messages and he distributed excess clothing items to the tribesmen.

At least one Indian agent thought Harney's pact was the best peace agreement ever bartered between the two parties. Even the Oglala, one of the most belligerent bands, came to the fort asking to be part of Harney's peace program.

Harney turned the official ratification, held on May 20, 1856, into a memorable occasion. Nearly 5,000 Sioux camped near the post to observe it. The Sioux turned over to Harney the warrior that had killed the Mormon's cow. In a major show, Harney arrested the man and locked him in the guardhouse—then released him the following day.

Following his extended discussions and successful treaty negotiations with the Sioux, Harney suggested that the government treat the Sioux bands as one nation and that it be kept in check by a separate army unit specifically assigned to that task. In later years, Ranald Mackenzie, Philip H. Sheridan and others would come to share his view that the Indians would struggle until every avenue of resistance was closed to them. They would surrender without fanfare, he believed, only when they had no other alternatives remaining.

Harney's victory at the Battle of the Blue Water and the agreement he negotiated in its aftermath kept the peace on the frontier for most of the following decade, until August 1864 saw the first in a series of massive uprisings that began at Plum Creek, Nebraska.

Like certain of his contemporaries—Custer, Mackenzie, and Miles foremost among them—Harney's legacy is difficult to place in balance. Of his courage, daring, organizational skill, and innovative leadership there can be no question. Yet apparent also were less positive traits, including an impulsive, vindictive personality prone to eruptions of brutality. Harney's lack of tact was legendary; the army court-martialed him four times. He was once tried in a civil court in St. Louis for allegedly bludgeoning a black female servant who had lost his keys. Forced to hurriedly leave town, he was later found not guilty of the charge.

Harney's record in combat was long and distinguished even before fate brought him to the frontier as the earliest of the major military leaders in the American West. From the time he was commissioned as a second lieutenant in 1818, he fought in all of the nation's conflicts, beginning with the struggle against Jean Lafitte's pirates, and extending through the Black Hawk War, the Seminole wars, and the war with Mexico. The army was apparently willing to overlook the contentious, at times violent, personality in return for his obvious skills as a combat leader. When the Civil War began, Harney was one of only four generals in the Regular Army, outranked only by Winfield Scott and John E. Wool.

Like Ranald Mackenzie, Harney exhibited a complex and at times seemingly contradictory personality. Like Mackenzie, Harney was an implacable foe of the Indians, believing that peace on the frontier was impossible unless the tribes were utterly crushed. However, when the Indians succumbed and moved to reservations, there was no stronger advocate for their care and well-being than William S. Harney. As a key member of several government commissions that negotiated treaties with the Plains Indians, Harney earned the Indian name "Man-who-always-kept-his-word." Renowned for his dash and ferocity on the battlefield, Harney's principal hobby as a young officer was raising flowers and vegetables. He was not an easy man to categorize.

Before and After

Harney was born April 22, 1800, near Nashville, Tennessee. His first of many experiences under fire took place in Louisiana, where as an 18-year-old newly commissioned second lieutenant, he helped force Jean Lafitte to move his operations out of the United States. The encounter with Lafitte provided affirmation to Harney that his career was well-chosen. He was tall, at 6 feet 4 inches, and ramrod-straight, with an impressive soldierly bearing. In later life, a well-trimmed white beard accentuated blue eyes that were sometimes described as fierce in appearance. He rather quickly earned a reputation—carried with him throughout his career—as a blunt, rough individual proud of his accomplishments and his reputation for exceptional leadership on the battlefield. His harsh, discourteous manner alienated many of his colleagues and subordinate officers. He was, however, solicitous of the well-being of his enlisted soldiers and was generally respected by them. Harney disliked military details and trivialities, but became known as one of the nation's most bold and effective soldiers.

Blue Water, the western battle that Harney would become most known for, was not his first experience on the frontier. Remarkably, thirty years earlier, in 1825, he accompanied General Henry Atkinson on an expedition up the Missouri that successfully concluded treaties with several tribes.

During the Seminole War, Harney was an advocate of what might in later years have been called civic action, seeking to win the Indians over rather than confronting them militarily.

Among other gestures, he was known for challenging Indian warriors to foot races near the fort. Still, when combat was required, he proved to be an innovative, aggressive leader.

During the second war with the Seminoles, Harney led forces on quick, canoe-borne raids that contributed substantially to the success of General William Worth's counter-insurgency campaign.

Eight years later when war erupted with Mexico, Harney was given command of the 2nd U.S. Dragoons, serving first in the north with John E. Wool's forces under the overall command of Zachary Taylor. Harney's excellent performance was well-noted. After the Battle of

Buena Vista, Winfield Scott ordered him south to serve as the army's senior cavalry officer during the campaign that captured Mexico City and ended the war. Harney fought with particular distinction at Cerro Gordo and soon after received a brevet promotion to brigadier general.

For a time immediately following the war, Harney served as commander of Military District Number Five, which comprised most of the settled portion of the new state of Texas.

In the late 1850s, Harney led troops charged with upholding federal authority in "Bleeding Kansas." He briefly commanded an expedition in the "Mormon War," but was recalled to Kansas when conditions there deteriorated.

In 1859, while commanding the Department of Oregon, he was involved in the international incident that became known as the Pig War. San Juan Island, off the coast of Washington near Vancouver, was at the time subject to competing claims by the British and the Americans. When a pig owned by a British national caused damage to an American's property, Harney sent troops led by George Pickett, later the Confederate general known for the famous charge at Gettysburg, to demand reparations. The British refused, nearly precipitating a shooting war. Tension continued until General Winfield Scott negotiated an agreement that allowed dual occupancy of the island until an international tribunal could adjudicate the competing claims. (An international court later ruled in favor of the United States.) Harney's impulsiveness and lack of tact did not contribute to the peaceful outcome and he was eventually recalled.

The run-up to the Civil War found Harney commanding the Department of the West with Headquarters at Jefferson Barracks. In Missouri, the sympathies of the political leadership of the state, like those of the populace, were split between pro- and anti-secessionists. In the shifting and ambiguous circumstances that followed, Harney, apparently trying to alleviate tensions, took actions that alienated the state's political hierarchy. Possibly also suspicious of Harney's Southern birth, Republican Party leaders demanded his replacement. Harney was recalled to Washington, D.C., for consultation. There, to his surprise, he was relieved of his command.

Harney spent the next two years in Washington in administrative duties before retiring from the army on August 1, 1863. Two years later he was made a brevet major general in recognition of his long service. Winfield Scott, Commanding General of the United States Army—no friend of the acerbic Harney—expressed his displeasure that Harney had been removed from command. Later, President Lincoln, desperate for much of the war for effective combat leaders, was alleged to have said that cashiering Harney had been one his administration's greatest mistakes.

Harney's service to the United States was not yet complete, however. He was recalled on various occasions to serve on Indian commissions and as an emissary to the northern tribes. In those duties he was consistent in his appeals to the government to honor its commitments and treat the Native tribes fairly. Considering his legendary lack of tact, Harney exhibited remarkable forbearance in his negotiations with Indian leaders, sitting patiently for hours listening to the ritual, rambling prologues that eventually led to substantive talks. In 1868, he was involved in the treaty discussions at both Fort Laramie and Fort Rice, and for a time was put in charge of disbursements to the tribes and administrative matters in the treaty area. By the time of his death the Indians regarded him as one of the most trusted and widely respected of the government's representatives: The-man-who-always-kept-his-word.

Harney died at Orlando, Florida on May 9, 1889. He is buried at Arlington National Cemetery.

A FAMILIAR NAME IN A LESSER KNOWN ROLE:
PHILIP H. SHERIDAN

Far better known for his Civil War service, Sheridan commanded an enormous frontier region for a longer time than any other officer. An aggressive leader who favored constant pursuit and multi-axes of attack, his forces, though typically small in number, eventually brought the major Indian wars to a close.

General Philip H. Sheridan is a transcendent figure in American military history. Known for his service during the Civil War, Sheridan, along with Ulysses S. Grant and William T. Sherman, emerged from the conflict as one of a triumvirate of the most famous Union generals.

Overshadowed is Sheridan's long post-Civil War service directing operations against warring tribes in the American West. In actuality, Sheridan commanded a large frontier region for a longer time than any other officer. For the better part of two decades, he led the Division of the Missouri, a vast theater comprising almost half of the nation's territory. Sheridan's zone of responsibility extended north to south from the Canadian border to the tip of Texas and east to west from Chicago to the Rockies. Inside that enormous region were 175,000 Natives of various tribes.

To pacify and secure the region, Sheridan had remarkably few resources. By the 1870s, the entire Army of the United States numbered less than 25,000 enlisted men, down from the more than two million that had served during the Civil War. Sheridan's force was chronically undermanned. Most infantry companies had only 40 men assigned; cavalry companies only 50. Across three departments in the Division of the Missouri—the Platte, Dakota, and the Missouri—Sheridan's force averaged one trooper for 75 square miles of territory. In Texas, the fourth department, the ratio was even more extreme: one for every 120 square miles. His always underpaid and often undersupplied soldiers faced a warrior culture whose core elements were riding and fighting and whose leaders knew every terrain feature and the location of every water hole.

During Sheridan's tenure, the western frontier was the venue for almost constant military action.

As division commander, Sheridan directed forces in the Red River War, the Ute War, and the Great Sioux War. Later still, as Commanding General of the United States Army, he oversaw operations against Geronimo's Apaches and other hostile tribes in the American Southwest.

The Red River War (1868–1869) first illustrated the concept of operations that would characterize Sheridan's generalship on the frontier. Using converging columns deployed from three locations, his forces struck the hostile tribes in their winter quarters, destroying food, shelter, and provisions.

Critics regarded Sheridan's form of warfare as harsh and unremitting. Supporters believed it to be necessary.

Though the strategy would be refined over time, Sheridan-directed operations almost always featured multiple columns and unremitting pressure, regardless of terrain and without respite during winter months. Hostile bands were deprived of shelter, sustenance, and mobility. Harassed incessantly, the tribes were eventually drained of their will to resist.

For the Natives the consequences were devastating. For the government, soldiers, and emigrants, the subjugation of the warring tribes opened an immense portion of the continent to unthreatened settlement and commerce.

Though Sheridan was known on occasion to speak in sympathetic terms about the Indians' plight, those remarks were reserved for ruminations about why the tribes were induced to fight and conditions on the reservations (which he urged be improved). Once the fighting began, he became an implacable foe, unapologetic for his actions or those of his men. While he recognized that breaking up the Indians' lifestyle was a major cause of the persistent warfare that plagued the Plains, Sheridan placed no moral judgment on that series of events. Rather, he spoke in favor of consistency in national policy, railing against programs that seemed to vacillate between benign humanitarianism and stern oversight.

Sheridan agreed with placing the tribes on reservations and attempting to convert them to modes of living more compatible with the greater U.S. population. Like almost all military officers, he disagreed with the government's approach. Sheridan advocated putting the reservations under military control. That, in his judgment, would result in fairer treatment, better administration, and eliminate the graft so prevalent in the Indian Bureau. Fairer treatment, though, did not mean milder treatment. Sheridan was appalled by the lax standards on many reservations. In his view, the tribes' warrior cultures predisposed them to violence; thus, every infraction needed to be addressed until the cultures were transformed.

Sheridan believed the clash between cultures was inevitable and that prosecuting war with extreme measures would serve to shorten the conflict. Perhaps drawing on his own experience as a junior officer in the Pacific Northwest serving under General George Wright—whose harsh tactics brought a quick and permanent end to a war—and his own actions in the Civil War, he concluded, like his friend and colleague William T. Sherman, that victory was not assured until the enemy had been defeated psychologically as well as militarily. The quickest, surest way to do that, in his view, was to punish the enemy with the utmost severity, making every aspect of his continued existence difficult and uncertain.

The "only good Indian is a dead Indian" comment that is often attributed to Sheridan is perhaps apocryphal. He denied ever saying it. Nonetheless, Sheridan was a "total war" soldier. When forces under his command were engaged in a shooting war, he may well have applied similar sentiments to any foe that happened to be facing him at the time.

For nearly three decades, Sheridan played a prominent role in shaping and employing the army that fought the Native tribes after the Civil War. The "winning of the West" (as seen from the settlers', soldiers', and government's perspective) may be credited to him as much as to any officer who saw service on the American frontier.

There is some dispute about Sheridan's date and place of birth. Most references cite March 6, 1831, at Albany, New York. Supposition persists, however, that he may have been born in Ireland (and that he, or perhaps his parents, fudged the location in the event he might later enter politics). Other suggested birthplaces have included Boston, Massachusetts, and Somerset, Ohio.

Sheridan was a diminutive 5 feet 4 inches tall. He had a swarthy complexion and a large head typically topped by a small, flat "pork pie" hat. President Lincoln described his as "a brown, chunky little chap with a long body, short legs, not enough neck to hang him and such long arms that if his ankles itch he can scratch them without stooping." To his men and the American public, he became "little Phil."

Perhaps in a foreshadowing of his later aggressiveness on the battlefield, during his third year at West Point, Sheridan was suspended after a fight with a classmate. After sitting out for a year, he graduated with the class of 1853, ranked 34th of 52 cadets.

After graduation, Sheridan served for a short time at Fort Davis, Texas, a small post situated near the Rio Grande. His time there was brief; a few months later he was transferred to the 4th Infantry and posted to Camp Reading, California, at the northern end of the Sacramento Valley.

The Yakima War of 1855 brought Sheridan's first experience under fire. In March 1856, he led 40 dragoons to the rescue of a group of settlers under siege near Oregon Cascades. Though outnumbered, Sheridan's company tore into the attackers and drove them away from the embattled party. Sheridan was later reassigned to western Oregon, where he and his men guarded the Grande Ronde Indian Reservation. Sheridan served through the Yakima and Rogue River Wars under the overall command of General Wright, whose use of superior firepower combined with harsh measures eradicated the threat—tactics no doubt recalled by the young officer in later years. Sheridan remained in the Pacific Northwest for nearly six years, helping Wright and other commanders tame the Yakimas, Cascades, and other warring bands.

Sheridan was a 30-year-old captain, still posted on the West Coast when the Civil War began. In September 1861, he was transferred east to join the 13th Infantry, but found himself shunted off to staff duties working on behalf of Generals Henry Halleck and Samuel Curtis. Though the duties were not to his liking, he performed them exceptionally well. Halleck, in particular, was reluctant to replace him. Eventually, Sheridan secured an appointment as commander of the Second Michigan Cavalry. From that point, his rise was meteoric. In some of the bloodiest fighting of the war, he earned a reputation for aggressiveness, tenacity, and personal courage. By September 1862, he was a brigadier general of volunteers.

After difficult struggles at Perryville and Stones River, where his counterattack turned an apparent defeat into an important, but costly, Union victory, he was promoted to major general of volunteers.

Sheridan and his unit fought well at the bloodbath at Chickamauga, but like Union forces other than those under George Thomas, were forced into a hurried retreat to Chattanooga. Sheridan apparently tried to rally his regiment to assist Thomas but was unsuccessful in stopping the panic-driven rush to safety.

If redemption was necessary, Chattanooga provided it. Surrounded for a time in the city, Union forces under the command of U.S. Grant launched an attack. Sheridan led a bold, surprisingly successful charge up Missionary Ridge, capturing Grant's attention and earning his esteem. When Grant soon after moved east to assume command of all

Union forces in the field, he took Sheridan with him, installing him as commander of the Army of the Potomac's cavalry.

Frustrated initially when the cavalry arm under General George G. Meade was confined to escort and reconnaissance roles, Grant eventually approved Sheridan's employment of the force as an offensive weapon. Sheridan quickly commenced a series of raids into Confederate territory. One, with as many as ten thousand horsemen, struck towards Richmond. Another killed Confederate cavalry leader J.E.B. Stuart at Yellow Tavern. Not all the raids were successful and at times took his cavalry away from their "eyes and ears" responsibilities to the Army of the Potomac. Nonetheless, their cumulative impact and potential led Grant to give Sheridan an independent command.

Sheridan was subsequently sent to the Shenandoah Valley with orders to defeat rebel General Jubal Early, who maintained a formidable presence there, on occasion threatening Washington, D.C. Two initial victories drove Early south. Then, on October 19, 1864, at Cedar Creek, Early's forces attacked while Sheridan was 14 miles away traveling to a meeting at Winchester, Virginia. Early's attack carried through the Union lines, sending the Federals into an all-out retreat. Sheridan heard the distant firing, raced back to the battlefield, rallying and collecting his disorganized soldiers along the way. His personal example, galloping toward the enemy, waving his hat, and calling to his men, turned the tide of battle. His reassembled troops slammed into the rebels, many of whom were busy looting the Union camp. Early's army was routed, forced from the valley for the final time. "Sheridan's Ride" made him and his horse Rienzi legends in the popular press. Sheridan's victory allowed him free rein to utterly destroy the food producing capacity of the valley, known as the "bread basket of the Confederacy." Grant had assigned him that task, advising him to demolish it to the point that "crows flying over it will have to carry their own provender."

Sheridan was with Grant during the closing actions of the war. At Five Forks on April 1, 1865, his forces captured the vital crossroads, contributing greatly to Lee's decision to abandon the Petersburg-Richmond area and attempt to move his army to North Carolina and there link up with the remaining major Confederate force in the field. Grant sent Sheridan to intercept Lee as the Confederates made a desperate attempt to escape.

Over the next several days as the armies moved west and slightly south across Virginia, Lee tried to slip past the Federals. In the end, Lee's genius was not enough. Sheridan's relentless pursuit was too much for Lee's starving, exhausted soldiers.

At Saylor's Creek on April 6, Sheridan caught an entire wing of the Confederate army and captured a quarter of the remaining rebel forces. A few days later, as Lee made a final attempt to reach a railroad, Sheridan blocked the way. Sheridan was with Grant in William McLean's parlor near Appomattox Court House when Lee surrendered.

After Appomattox, Sheridan was sent initially to the Texas border. With 50,000 troops, he provided moral and material support to the forces of Benito Juarez who were battling 40,000 French troops serving Emperor Maxmilian's bid to maintain control of Mexico.

His next stop was also a brief one. Assigned to Reconstruction duties in Louisiana and Texas, he was replaced on July 31, 1867, after charges that his administration was too harsh in its treatment of former Confederate officials.

His subsequent posting, as Commander of the Department of the Missouri, brought him directly into the Indian wars, an involvement that in some degree would continue through the remainder of his long career.

Although the Medicine Lodge Treaty, signed in October 1867, seemed to hold initial promise for pacifying the southern Plains, most of the tribes failed to settle on new territory provided to them by the government. In addition to the usual contentions, for a considerable time Congress—tied up with impeachment proceedings for President Andrew Johnson—failed to appropriate funds for food, clothing, and other essentials promised by the treaty. Tribal leaders seldom had full control of their aggressive young warriors even under the best of circumstances. By the time the bill finally passed in July 1868 it was too late. A Cheyenne war party was the first to leave the reservation. In the coming weeks they were joined by Oglalas, Brules, and other Cheyenne bands, all combining in a series of raids on farms and settlements. Fifteen white men were killed, five women raped and others taken captive during the attacks. Farm buildings and other dwellings were burned over a widespread area.

Seeking to stop further violence, Sheridan sent two emissaries to discuss grievances with tribal leaders. The negotiators were attacked along the Solomon River. One was killed and the second wounded before fleeing the area.

Sheridan then ordered the Cheyenne and Arapaho to return to their reservations as required by the treaty. They were to turn over the leaders of the raids in Kansas—also a stipulation of the treaty. Both requests were refused. Believing at the time that he had too few soldiers to mount a summer campaign, Sheridan assigned his available forces to protect the Kansas Pacific Railroad and nearby settlements.

As he prepared for a campaign later in the year, in May 1868, Sheridan sent Colonel Benjamin Grierson from Fort Riley, Kansas, to reconnoiter and establish a post closer to the potential area of hostilities. At the junction of two waterways near a crossing point often used by Comanches on their raids into Texas, Grierson constructed the future Fort Sill.

In the meantime, hoping to distract the hostiles, Sheridan sent Lieutenant Colonel Alfred Sully with a sizable combined force of cavalry and infantry to strike Cheyenne and Arapaho camps south of the Arkansas River. A few skirmishes followed, but Sully did not move fast enough to close with the renegade bands. His expedition returned to Fort Dodge on September 18 without achieving significant results.

Conditions continued to deteriorate through the summer and fall. Subsequent to the earlier raids in Kansas, more than a hundred settlers had been killed and many more women violated. Farmsteads and stage stations were burned and livestock numbering in the hundreds stolen. Throughout the Department of the Missouri, 18 soldiers were killed and another 43 wounded.

With public outrage building, Sheridan decided on a winter campaign. First, though, he wanted his main strike force to be commanded by an officer of his choice. George Armstrong Custer, a colleague from the Civil War, had been court-martialed in October 1867 and suspended from active duty for a year. Intervening on his behalf, Sheridan succeeded in having Custer restored to duty before his suspension ended. On September 24, 1868, Sheridan telegraphed Custer at his home in Monroe, Michigan, advising him to report immediately.

Custer was assigned 11 companies of the 7th Cavalry, four companies of infantry, and the 19th Kansas Volunteer Cavalry. In a trek led personally for a time at the outset by Sheridan, on the 22nd of November, Custer's column reached Fort Supply in present-day Woodward County, Oklahoma, 100 miles south of Fort Dodge, Kansas.

Sheridan's idea for a winter campaign was not entirely new, but it did have numerous skeptics, including among them even some veteran frontiersmen. Sheridan, though, believed that well-clothed, well-fed soldiers could subsist in the bitter conditions long enough to find and strike the Native camps. His prospects for success were aided by the steady advance of rail lines across the Plains. Before the railroads, weather and distance considerations had favored the Indians, tucked away nearly out of reach on the vast expenses of the American West. Now, the progress of the rails allowed the buildup of supplies at distant depots, greatly increasing the army's mobility and staying power.

As would be typical of Sheridan-conceived campaigns over the years, he envisioned several columns moving in concert. Major Andrew W. Evans with 500 men would move eastward from Ft. Bascom, New Mexico, to the Canadian River region of the Texas Panhandle. Major (brevet brigadier general) Eugene A. Carr would push south from Fort Lyon, Colorado, with seven companies of the 5th Cavalry. Along the way Carr's column would be joined by five more companies already operating in the field. Together the combined force would the march further south and east.

Carr's and Evan's columns were intended to push the Indians towards Sheridan's main column, led by Custer, coming towards them from the east. Once Custer's larger force made contact, Carr and Evans would block the Indians' escape to the west and north.

As events played out, supply snafus, organizational delays, and horrific weather prevented Evans and Carr from having much impact on the campaign. On November 27, Custer found Black Kettle's Southern Cheyenne camp, the westernmost of a series of villages strung along the Washita River. In a costly, controversial encounter, Custer claimed 103 Cheyennes killed, including Black Kettle, and 53 captives taken. Custer lost 21 killed and 14 wounded.

On Christmas Day, Evans struck a combined Kiowa-Comanche village several miles south of the Washita battlefield along Soldier Spring.

Evans' men destroyed food caches, lodges, and camp supplies. In the midst of a bitter winter, many of the hostiles returned to the reservation.

By the spring and summer of the following year, 1869, most of the renegade Sioux and Cheyenne had surrendered. The one major exception was perhaps the most fearsome band of all—the Cheyenne Dog Soldiers led by Chief Tall Bull. After destructive raids along the Republican River Valley in Kansas and Nebraska, the Cheyenne moved north to join hostile bands of Sioux.

Sheridan sent Carr from his post at Fort Lyon to Fort McPherson in preparation for a major campaign to be launched from that location. After a legendary chase covering a hundreds-of-miles-long horseshoe-shaped track the extended from central Nebraska into northern Kansas and eastern Colorado, Carr caught and defeated Tall Bull at Summit Springs, Colorado, on July 11, 1869. Tall Bull and 51 other warriors were killed, and all of the band's lodges, weapons, and supplies were destroyed. Carr's victory at Summit Springs broke the power of the Cheyenne. Nearly all of the few hostiles still in the field soon surrendered.

As conditions would show, Sheridan's campaign succeeded in achieving his three announced goals. The southern Plains tribes had been forced onto reservations. Hostiles had essentially been removed from the area between the Platte and Arkansas Rivers, assuring the security of railroads and settlements. Lastly, the Indians that had precipitated the raids had been severely punished.

While successful far beyond most past expeditions, the campaign had not yet been decisive. A few years later, the Red River War of 1874–1875 would complete the subjugation of the southern Plains tribes.

Meanwhile, still at large elsewhere were about 11,000 "non-treaty" hostiles who had been pushed westward from the Dakotas, Wyoming, and Nebraska, deeper into Montana. For the next several years, these bands would engage in a life and death struggle with the frontier army.

The westward march of the Northern Pacific Railroad provoked recurring clashes as tracks pushed further into the historic grounds of the Sioux nation. Sherman, Commanding General of the United States Army and Sheridan's immediate superior, believed that the railroads would advance settlement and ultimately help solve the "Indian problem." As white habitation increased, the tribes would be generally confined within the tracks of the Union and Northern Pacific railways, and the buffalo herds that sustained them would be split and diminished as well.

Like Sherman, Sheridan anticipated that the Sioux and their allies would eventually react with violence to the incursion. In a series of preemptive moves, Sheridan sent two powerful strike forces into the field in the spring of 1872. Colonel David S. Stanley, with 600 infantrymen, a battery of Gatling guns and 12-pounders, moved from Fort Rice to the mouth of the Powder River, while Major E.M. Baker with 400 soldiers patrolled further west of Stanley.

When Baker was forced to pull back after confronting hostiles in numbers seldom seen before, army leaders took it as a signal that the task would be difficult and bloody. Shortly after, the tribes underlined their resolve with a direct attack on Fort Abraham Lincoln.

Sheridan responded by transferring Custer and the 7th Cavalry to man the fort and others on the Upper Missouri. In doing so, Sheridan introduced a new dynamic into the conflict. Henceforth, the forts were changed from defensive bastions into bases of supply for cavalry forces that under aggressive commanders would range far and wide in pursuit of hostile tribesmen.

When violence flared again in the south, Sheridan's strategy was similar to that he had employed on the northern Plains in 1868–1869. Using climate as an ally, converging columns would keep the hostile bands constantly on the move causing them to expend their supplies. Eventually, Sheridan believed, the bands would be exhausted by the relentless pursuit and lose their will to resist. That, as well as his confidence that sooner or later one of the columns would find and defeat the war parties, would ultimately cause them to surrender.

To launch what would be known as the Red River War, Sheridan sent three columns from posts in Texas and Indian Territory toward the "Staked Plains" of West Texas, a historic and previously unconquered stronghold of the southern Plains tribes. Meanwhile, from forts in New Mexico and Kansas, two columns would press the Indians from the north and west. The five columns, totaling about 2,000 soldiers, would remain constantly on the move, harassing the tribes and battering them when they came in contact.

On August 31, 1874, Nelson Miles destroyed a village and all its associated property after a difficult, masterfully fought battle deep in West Texas. Miles used Gatling guns, howitzers, and repeated flanking movements to dislodge a combined force of 600 or so of Kiowa and Cheyenne. After fixing some momentary supply problems, Miles chased the tribes through blizzards and the depths of a bitter cold winter.

On September 28, Ranald Mackenzie, after moving a force across the supposedly impregnable "Staked Plains," defeated a large, combined camp in the Palo Duro canyon. Of the 25 engagements fought during the war, Palo Duro was the largest and would have the most far-reaching consequences. Spurred by the efforts of Mackenzie and Miles, the five columns in the field eventually achieved the result Sheridan intended. During February and March 1875, hostile bands surrendered in droves at Fort Sill and the nearest Indian agencies. When the last war party surrendered in June, the war on the southern Plains was over.

Sheridan had defeated the tribes not by inflicting significant losses in battle, but through subjecting them to exposure and starvation, destroying their property and killing their livestock. In considerable measure, it was the sufferings of the tribe in total that induced warriors to seek solace on reservations. Quick results, Sheridan believed, could only be achieved by making war on the entire tribe. It was total war, and it was brutally effective. In a sense, it was the Shenandoah Valley all over again.

As the war in the south was dying down, the focus of action was shifting further north. Gold had been discovered in the Black Hills, a region granted to the Sioux by the Fort Laramie Treaty of 1868. At the cash-strapped government's behest, Sheridan sent George Armstrong Custer with six companies of the 7th Cavalry from Fort Abraham Lincoln to accompany mining experts and other interested parties. The expedition's reports of gold and glowing descriptions of remarkable landscape ratcheted up pressure from commercial interests to open the region.

Though economic considerations and commercial pressure may have weighed in Sheridan's assessment, his stated justification focused primarily on protection for the region's civilian population. The ostensible reason for the expedition was to explore suitable sites for the establishment of a fort. Sheridan had long favored a post in the area, believing it would control marauding Sioux who struck from the sanctuary to raid into Nebraska, Dakota, and Wyoming.

On November 3, 1875, Sheridan attended a meeting at the White House that established a policy toward the region that would shift considerably over the following months. Initially, the attempt was made to rigidly enforce the provisions of the Fort Laramie Treaty. Soldiers were ordered to prevent miners and other emigrants from entering the Black Hills. In the meantime, the government launched an ultimately unsuccessful attempt to buy the Black Hills, the Paha Sapa sacred ground, from the Sioux. Later, though white incursions remained officially prohibited, a decision was made to not restrict prospectors and others from entering the region—a task that the stretched, undermanned army had difficulty carrying out under the best of circumstances.

A further decision, made late in the year, required all Indians to report to their agencies by January 31, 1876. Those who failed to comply would be regarded as hostile. In reality, given conditions of distance and weather, compliance was in most cases difficult and in many nearly impossible, even among bands that were disposed towards a peaceful outcome. Many, angered by the Black Hills imbroglio, were not.

Anticipating widespread non-compliance from the largest and most warlike tribes on the Plains, Sheridan initially planned on a winter campaign. The initial blow was to be struck by a force led by Colonel Joseph Reynolds under the overall command of General George Crook. However, Reynolds' defeat at Powder River on March 17, 1876 made a summer campaign inevitable.

Sheridan's plan for the summer involved a sizable portion of the U.S. Army forces in the west. General Alfred Terry with 1,200 men would move from Fort Abraham Lincoln. Terry's column included much of the 7th Cavalry under the command of George Armstrong Custer. Coming from the opposite direction, Colonel John Gibbon would bring 440 troopers from Fort Ellis, Montana. Finally, General George Crook with 1,100 men would press north from Fort Fetterman, Wyoming. The columns would converge in south central Montana in the vicinity of the Yellowstone and Powder Rivers.

The campaign was mishandled from the outset, beginning with Crook's withdrawal after a June 17 battle at Rosebud Creek. A litany of misadventures followed; Gibbon deferred a fight on his way east; communications between the columns was lacking; Terry's guidance to Custer was, perhaps intentionally, ambiguous; and Custer's decisions as he approached and entered into battle at the Little Bighorn have been questioned for more than a century and a quarter.

Sheridan was an indomitable, aggressive commander who was not daunted by adversity. Three weeks after Custer's defeat, Wesley Merritt and the 5th Cavalry—placed near Warbonnet Creek by Sheridan's foresight—turned back Sioux and Cheyennes attempting to join Crazy Horse and other hostiles in the north. He followed by sending Lieutenant Colonel Elwell S. Otis and Colonel Nelson Miles to reinforce the remnants of Terry's column and dispatched Wesley Merritt and the 5th Cavalry to join Crook.

In the months that followed, Crook, Miles, and Mackenzie chased down and defeated Crazy Horse, Sitting Bull, Lame Deer, and Dull Knife in a string of victories that ended the Great Sioux War. The campaign was model Sheridan: fast-moving, independent commands; multiple axes of attack; constant pursuit, even under bitter conditions; elimination of pony herds, thus immobilizing the nomadic tribesmen; destruction of shelters and food supplies. By the end of 1877, there was not a hostile Indian left in the "Big Open."

Far away from the Little Bighorn battlefield, conditions across the Great Plains remained unsettled. In the fall of 1876, the government made another attempt to acquire the Black Hills from the Sioux. In late September commissioners claimed questionable title to the region after the majority of the assembled chiefs—though some were no doubt confused or induced to agree by the promise of goods—signed the treaty. Problems immediately arose. Red Cloud, a powerful and venerated Sioux chief, along with Red Leaf, another Sioux leader, protested by removing their bands from the Red Cloud Agency, not far from Fort Robinson in the northwest panhandle of Nebraska. They moved their followers north, setting up new camps about 30 miles away along Chadron Creek. Once established there, they demanded that the government deliver their rations to them at those locations.

Sheridan sent Ranald Mackenzie to Fort Robinson to help quell the incidents that threatened the fragile peace in the region. Sheridan shared department commander George Crook's concern that acquiescing to the chiefs' demands might lead to a breakdown in the government's reservation system. More immediate was the threat that the bands might break away and join the hostile groups still operating in the north.

Crook dispatched Mackenzie toward the camps with eight companies of cavalry and a contingent of Frank North's Pawnee Scouts. After a night march, Mackenzie surrounded the camp, captured the pony herd, and ended the incipient uprising without a shot being fired. On November 25 1876, Mackenzie's victory over the Cheyenne on the Powder River—called the Dull Knife Fight—ended the tribe's participation in the war.

The Little Bighorn campaign and the Great Sioux War caused Sheridan to further refine his strategy. Though converging columns would remain a central feature in his planning, the greater distances and the harsher climate on the northern Plains made that approach less effective than it had been further south—a circumstance for which Sheridan is sometimes criticized for not having recognized more quickly. To complement that tactic, Sheridan placed troops on the tribes' favorite hunting grounds and established posts from which the Indians could be continuously watched and harassed until hunger drove them to the agencies.

Reservations were then ringed with posts to prevent breakout raids.

In 1883, with William T. Sherman's retirement, Sheridan was appointed Commanding General of the United States Army. Conditions on the central and northern Plains were benign by that time, the Indians having been suppressed by a series of campaigns over the past two decades. In the Southwest, however, small bands, mostly Apaches, continued to cause periodic disruptions. Led by Geronimo and others, the Apaches went through recurring cycles of subjugation, surrender, reservation domicile, break-out, and resumption of warfare. General George Crook had succeeded by varying means, not all of them military, in whittling down the frequency of the raids and the size of the renegade parties.

In late March 1886, yet another breakout by Geronimo and about 40 followers caused Sheridan to fire off a caustic note to Crook, while at the same time rejecting Crook's negotiated settlement with a large band of Apaches who had recently surrendered. Contrary to Crook's terms, Sheridan demanded unconditional surrender.

The two officers already disliked one another. Among other things, Sheridan was not enamored of Crook's considerable use of Indian auxiliaries, and thought Crook's treatment of the Apaches was too moderate. Greatly angered, on April 1 Crook asked to be reassigned. Sheridan immediately complied, transferring Crook to the Department of the Platte and naming Nelson Miles as his replacement. Miles, using many of Crook's tactics, albeit with a harsher edge, eventually quelled the uprising and shipped Geronino and others off to prison in Florida.

Although he lobbied for improved weapons and supported creating professional schools for artillery, cavalry, infantry, and engineer training, Sheridan was rather conservative by nature. His tenure as commanding general was not known for radical reorganization or innovation.

Several lesser known facets of Sheridan's service highlight an exceptionally diverse career. In 1870, President Grant sent him to Europe to observe and report on the Franco-Prussian War, and Sheridan was present at Napoleon III's surrender. In 1871, from his headquarters in the city, Sheridan coordinated relief efforts during the Great Chicago Fire. He was eventually placed in complete charge when the mayor placed the city under martial law.

To a considerable extent, it was through Sheridan's efforts that Yellowstone was conserved as a national park. Acting first in the mid-1870s, he advocated military control to prevent the loss of wildlife and natural features unique to the region. Later, when land developers and railroad interests threatened the park, Sheridan lobbied successfully to protect it. His efforts expanded the park's boundaries, constricted commercial ventures, and prohibited leases near the natural attractions. In 1886, after the park had suffered through a series of incompetent and nefarious superintendents, Sheridan sent a cavalry unit to take control. The military operated Yellowstone until 1916 when the newly formed National Park Service took over.

In the summer of 1888, about two months before his death, Sheridan finished writing his memoirs. Soon after, he was stricken with a massive heart attack in Washington, D.C., and was moved to his summer home in Norquitt, Massachusetts. On June 1, Congress, reacting to his fragile condition, promoted him to four-star general. Sheridan died at his summer residence on August 5 at age 57. He was buried at Arlington National Cemetery near the Custis-Lee Mansion.

CLOSING THOUGHTS

The military leaders whose stories are told on these pages fought on battlefields that spanned the continent. From the Pacific Northwest to New England, down the Eastern Seaboard to Florida, then back west toward the Mississippi and across the frontier to the Great Plains, Mountain West, and American Southwest, they led the forces that helped shape the nation's appearance, progress, and future.

Some of those battlefields are marked by impressive monuments. Others, less well remembered, are barely identified or noted not at all. All, though, formed milestones on the nation's journey.

From the beginning, America's sailors were equally the stuff of legends, audaciously taking on the world's most formidable naval power despite possessing only a few superb, well-captained ships. A few years later the Barbary Wars provided the first occasion for the infant republic to project its growing power beyond its own shores. Later still, the Civil War brought actions on the country's great river systems and control of 3,500 miles of coastline that contributed quietly but substantially to the final Union victory.

The commanders of the units that fought on the nation's soil and the ships that protected its shores are interred across the vast landscape of the great, sprawling nation they helped create. As might be expected, Arlington National Cemetery contains the most, even though that site came into existence only at the time of the Civil War.

With the exception of the war with Mexico and the navy's actions on the oceans of the world, the conflicts described in this volume have a unique feature in common: all were waged on American soil. They would be the last to share that circumstance. All of the nation's future wars—the Spanish-American War, the Philippine Insurrection, World War I, World War II, Korea, Vietnam, the Gulf War, and the conflicts in Iraq and Afghanistan—would be fought in places far from the nation's coasts. Like America's earlier conflicts, they too would have ample numbers of leaders "in the shadows of victory." Their stories will be told in a future volume.

Even the most recent of the major conflicts that took place during America's first century of existence is now more than a century and a quarter in the past. The passage of time has further muted the faint recollections of those whose services to the nation have long been undervalued or overlooked. That is unfortunate. Fairness and an accurate appreciation of their contributions to the nation's history challenge us to bring them out of the shadows and into the light.

REFERENCES

Nathanael Greene
"I never saw such fighting since God made me..."
>   Buchanon, John. *The Road to Guilford Court House: The American Revolution in the Carolinas.* New York: John Wiley & Sons, 1997, p. 381.

"We fight, get beat, rise, and fight again."
>   Galway, Terry. *Washington's General: Nathanael Greene and the Triumph of the American Revolution.* New York: Henry Holt and Company, Inc., 2005, p. 271.

"Greene is as dangerous as Washington..."
>   Kieron, Francis. *The Battle of Guilford Court House.* The Journal of American History, VIII, 1913, extracted in New River Notes, North Carolina Historical File.

"forgotten victory"
>   Fleming, Thomas. *The Forgotten Victory: The Battle for New Jersey— 1780.* New York: Reader's Digest Press, 1973.

John Stark
"There are your enemies, the Red Coats and Tories..."
>   Crockett, Walter Hill. *Vermont: The Green Mountain State, Vol. II.* New York: The New Century Company, 1921, p. 125.

"Live free or die. Death is not the worst enemy."
>   "The Papers of John Stark." Concord, NH: The New Hampshire State Historical Society, Letter, July 31, 1809.

"Light Horse Harry" Lee
"an active and daring officer, high-spirited and meticulous..."
>   Ward, Christopher. *The War of the Revolution.* New York: Skyhorse Publishing, 2011, p. 604.

"First in war, first in peace…"
"Papers of George Washington" GWpapers.virginia.edu Accessed at http:// gwpapers.virginia.educ/project/exhibit/ing/respone.html, April 15, 2014.

Francis Marion
"As for this damned old devil…"
    Crawford, Amy. *The Swamp Fox*, Smithsonian.com, July 1, 2007.
"Marion has so wrought…"
    Wickwire, Franklin and Mary Wickwire. *Cornwallis and the War of Independence*. London: Faber & Faber, 1971, p. 190–191.
"void of ruthlessness…" Ward, p. 604.

Andrew Pickens
"low and deliberately"
    Ward, p. 757.
"little bands of outraged patriots…"
    Stokesbury, James L. *A Short History of the American Revolution*. New York: William Morrow and Company, 1991, p. 232.

Jacob Brown
"Those are regulars, by God"
    Borneman, Walter R. *1812: The War that Forged a Nation*. New York: Harper Perennial, 2004, p. 188.
"… in the late war, [Brown] contributed perhaps more than any man…"
    Morris, John D. *Sword of the Border: Major General Jacob Jennings Brown 1775–1828*. Kent, OH: Kent State University Press, 2000, p. 1.

William Worth (Seminole War)
"a splendid horseman; he was physically the ideal soldier"
    Korda, Michael. *Clouds of Glory: The Life and Legend of Robert E. Lee*. New York: HarperCollins Publishers, 2014, p. 113.

William Worth (War with Mexico)
"His fame will endure when his monument shall have crumbled."
> Wallace, Edward J. *General William Jenkins Worth: Monterrey's Forgotten Hero*. Dallas, TX: Southern Methodist University Press, 1953, p. 201.

George H. Thomas
"...may have been the best of them all..."
> Bobrick, Benson. *Master of War*. New York: Simon & Schuster, 2009, p. 336.

"...on the eve of battle"
> Piatt, Don and H.V. Boynton. *General George H Thomas: A Critical Biography*. Cincinnati, OH: Robert Clarke, 1893, p. 171.

"My army is whipped and dispersed."
> Bobrick, p. 184.

"Atlanta is ours..."
> O'Connor, Richard. *Thomas: Rock of the Chickamauga*. New York: Prentiss Hall, 1948, p. 287.

"make Georgia howl"
> Sherman, William T. *Memoirs*. New York: Penguin, 2000, p. 429.

"self-lauding fiction," "charming indifference to fact"
> O'Connor, p. 376.

"Time and history will do me justice"
> Bobrick, p. 4.

"intolerable"
> O'Connor, p. 56.

"What a general could do, Thomas did; no more dependable soldier..."
> Catton, Bruce. *Hallowed Ground*. Garden City, NY: Doubleday, 1956, p. 283.

David J. Porter
"unvexed to the sea"
> Winschel, Terrence J. "Vicksburg Campaign: Unvexing the Father of Waters," *Hallowed Ground Magazine*, 2004.

Patrick Cleburne
"the Stonewall of the West"
> Wagner, Margaret E. (ed.). *The Library of Congress Civil War Desk Reference.* New York: Simon & Schuster, 2002, p. 408.

"A meteor shining from a clouded sky"
> Dufour, Charles L. *Nine Men in Gray.* Lincoln, NE: University of Nebraska Press, 1993, p. 118.

"the perfect type of perfect soldier"
> Dufour, p. 118.

Ranald Mackenzie
"the best light cavalry in the world"
> Leckie, Robert. *The Wars of America.* New York: Harper & Row, Publishers, 1982, p. 12.

"alone and aloof," "cold and efficient"
> Robinson, Charles M. III. *Bad Hand: A Biography of General Ranald S. Mackenzie.* Austin, TX: State House Press, 1993, p. 20.

"They never loved him..."
> Robinson, p. xvi.

"You were the one I was afraid of."
> Robinson, p. 235.

Eugene A. Carr
"a particularly sharp conflict"
> Paul, R. Eli (ed.). *The Nebraska Indian Wars Reader, 1865–1877.* Lincoln, NE: University of Nebraska Press, 1958, p. 3.

"skill, fighting, and marksmanship"
> King, James T. "The Republican River Expedition June–July 1869," *Nebraska History Magazine*, September 1960, p. 170.

"those whose horses were fit for service..."
> King, p. 198.

Wesley Merritt
"timely, professionally executed, and desperately needed"
> Hedron, Paul. *First Scalp for Custer: The Skirmish at Warbonnet Creek, Nebraska, July 17, 1876.* Lincoln, NE: University of Nebraska Press, 1980, p. 84.

"boy generals"
> Hedron, p. 53.

Nelson Miles
"fought with almost scientific skill..."
> Josephy, Alvin M. Jr. *The Nez Perce Indians and the Opening of the Northwest.* New Haven, CT: Yale University Press, 1965, p. 632.

William S. Harney
"about 20 feet wide...", "abrupt and 3 to 4 feet high"
> Journal of Lieutenant G.K. Warren in Mattes, Merrill J. *The Great Platte River Road.* Lincoln, NE: The Nebraska State Historical Society, 1969, p. 318.

"There was much slaughter in pursuit..."
> Werner, Fred H. *With Harney on the Blue Water: Battle of Ash Hollow, September 3, 1855.* Greeley, CO: Werner Publications, 1988, p. 28.

"indefatigable in his attention to suffering..."
> Mattes, Merrill J. *The Great Platte River Road.* Lincoln, NE: The Nebraska State Historical Society, 1969, p. 325.

Philip H. Sheridan
"a brown, chunky little chap ellipses character"
> Robertson, James I. Jr. *For Us The Living.* New York: Fall River Press, 2010, p. 207.

"crows flying over it..."
> www.encyclopediavirginia.org/Hard War in Virginia During the Civil War. Accessed December 18, 2012.

SELECTED BIBLIOGRAPHY

War of Independence

Alden, John R. *A History of the American Revolution*. Cambridge, MA: Da Capo Press, 1989.

Chambers, John Whiteclay II, Editor. *The Oxford Companion to American Military History*. New York: Oxford University Press, 1999.

Countryman, Edward. *The American Revolution. Revised Edition*. New York: Hill and Wang, 2003.

Dupuy, R. Ernest and Trevor N. Dupuy. *The Encyclopedia of Military History. Second Revised Edition*. New York: Harper & Row, Publishers, 1986.

Ferling, John E. *Almost a Miracle: The American Victory in the War of Independence*. New York: Oxford University Press, USA, 2007.

Ferling, John E. *Independence: The Struggle to Set America Free*. New York: Bloomsbury Press, 2011.

McCullough, David. *1776*. New York: Simon & Schuster, 2006.

Middlekauff, Robert. *The Glorious Cause: The American Revolution 1763–1789*. New York: Oxford University Press, USA, 2007.

Stokesbury, James L. *A Short History of the American Revolution*. New York: William Morrow and Company, Inc., 1991.

Ward, Christopher. *The War of the Revolution*. New York: Skyhorse Publishing, 2011.

Wood, Gordon S. *The American Revolution: A History*. New York: Modem Library, 2003.

Nathanael Greene

Buchanon, John. *The Road to Guilford Court House: The American Revolution in the Carolinas*. New York: John Wiley and Sons, 1997.

Charbone, Gerald M. *Nathanael Greene: A Biography of the American Revolution*. New York: Palgrave Macmillan, 2008.

Flood, Charles Bracelen. *Rise and Fight Again: Perilous Times Along the Road to Independence*. New York: Dodd Mead and Company, 1976.

Golway, Terry. *Washington's General: Nathanael Greene and the Triumph of the American Revolution.* New York: Henry Holt and Company, 2004.

Lumpkin, Henry. *From Savannah to Yorktown: The American Revolution in the South.* Columbia, SC: University of South Carolina Press, 1981.

Morrill, Dan L. *Southern Campaigns of the American Revolution.* Mount Pleasant SC: Nautical & Aviation Publishing Company, 1993.

Tucker, Spencer C. *Rise and Fight Again: The Life of Nathanael Greene.* Wilmington DE: Intercollegiate Studies Institute, 2009.

Daniel Morgan

Babits, Lawrence E. *A Devil of a Whipping: The Battle of Cowpens.* Chapel Hill, NC: The University of North Carolina Press, 1998.

Buchanon, John. *The Road to Guilford Court House: The American Revolution in the Carolinas.* New York: John Wiley and Sons, 1999.

Callahan, North. *Daniel Morgan: Ranger of the Revolution.* New York: AMS Press, 1961.

Davis, Burke. *The Cowpens-Guilford Court House Campaign.* Philadelphia: University of Pennsylvania Press, 2002.

Higginbotham, Don. *Daniel Morgan: Revolutionary Rifleman.* Chapel Hill, NC: University of North Carolina Press, 1979.

La Crosse, Richard B., Jr. *Revolutionary Rangers: Daniel Morgan's Riflemen and Their Role on the Northern Frontier, 1778–1783.* Westminster, MD: Heritage Books, Inc., 2002.

Withrow, Scott. *The Battle of Cowpens.* U.S. Department of the Interior: National Park Service, 2005.

John Stark

Crockett, Walter Hill. *Vermont; The Green Mountain State, Vol IL.* New York: The New Century Company, 1921.

LaBree, Clifton. *New Hampshire's General John Stark: Live Free or Die: Death is not the Worst of Evils.* Portsmouth, NH: Peter E. Randall Publisher LLC, 2007.

Langguth, A. J. *Patriots: The Men Who Started the American Revolution.* New York: Simon & Schuster, 1988.

Moore, H.P. *A Life of General John Stark of New Hampshire.* New York: H.P. Moore, 1949.

"The Papers of John Stark." Letter, July 31, 1809. Concord, NH: The New Hampshire State Historical Society.

Rose, Ben Z. *John Stark: Maverick General.* Enfield, NH: Treeline Press, 2007.

Special thanks to Malia Ebel, Librarian/Archivist, New Hampshire Historical Society for her assistance with information related to John Stark.

John Glover

Billias, George Athan. *General John Glover and his Marblehead Mariners.* New York: Henry Holt and Company, 1960.

Upham, William P. *A Memoir of General John Glover of Marblehead.* Whitefish, MT: Kessinger Publishing LLC, 2007.

"Light Horse Harry" Lee

Boyd, Thomas. *Light-Horse Harry Lee.* New York: Scribner's Sons, 1931.

Gerson, Noel B. *Light-Horse Harry: A Biography of Washington's Great Cavalryman, General Henry Lee.* New York: Doubleday, 1966.

Lee, Henry. *The Revolutionary War Memoirs of General Henry Lee.* New York: Da Capo Press, 1998.

Royster, Charles. *Light-Horse Harry Lee and the Legacy of the American Revolution.* New York: Knopf, 1981.

Francis Marion

Bass, Robert. *Swamp Fox.* Orangeburg, SC: Sandlapper Publishing Co., 1989.

Hartley, Cecil B. and G.G. White. *Heroes and Patriots of the South: Comprising Lives of General Francis Marion, General William Moultrie, General Andrew Pickens and Governor John Rutledge.* Whitefish, MT: Kessinger Publishing, LLC, 2008.

James, William Dobein. *Swamp Fox: General Francis Marion and His Guerilla Fighters of the American Revolutionary War.* Charleston, SC: CreateSpace, 2010.

Sims, William Gilmore. *The Life of Francis Marion.* Whitefish, MT: Kessinger Publishing LLC, 2010.

Andrew Pickens

Boatner, Mark Mayo. *Encyclopedia of the American Revolution.* Mechanicsburg, PA: Stackpole Books, 1994.

Buchanon, John. *The Road to Guilford Court House: The American Revolution in the Carolinas.* New York: John Wiley & Sons, 1997.

Hartley, Cecil B. and G.G. White. *Heroes and Patriots of the South: Comprising Lives of General Francis Marion, General William Moultrie, General Andrew Pickens and Governor John Rutledge.* Whitefish, MT: Kessinger Publishing, LLC, 2008.

Waring, Alice. *The Fighting Elder: Andrew Pickens.* Columbia, SC: University of South Carolina Press, 1962.

The Barbary Wars

Boot, Max. *The Savage Wars of Peace: Small Wars and the Rise of American Power.* New York: Basic Books, 2002.

Lambert, Frank. *The Barbary Wars: American Independence in the Atlantic World.* New York: Hill and Wang, 2005.

Smethurst, David. *Tripoli: The United States' First War on Terror.* New York: Presidio Press, 2006.

Wheelan, Joseph. *Jefferson's War: America's First War on Terror, 1801–1805.* New York: Carroll and Graf, 2003.

Stephen Decatur

Allison, Robert J. *Stephen Decatur: American Naval Hero, 1779–1820.* Amherst, MA: University of Massachusetts Press, 2005.

Brady, Cyrus Townsend. *Stephen Decatur.* Whitefish, MT: Kessinger Publishing, LLC, 2006.

Leiner, Frederick C. *The End of Barbary Terror.* New York: Oxford University Press, 2006.

Miller, Nathan. *The U.S. Navy: An Illustrated History.* New York: American Heritage, 1977.

Special thanks for Stephen Decatur information provided by Karen Hill, Director of Education and Public Programs, National Museum of the United States Navy and L.C.D.R. Jourdan Travis Moger, U.S.N., Department of History, United States Naval Academy.

The War of 1812

Borneman, Walter R. *1812: The War That Forged a Nation*. New York: HarperCollins, 2004.

Elting, John R. *Amateurs to Arms: A Military History of the War of 1812*. Chapel Hill, NC: Algonquin Books, 1991.

Hitsman, J. Mackay and Donald E. Graves. *The Incredible War of 1812. Revised Edition.* Toronto: Robin Brass Studio, 1999.

Malcomson, Robert. *Lords of the Lake: The Naval War on Lake Ontario.* Annapolis, MD: Naval Institute Press, 1999.

Quimby, Robert S. *The U.S. Army in the War of 1812: An Operational and Command Study.* East Lansing, MI: Michigan State University Press, 1997.

Jacob Brown

General Books, LLC. *Life of General Jacob Brown: To Which Are Added Memoirs of Generals Ripley and Pike.* 2010.

Latham, Frank Brown. *Jacob Brown and the War of 1812.* Spokane, WA: Cowles Book Co., 1971.

Morris, John D. *Sword of the Border: Major General Jacob Jennings Brown, 1775–1828.* Kent, OH: Kent State University Press, 2000.

Thomas MacDonough

Forester, C.S. *Victory on Lake Champlain.* American Heritage, Vol. 15, 1963.

Muller, Charles G. *The Proudest Day: Thomas MacDonough on Lake Champlain.* New York: The John Day Co., 1960.

Skaggs, David Curtis. *Thomas MacDonough: Master of Command in the Early U.S. Navy.* Annapolis, MD: U.S. Naval Institute Press, 2003.

Isaac Hull

Allen, Gardner Weld, ed. *Commodore Isaac Hull: Papers of Isaac Hull, Commodore of United States Navy.* Whitefish, MT: Kessinger Publishing, LLC, 2010.

Biographies in Naval History—Captain Isaac Hull, USN Annapolis, MD: Naval Historical Center, 2007.

Isaac Hull. MSN Encarta Encyclopedia, 2007.

Maloney, Linda M. *The Captain from Connecticut: The Life and Naval Times of Isaac Hull.* Boston: Northeastern University Press, 1986.

Winfield Scott

Eisenhower, John S. D. *Agent of Destiny: The Life and Times of General Winfield Scott*. New York: Free Press, 1997.

Elliott, Charles Winslow. *Winfield Scott, the Soldier and the Man*. New York: Macmillan, 1937.

Johnson, Timothy D. *Winfield Scott: The Quest for Military Glory*. Lawrence, KS: The University of Kansas Press, 1998.

Peskin, Allan. *Winfield Scott and the Profession of Arms*. Kent, OH: Kent State University Press, 2003.

The Seminole Wars

Chambers, John Whiteclay, Jr. Ed. *The Oxford Companion to American Military History*. New York: Oxford University Press, 1999.

Knetsch, Joe. *Florida's Seminole War 1817–1858*. Mt. Pleasant, SC: Arcadia Publishing, 2003.

Mahon, John K. *History of the Second Seminole War 1835–1842*, Revised Ed. Gainesville, FL: University of Florida Press, 1985.

Missal, John and Mary Lou Missal. *The Seminole Wars: America's Longest Indian Conflict*. Gainesville, FL: The University of Florida Press, 2004.

William Worth

Aztec Club of 1847: Biographies. http://www.aztecclub.com/bios/worth.html. Extracted August 25, 2010.

The Handbook of Texas Online. http://www.tshaonline.org/handbook/online/articles/view/ww/fwo28.html. Extracted August 25, 2010.

Wallace, Edward S. *General William Jenkins Worth*. Dallas, TX: Southern Methodist University Press, 1953.

The War with Mexico

Chambers, John Whiteclay II. *The Oxford Companion to American Military History*. New York: Oxford University Press, 1999.

Dugard, Martin. *The Training Ground* New York: Little, Brown, and Company, 2008.

Eisenhower, John S. D. *So Far from God: The U.S. War with Mexico, 1846–1848*. New York: Random House, 1989.
Henderson, Timothy J. *A Glorious Defeat: Mexico and its War with the United States*. New York: Hill and Wang, 2007.

William Worth
See William Worth references in the Seminole Wars section.

John E. Wool
General John Wool. www.sonofthesouth.net. Extracted August 25, 2010.
Sylvester, Nathaniel Bartlett. *Major General John Ellis Wool*. History of Rensselaer County, New York. Rensselaer County GenWeb, 2004.

David Conner
Commodore David Conner. http://www.pbs.org/kera/usmexicanwar/biographies/david_connor.html. Extracted August 25, 2010.

The Civil War

Catton, Bruce. *The Civil War*. New York: Random House, 1986.
Dupoy, R. Ernest and Trevor Dupoy. *The Encyclopedia of Military History 2nd Revised Edition*. New York: Harper and Row Publishers, 1986.
Foote, Shelby. *The Civil War: A Narrative Volume I: Fort Sumter to Perryville* (1958) *The Civil War: A Narrative Volume II: Fredericksburg to Meridian* (1963) *The Civil War: A Narrative Volume III: Red River to Appomattox* (1974) New York: Random House.
Keegan, John. *The American Civil War: A Military History*. New York: Knopf, 2009.
McPherson, James M. *Battle Cry of Freedom: The Civil War Era*. New York: Oxford University Press, 1988.
Wagner, Margaret E. Ed. *The Library of Congress Civil War Desk Reference*. New York: Simon & Schuster, 2002.

George H. Thomas
Bobrick, Benson. *Master of War*. New York: Simon & Schuster, 2009.
Buell, Thomas B. *The Warrior Generals: Combat Leadership in the Civil War*. New York: Three Rivers Press, 1997.

Cleaves, Freeman. *Rock of Chickamauga: The Life of George H. Thomas.* Norman, OK: University of Oklahoma Press, 1949.

Einolf, Christopher J. *George H. Thomas: Virginian for the Union.* Norman, OK: University of Oklahoma Press, 2007.

O'Connor, Richard. *Thomas: Rock off Chickamauga.* New York: Prentiss-Hall, 1948.

David Porter

Bearss, Edwin C. and J. Parker Hills. *Receding Tide: Vicksburg and Gettysburg, The Campaign That Changed the Civil War.* Washington D.C.: National Geographic, 2010.

Hearn, Chester G. *Admiral David Dixon Porter: The Civil War Years.* Annapolis, MD: Naval Institute Press, 1996.

Lewis, Paul. *Yankee Admiral: A Biography of David Dixon Porter.* Philadelphia: David McKay Co., 1968.

Musicant, Ivan. *Divided Waters: The Naval History of the Civil War.* New York: HarperCollins, 1995.

Porter, David D. *Memoir of Commodore David Porter of the United States Navy.* Whitefish, MT: Kessinger Publishing, LLC, 2008.

Wagner, Margaret E. Ed. *The Library of Congress Civil War Desk Reference.* New York: Simon & Schuster, 2002.

Patrick Cleburne

Dufour, Charles L. *Nine Men in Gray.* Lincoln, NE: University of Nebraska Press, 1993.

Eicher, John H. and David J. Eicher. *Civil War High Commands.* Palo Alto, CA: Stanford University Press, 2002.

Joslyn, Maur. *A Meteor Shining Brightly: Essays on the Life and Career of Major General Patrick Cleburne.* Macon, GA: Mercer University Press, 2000.

Stewart, Bruce H., Jr. *Invisible Hero, Patrick R. Cleburne.* Macon, GA: Mercer University Press, 2009.

Symonds, Craig L. *Stonewall of the West: Patrick Cleburne and the Civil War.* Lawrence, KS: University Press of Kansas, 1997.

Emery Upton

Ambrose, Stephen E. *Upton and the Army.* Baton Rouge, LA: Louisiana State University Press, 1964.

Coles, David J. and David S. Heidler, Jeanne T. Heidler, James M. McPherson, (eds.). *Encyclopedia of the American Civil War: A Political, Social, and Military History*. New York: W.W. Norton & Company, 2002.

Eicher, John H. and David J. Eicher. *Civil War High Commands*. Palo Alto, CA: Stanford University Press, 2002.

Faust, Patricia L. (ed.). *Historical Times Illustrated Encyclopedia of the Civil War*. New York: Harper & Row, 1986.

Winik, Jay. *April 1865*. New York: Harper Collins, 2001.

Benjamin F. Isherwood

Bureau of Steam Engineering. http://en.academic.ru/dic.nsf/enwiki/ 75277639. Extracted August 25, 2010.

Sloan, Edward. *Benjamin Franklin Isherwood Naval Engineer: The Years as Engineer in Chief 1861–1869*. Annapolis, MD: United States Naval Institute, 1965.

United States Navy PAO Biography. *B.F Isherwood*. August 25, 2010.

Montgomery C. Meigs

Eicher, John H. and David J. Eicher. *Civil War High Commands*. Palo Alto, CA: Stanford University Press, 2002.

Miller, David W. *Second Only to Grant: Quartermaster General Montgomery C. Meigs*. Shippensburg, PA: White Mane Publishing Company, 2001.

U.S. Army Quartermaster Foundation, Fort Lee, Virginia. www. gmkfound.com/BG-Montgomery-Meigs.htm March 18, 2011.

Weigley, Russell F. *Quartermaster General of the Union Army: A Biography of M. C. Meigs*. New York: Columbia University Press, 1959.

Joshua Lawrence Chamberlain

Eicher, John H. and David J. Eicher. *Civil War High Commands*. Palo Alto, CA: Stanford University Press, 2001.

Longacre, Edward G. *Joshua Lawrence Chamberlain: The Soldier and the Man*. Cambridge, MA: Da Capo Press, 2003.

Pullen, John S. *Joshua Chamberlain, A Hero's Life and Legacy*. Mechanicsburg, PA: Stackpole Books, 1999.

Shaara, Michael. *The Killer Angels*. Philadelphia: David McKay Publishers, 1974.

Wallace, Willard M. *Soul of the Lion: A Biography of Joshua L. Chamberlain.* Gettysburg, PA: Stan Clark Military Books, 1991.

Winfield Scott
See Winfield Scott references in the War of 1812 section.

Indian Wars of the West

Greene, Jerome A. *Battles and Skirmishes of the Great Sioux War, 1876–1877: The Military View.* Norman, OK: University of Oklahoma Press, 1998.

Josephy, Alvin M. *War on the Frontier.* New York: Time-Life Books, 1986.

McDermott, J.D. *A Guide to the Indian Wars of the West.* Lincoln, NE: University of Nebraska Press, 1998.

Michno, Gregory F. *Encyclopedia of Indian Wars.* Missoula, MT: Mountain Press Publishing Company, 2003.

Phillips, Thomas D. *Boots and Saddles: Military Leaders of the American West.* Caldwell, ID: Caxton Press, 2015

Robinson, Charles M. III. *A Good Year to Die: The Story of the Great Sioux War.* Norman, OK: University of Oklahoma Press, 1996.

Sauers, Richard Allen. *America's Battlegrounds.* San Diego, CA: Tehabi Books, 2005.

Wellman, Paul I. *The Indian Wars of the West.* Garden City, NY: Doubleday & Company, Inc., 1956.

Utley, Robert. *Indian Wars.* New York: Bonanza Books, 2002.

Ranald Mackenzie

Bourke, John Gregory. *Mackenzie's Last Fight with the Cheyennes: A Winter Campaign in Wyoming and Montana.* London: Argonaut Press, 1966.

Buecker, Thomas R. *Fort Robinson and the American West: 1874–1899.* Norman, OK: University of Oklahoma Press, 1999.

Moore, Fred H. and Ella Mae Moore. *On the Border with Mackenzie; or, Winning West Texas from the Comanches.* Texas State Historical Association, 2007.

Pierce, Michael D. *The Most Promising Young Officer: A Life of Ranald Slidell Mackenzie.* Norman, OK: University of Oklahoma Press, 1993.

Robinson, Charles M. III. *Bad Hand: A Biography of General Ranald S. Mackenzie.* Buffalo Gap, TX: State House Press, 1993.

Thompson, Richard A. *Crossing the Border with the 4th Cavalry: Mackenzie's Raid into Mexico 1873.* Waco, TX: Texian Press, 1986.

Wallace, Ernest. *Ranald S. Mackenzie on the Texas Frontier.* West Texas Museum Association, 1964.

Eugene A. Carr

"Carr, Eugene A." *The Handbook of Texas Online.* www.tshaonline.org. handbook/online/articles/CC/fcadd.html. Extracted March 1, 2010.

Eicher, John H. and David J. Eicher. *Civil War High Commands.* Palo Alto, CA: Stanford University Press, 2000.

King, James T. "The Republican River Expedition June-July 1869". *Nebraska History*, September, 1960.

King, James T. *War Eagle: A Life of General Eugene A. Carr.* Lincoln, NE: University of Nebraska Press, 1963.

Phillips, Thomas D. *Battlefields of Nebraska.* Caldwell, ID: Caxton Press, 2009.

Wesley Merritt

Alberts, Don E. *General Wesley Merritt: Brandy Station to Manila Bay.* General's Books, 2001.

Eicher, John H. and David J. Eicher. *Civil War High Commands.* Palo Alto, CA: Stanford University Press, 2001.

Hedron, Paul. *First Scalp for Custer: The Skirmish at Warbonnet Creek, Nebraska, July 17, 1876.* Lincoln, NE: University of Nebraska Press, 1980.

Phillips, Thomas D. *Battlefields of Nebraska.* Caldwell, ID: Caxton Press, 2009.

Robinson, Charles M. III. *A Good Year to Die: The Story of the Great Sioux War, 1876–77.* Norman, OK: University of Oklahoma Press, 1993.

Werner, Fred H. *The Slim Buttes Battle.* San Luis Obispo, CA: Werner Press, 1981.

Nelson Miles

Demontravel, Peter R. *A Hero to his Fighting Men: Nelson A. Miles, 1839–1925.* Kent, OH: Kent State University Press, 1998.

Greene, Jerome A. *Yellowstone Command: Colonel Nelson A. Miles in the Great Sioux War, 1876–1877*. Norman, OK: University of Oklahoma Press, 2006.

Hedron, Paul. *Great Sioux War Order of Battle: How the United States Army Waged War on the Northern Plains, 1876–1877*. Norman, OK: The Arthur H. Clarke Company, 2011.

Hutton, Paul Andrew and Durwood Ball. *Soldiers West: Biographies from the Military Frontier:* Norman, OK: University of Oklahoma Press, 2009.

Wooster, Robert. *Nelson A. Miles and the Twilight of the Frontier Army*. Lincoln, NE: University of Nebraska Press, 1996.

William S. Harney

Adams, George Rollie. *General William S. Harney: Prince of Dragoons*. Lincoln, NE: University of Nebraska Press, 2001.

Archer, Jules. *Indian Foe, Indian Friend: The Story of William S. Harney*. New York: Atheneum, 1970.

Werner, Fred H. *With Harney on the Blue Water: Battle of Ash Hollow, September 3, 1855*. Greeley, CO: Werner Publications, 1988.

Philip H. Sheridan

Drake, William F. *Little Phil: The Story of General Philip Henry Sheridan*. Prospect, CT: Biographical Publishing Company, 2005.

Hutton, Paul Andrew and Durwood Ball (Eds.). *Soldiers West: Biographies from the Military Frontier*. Norman, OK: University of Oklahoma Press, 2009.

Keim, DeBenneville Randolph and Paul Andrew Hutton. *Sheridan's Troopers on the Borders: A Winter Campaign on the Plains*. Lincoln, NE: University of Nebraska Press, 1985.

Morris, Roy, Jr. *Sheridan: The Life and Wars of General Phil Sheridan*. New York: Vintage, 1997.

Rister, Carl Coke. *Border Command: General Phil Sheridan in the West*. London: Greenwood Press, 1974.

INDEX